Defeating Islamic Terrorism

THE WAHHABI FACTOR

Father Patrick Bascio, C.S.Sp.

Branden Publishing Co
Boston

© Copyright 2007
Branden Publishing Company, Inc.

Library of Congress Cataloging-in-Publication Data

Bascio, Patrick, 1927
  Defeating Islamic Terrorism : the Wahhabi Factor / Patrick
Bascio. p. cm.
  Includes bibliographical references and index.
  ISBN-13: 978-0-8283-2152-5 (pbk. : alk. paper)
  1. Terrorism--Religious aspects--Islam.
  2. Wahhābīyah.
  3. Terrorism--Government policy --United States.
  4. United States--Relations--Asia, Central.
  5. Asia, Central--Relations--United States.
  I. Title.
HV6431.B3365 2007
363.325'16--dc22

2006031904

B|B

BRANDEN BOOKS
www.brandenbooks.com
PO Box 812094
Wellesley MA 02482

ACKNOWLEDGMENT

I wish to thank the following kind people who assisted, housed and fed me while I focused on this work:
—The Holy Ghost Fathers, Province of Trinidad, especially Father Neil Rogriguez and Nyron Rolingson. Nyron kept me in business by fixing the many computer problems I had.
—Dexter and Sue Hurst of Aurora, Indiana
—Denese Denman of Aurora, Indiana who edited this work
—Mary Ashcraft and her son, John, of Birmingham, Michigan, whose lives inspired me to attempt to make a contribution to American foreign policy.
—Evgueny Novikov, former member of the Soviet Central Committee, Soviet expert on things Arabic, and my co-author in a previous book. He planted the seeds of this work in my mind and helped me to understand the nature of Central Asia's potential contribution to defeating Islamic terrorism.
—Hugh Auchincloss of Newport, Rhode Island and stepbrother of Jackie Kennedy, who has all of her charm plus a deep abiding knowledge of and friendship with the Arab nation, in particular the Palestinian people. I am very grateful that he agreed to write the Foreword to this work.

DEDICATION

To Father Lenny Sansone, a Holy Priest,
my lifelong friend, and air force companion.

CONTENTS

FOREWORD

In this book, Father Pat has made a contribution to our understanding of the problems we are experiencing in the war on terrorism, and offers a viable solution to solving those problems. As Director of the PhD program for American and Allied military who were studying out of the United States Naval War College in Newport, he offered these men a broader understanding of the economic and political framework of the wider world. It was during this time that I came to know him and worked with him on his PhD program, as we became friends and colleagues.

Father Pat offers an alternative to diplomatic business-as-usual that calls for direct communication with the Islamic peoples, especially those of Central Asia who share with us a common desire to get at the root causes of and eliminate an Islamic terrorism that has been disrupting their lives long before 9/11. His approach preserves the dignity and value of the Islamic cultural and religious ethos, substituting understanding and patience in the place of anger, and the prudent and selective use of military force in place of "shock and awe."

Hugh Auchincloss
Newport Rhode Island
September, 2006

PART ONE

WAHHABISM

INTRODUCTION

Problem:
*Wahhabism is the angry form of Islamism...the soil
in which anti-Western and anti-American terrorism
grows.*
Ex-CIA Director, R. James Woolsey
Solution:
*It is "critical to the national interests of the United
States that we greatly enhance our relations with the
five Central Asian countries."*
**Report to U.S. Senate Committee on
Foreign Relations, June 27, 2002**

N ever before in history have so many been so fearful of so few because Islamic terrorism plagues a very large section of the world's population. This phenomenon is now drawing together, in common cause, the major powers that, at times, have had notable differences in their world outlooks. To understand these shifts in international relations, we need to observe and study the fact that three major powers, Russia, China and the United States, and at least five Central Asian nations, plus at least three European nations, plus a host of South East Asian nations, share a common enemy, the terrorism aided and abetted by the Wahhabi sect of Saudi Arabia and the terrorist allies they have spawned around the world. Our Iraq policy, no doubt well-intentioned, has produced the exact opposite of what we hoped to achieve. The very liberation by the United States armed forces of Shiite politics in Iraq has ignited and empowered the rise of radical Shiism from Iran to potentially explosive sectarian Civil War in Iraq, to the strengthening of Hezbollah,

8 Father Patrick Bascio, C.S.Sp.

Hamas and their look-alikes around the globe. Ironically, Saddam Hussein developed the most technologically and socially advanced Arab nation in the Middle East. Unfortunately for the Iraqis and the rest of the world he also came to embody the expression: Power corrupts, and absolute power corrupts absolutely. It is not shameful that we tried and failed to fight terrorism in Iraq, where, in fact, it was not but now is as a result of our invasion. It is shameful, however, that many in authority refuse to face up to the reality of that failure and chart a different course.

I am suggesting a rather bold but very realistic alternative to our failed policy in Iraq, namely an alliance with the Central Asian (CA) nations, former Muslim republics of the old Soviet Union that have been battling the same Islamic terrorism long before 9/11. They are: Kazakhstan, Kyrgyzstan, Turkmenistan, Tajikistan, and Uzbekistan, nations geographically isolated but strategically situated in the heart of Central Asia, with reasonably certain potential for economic growth based on expanded exploration and use of existing gas and oil resources. Considering the fact that they were ruled by Soviet Union for about 70 years and that prior to Russian occupation they had not developed nation-state status as we understand it today, they are making good progress in developing democratic institutions, working out their future within the context of the ethos of their Islamic religion, culture and history.

This is important to stress because the first significant diplomatic initiative these nations took upon becoming independent from the Soviet Union was to reach out to the United States as a partner both in the development of their natural resources and as a protection against what they perceived to be the real possibility that Russia might wish to reclaim its former position of dominance in the region. Our first reaction to their initiative was very positive. However, the Uzbekistan government's swift and decisive response to a terrorist act on their soil in the city of Andijon drew equally swift and pervasive condemnation from the United States, European governments and a plethora of NGOs around the world. These harsh assessments of Uzbek determination to put down the Andijon terrorist actions immediately triggered a wave of shock and disbelief in Central Asia. The previous good will toward the United States evaporated overnight. We failed to understand both the historical cultural and political evolutions taking place in Central Asia, thereby throwing away the enormous amount of good will and affection for America and its institutions. In the interest of our national security and the reputation we wished to have for patiently nurturing countries from less democracy to more democracy, the United States needs to make amends for its rash judgments in that part of the world. It will not be easy but it can be done. It is in the interest of our national security because only in Central Asia has Wahhabism, the chief architect of anti-Western terrorist activity, been confronted and contained successfully, and all of this happened before 9/11. This is not surprising since Islam is the cultural ethos of Central Asia enabling it to speak the language of Wahhabism and understanding its mindset. We are in desperate need of their assistance. We need to apologize for our past mistakes in the area and recognize how far they have come to democracy since their independence from the Soviet Union, in spite of a debilitating history of being dominated by foreign powers.

The net result of Czarist, then Soviet, then Russian colonial rule in Central Asia is similar to the net results of European colonial rule in Asia and Africa; i.e., weak and sometimes corrupt political institutions. There has been and will continue to be political unrest as they work out their problems, but they need to be praised for their efforts. We need to form with them an institutional grouping that would foster economic, social and political cooperation. There needs to be close coordination on policy and strategy not only within the U.S. government but also with EU nations and agencies so as to encourage and promote broad-based economic and social reforms in Central Asia.

Fifty Nine Million Muslims

We need to win their friendship and respect, thereby breaching this terrible divide between the Muslim world and ourselves, while at the same time dealing seriously with the scourge of Islamic terrorism that afflicts them as well. An alliance with 59 million Central Asian Muslims is the most productive way out of our dilemma. One can only imagine the electric effects that a united front between the United States and 59 million Muslims would have on the rest of the world, especially the Arab world! It would be at this time in our history the best thing that could happen to the United States. It would bring peace and harmony with the Arab nation and it would dissipate the threat of Islamic terrorism. When Uzbekistan, in July 2005, ordered the eviction of U.S. military personnel from the Karshi-Khanabad airbase the dimensions of our loss of face and influenced in Central Asia became evident. We must reclaim that good will, and do so by honest and patient dialogue with Central Asian leaders. They would respect our desire to reverse the harm we did by our hasty judgments. It is an historic opportunity both to eliminate the dangers of Islamic terrorism and to strengthen our ties with Arab nations around the globe. Let us seize that opportunity while there is till time. In an address at Johns Hopkins University's School of Advanced and International Studies, Olivier Roy, Research Director for Humanities and Social Studies at the National Center for Scientific Research in Paris, warns that the main threat in Central Asia is the growth of Wahhabism. He said that the challenge of radical Islam in Central Asia must be examined through the prism of Wahhabi militancy worldwide. They need our help in this endeavor. By helping them we will be helping ourselves. At the same time we also need to admit publicly that the major financial source for international terrorism is the Saudi Arabian religious establishment. Since Saudi Arabia is, on paper, an ally of the United States, this is very disturbing. The Saudi religious establishment builds mosques and madrasas all over the United States and the Western world, and place an imam in each who teaches the young their duty to carry on jihad against the infidels, i.e., the West. That they are allowed to do this in America and in most, if not all, Western nations is a fact that needs to be dealt with urgently. Wahhabism is a dangerous cancer metastasizing in the international body politic. It is not coincidental that fifteen of the nineteen September 11, 2001 murderers were Wahhabi from Saudi Arabia, or that the Taliban was an ideal form of Wahhabi government, or that bin Laden himself is a Wahhabi.

There is something wrong with a foreign policy that is so lacking in knowledge of the Wahhabi that the average American citizen, upon hearing the term, has no idea what it means. No mention of it is made on television news, which says a lot about the ability of the worlds most financed and universal news programs to miss the point. With very rare exception, there is not a word about the Wahhabi from the Rumsfelds or the Kennedys or the dozens of Arabian and Islamic experts on the endless talk shows that are designed to inform public opinion. It is difficult to explain. Nor is there a word about the history of the Central Asian republics' successful struggle with our major enemy or their willingness to help us defeat them. The story of this lack of knowledge is worthy of a Kafka novel; it is Kafkaesque.

We can reverse all of these mistakes, but time is running out and we must do it now. We still have time, but if we do not move quickly events in the region may move so rapidly and so radically that, by default, the Central Asian extremists can gain political and religious control. In that case, given the distance from our shores and the enormous land mass of the area, we could be in a position where we can no longer either monitor or influence events. Such an event would signal the final loss of our ability to defeat Islamic terrorism and also signal the onset of a long dark night of chaos and mayhem in the world.

Chapter One

ASTANA

An important meeting of the Shanghai Cooperation Organization took place in May 2005, in Astana,[1] a lovely city of the Central Asian republic of Kazakhstan. However, the meeting was a bitter disappointment and a significant setback for the United States. The Shanghai Cooperation Organization (SCO) is an intergovernmental group, founded in Shanghai on June 15, 2001, whose members are China, Russia, Kazakhstan, Kyrgyzstan, Tajikistan and Uzbekistan. In June 2002, the heads of SCO member states met in St. Petersburg, Russia, and signed the SCO Charter, outlining in great detail SCO purposes and principles, organizational structure and form of operation. Its lofty goals include working together to insure regional security and stability by creating a new international political and economic order that is characterized by democracy, justice and rationality.

SCO member states cover an area of over 30 million km, with a population of 1.455 billion. Significantly, its working languages are Chinese and Russian, giving us pause to wonder at the enthusiasm with which they gravitated toward the United States as soon as they became independent. Originally designed to lessen fears on all sides when border clashes and incursions occurred, the SCO now focuses on attacking and destroying the Wahhabi, or any Islamic terrorist organization that Wahhabism has spawned and continues to financially support. The SCO's main resolution and determination is to coordinate its activities for mutual security. The SCO was among the first international organizations to advocate explicitly the fight against terrorism by spelling out for the first time in international forums its separatism and extremism. This part of its work laid a solid legal foundation for SCO security cooperation, for each member is inundated by terrorist violence.

In October 2002 they conducted a joint anti-terrorism military exercise, and another such exercise in August 2003. They have been active, vocal and knowledgeable participants in major conferences on terrorism held by the United Nations in Vienna, New York and Lisbon.

The May 2005 meeting in Astana was held primarily to discuss the progress made to date in the war on Islamic terrorism, the U.S. presence in the region and the annoyance they felt toward U.S. criticism on the manner in which the SCO is bringing the fight to Islamic terrorism. It was clear that American attitudes and actions, intentionally or not, have impacted negatively on American influence in the region. That is not good news for either the U.S. or its allies. Martha Brill Olcott, an expert on Central Asia at the Carnegie Endowment for International Peace in Washington, cautions U.S. polity makers: "If our policy response fully isolates those members of the ruling elite, those who serve in the administration who are inclined to change, are we making the process of regime transfer even more difficult?"

At the SCO meeting, for the first time, all six members asked the United States to submit a timetable for the withdrawal of all its military bases. The summit members also, in no uncertain terms, strongly censured the United States for what it called foreign interference in their internal affairs. Uzbekistan's President Karimov implied that the United States was fomenting and instigating anti-government activity in Uzbekistan and throughout the region. He argues that the measures they employ are necessary to fight militant Islamic groups that vow to overthrow the region's governments. What structures these groups would replace the current governments with is not clear, but the presidents are taking no chances.

Political observers believe that either Karimov, or Russian President Vladimir Putin or China's President Hu Jintao was behind the communiqué. Russia has publicly complained about the American military presence in Central Asia, saying that conditions on the ground in Afghanistan no longer warrant such a presence. The Russian and Central Asian press continue to speculate that the U. S. was behind the Kazak and Kyrgyz revolutions. It is in Moscow's best interest, of course, to rid Central Asia of American presence so that the Russians can regain the dominant position they formerly held in the region. China needs Central Asia's oil. And, we must not forget that, in any case, from the Russian perspective it is not desirable to have American superpower on its borders. We didn't like it when they were in Cuba and they don't like our proximity either. Fair enough. Russia and China often see the United States as an outsider intruding on their spheres of influence. In 2004, Putin suggested that Russia, China, and India should work together economically and politically to counterbalance U.S. hegemony.[2] Essentially, he was advocating a new axis, or "strategic triangle," to offset Russia's own weaknesses.

On August 18, 2005, the Associated Press reported an interesting interview with Sergay Pashevich, a former Soviet Army colonel who also possesses a PhD in Chinese history. The report said that Pashevich, at his office in Almaty, Kazakhstan, aimed his Kalishnakov rifle at a map of Central Asia hanging on the wall. He warned that a 21st century Great Game is being played out in Central Asia, with China and Russia on the one side and the U.S. on the other. The Great Game is the rivalry over trade, oil and the war on terrorism. The term was invented to define the imperial rivalries and ambitions of 19th century Russia and Britain. Pashevich simply sees the same game with a slightly different cast of characters. The Associated Press also talked to General Galyamova, a researcher at the Kazakhstan Institute for Strategic Studies. She agrees with Pashevich and adds "The Russian/Chinese military exercises that took place in August 2005 on the Shandong Peninsula and the Yellow Sea are a sign of things to come." Certainly, the exercises, combined with the July 2005 Shanghai Cooperation Organization meeting demand that the United States remove its presence from Central Asia, was a challenge the Russian and Chinese and, to some extent, the Central Asian nations have made to the U.S. while looking us squarely in the diplomatic eye. The United States replied that it could not give a date as yet because U.S. military presence in the region was needed for operations in Afghanistan. The President of Uzbekistan was not satisfied with Washington's response, so he bluntly said. "You have 180 days to withdraw." The Uzbek base has been a key hub for U.S. troops, so the Senate retaliated by blocking a $23m payment to Uzbekistan. The payment, for past use of the base, will be postponed for at least a year. Republican Senator John McCain sponsored the amendment bringing about the blocking of funds. He said that the actions of Uzbek President Islam Karimov were so alarming that the Senate should be considering sanctions against him, "not how to transfer millions of taxpayers' dollars to his government." The Senate was stung because the Karshi-Khanabad base has been an integral part of U.S. military operations in the region for nearly four years. Its location in a secure area, a short journey from the Afghan border, made it an ideal center for air operations.

If one has been observing the political wind in Central Asia, one could have seen this coming. In May 2005, China gave a red-carpet welcome to the president of Uzbekistan just days after his bloody crackdown on protesters, in which hundreds of Uzbeks were killed. At that welcoming, Karimov was congratulated on his handling of the riot.

Apart from any moral discussions about particular actions taken by particular Central Asian governments in riot situations, one thing is eminently clear. Karimov's switch from American friend to American foe is a direct result of being annoyed and even insulted by what he sees as Washington's preoccupation with human rights and democracy at a time when Uzbekistan is taking very strong measures to control the spread of Wahhabism. The timing was deeply resented. Cory Welt, a fellow at the Center for Strategic and International Studies in Washington, cautions the U.S. government to tread softly. He said that any move by Washington to retain the base in Uzbekistan could undermine its democratization initiative. "...if we intend to keep the U.S. military presence in Uzbekistan because of traditional geopolitical concerns then this simply runs the democracy promotion strategy straight into the ground."

At the same time, the CA nations do not want to be hugged too tightly either by the Russian or the Chinese bear. Their security guarantee will consist, not in Russia defending them against a foreign invasion, but in Russia working with them in trade, combating terrorism, and receiving from them the technology they so desperately need. The unexpected collapse of the ruble zone in 1993 put the Central Asian republics' leaders in a difficult position and forced them to adopt radical steps in both economic and social fields. After 1993, the CA governments were forced to implement unpopular economic measures (such as closing down unprofitable enterprises and removing subsidies for food and transportation, etc.). Having multiple discussions about the best "model of development" allowed them to identify with the experience of economic reforms in the Newly Industrialized Countries (NICs) and formed an intellectual and political base for these painful and unpopular reforms.

On the whole, the discourse had some important practical implication in promoting economic reforms. These debates have played a significant role in creating an intellectual environment for introducing and advancing economic changes in CA nations. For example, President Karimov of Uzbekistan had clearly indicated that he is not going to follow Russia's "shock therapy" approach and he introduced his "own model." President Adayev, of Kazakhstan, for example, declared that the Malaysian economic policy "is a good example to follow." It is hoped that because the CA nations are quite rich in natural resources they will not have to pay a high social price for implementing such reforms.

Chapter Two

THE ANDIJON EVENT

No government and no security arrangements are ever secure from a sudden change brought about by a particular event in a nation's life. The 9/11 event has caused a sea change in mood that Americans have not experienced since Pearl Harbor. The events in a London subway and aboard a London bus in July 2005 dramatically changed England from its historical role as the world's most popular haven for exiles, to a nation ready to deport any person whom the authorities deem a present or future danger to national security. In Andijon, Uzbekistan just such an epoch-making event made a dramatic change in the relations between the U.S. and the nations of Central Asia. Prior to the event the United States presence in Central Asia was so secure that we maintained a number of large military bases there, and enjoyed the prospect of a growing friendship on the part of huge numbers of Central Asian Muslims. Russia and China, sitting right on CA's borders could only be envious of our special relationship in the region. That all changed, almost overnight because of one event lasting less than 72 hours. The event took place in May 2005 and, by July America's relationship with all five Central Asian nations took a steep tumble and was in total disarray. Our presence on their land was no longer welcome. It is absolutely critical to understand the reasons behind this sudden loss of influence, especially because the CA nations are natural allies in the war against Islamic terrorism. The Andijon event and American reaction to it may just be a decisive turning point in our ability to control the international terrorism that is, one could reasonably argue, the greatest threat to our homeland since the Founding Fathers put pen to the pages of Independence. Ironically, a NATO Advanced Research Workshop on Global Security Challenges in Central Asia entitled "Impact of Aggressive Religious Extremism and Terrorism on Central Asian States" was scheduled to take place in Tashkent May 26-28, 2005. As soon as word of the event was received the NATO Council made a decision to postpone the meeting 'indefinitely.'

The Andjion Event

In the late evening hours of May 12 and the early morning hours of May 13, 2005, in Andijon there took place a bloody incident that sent chills and tremors throughout the world, and resulted in hurried discussions in world capitals. It was an event that overshadowed the usual diplomatic and economic discussions that occupy policy makers. The boldness of the government in the event was a surprise, but perhaps it should not have been. Uzbekistan and its CA neighbors are a great landmass that has been sleeping for centuries. For more than one hundred years an outside power has been telling them what to do, how to think and what policies they should adopt. And now, suddenly and powerfully they are asserting their own wishes and desires. Andijon is not an obscure sleepy hamlet sitting on the side of a mountain. It is a busy industrial center, the home of a number of joint ventures with foreign companies, including an Uz DaeWoo (Japanese) auto assembly plant.

Even more importantly, Central Asia is not an ordinary place. It is fast becoming the staging area, a new battleground for economic wealth and political domination. Central Asia, and more specifically, Uzbekistan, where this terrible event occurred, may well be the key to winning or losing the batter against Islamic terrorism. The action of the perpetrators and the immediate and powerful reaction of that night has become both an omen of the future and a measure by which every nation's reaction can be interpreted in terms of the mind and heart of that nation.

A Night of Terror

In the dark of night, around, midnight, the residents of Andijon awakened to the chilling sounds of shrill voices piercing the night air with shouting and the firing of automatic weapons. Peering out their windows and from balconies, they saw armed men droving along Andijon's winding streets, heading directly for the local prison in a cavalcade of 15-20 cars[3], containing perhaps 50 armed men.[4] The men drove up to the prison, exited their cars, spread out in what appeared to be a pre-planned formation and began firing in the direction of the prison. Local inhabitants came out onto their balconies and called to each other in confusion. A few men gathered in the street to see what was causing this turmoil. Members of the local mahalle committee (neighborhood watch) told the men to stay calm and go back inside their homes. That seemed to indicate that the insurgents had local help.

Other residents stood on balconies in their night clothing, looking out at the dark, wondering what could be disturbing their peaceful enclave. They shouted at their curious children tumbling from their beds in excitement and fear to return to their beds. Men and women called to each other asking what was happening. Confusion and a growing fear filled the night air. And then, as if appearing through a mist, a large army truck ripped through the city streets, past the homes, heading straight for the prison gate and, without hesitation, rammed the gate, scattering shattered wood and metal fragments along its path. The flimsy metal gate was easy to penetrate and was not backed up by anything else to prevent a forced entry, such as cement barriers.

For the insurgents, the task was easy. From both eyewitness accounts and the evidence of bullet-riddled walls it is clear that a fierce gun battle took place. At the same time the insurgents attempted to overcome two army barracks, one containing about 300 troops and another 100 troops. They were repulsed but they did manage to overcome a police patrol post, making off with a variety of weapons and ammunition. The insurgents entered the jail, broke into the cells and began releasing about 500 prisoners. Three prison guards were killed and a number of others wounded. There were another 200 more in a separate building, but since they were not released it is assumed that the insurgents did not know of their presence. Some of the prisoners who tried to hide were killed on the spot. The insurgents then gathered the prisoners at the refectory and distributed arms to some of them, perhaps to fellow-members of their fundamentalist religious group.

The release of the prisoners, both male and female, the insurgents' goal, took place very quickly amid the sounds of gunfire emitting from the prison walls. The female prisoners could be seen pouring out of the prison shouting "freedom," and disappearing into the dark night as they raced behind the prison compound. The male prisoners roamed the streets, and the night air was filled with the shouts of 'Allah Akbar.' To the horror of those residents watching from their balconies, an unlucky threesome driving by, unaware of what was taking place, were shot dead. Some onlookers described the unfolding scene as the equivalent of watching a movie. The residents could hear the armed men shouting and talking among themselves. The residents identified their accents as a mixed nationality group comprising Andijons, and men from Tashkent and Bukhara[5]. Some residents reported that the gunmen were speaking Russian, but poorly, perhaps a ploy to confuse the authorities. In all, about 500 prisoners were released. Three prison guards lost their lives and a few others were wounded. Finally, the prisoners were forced into a long march to the National Security Service building in downtown Andijon.

A few prisoners on whose behalf the raid was made were members of the Akromiya fundamentalist Islamic group, which began its missionary work in Uzbekistan in the 1990s. Their missionary activity was a bit unusual but effective. They opened small shops and hired young people to work in those shops, on the condition that they would attend religious lectures after work. To a young man without a job, living in poverty, this was an attractive proposition. Some of the businessmen, 23 of them, who hired the youths, had been imprisoned for using the lure of a job in exchange for a "course" in terrorist activity. For four months, protestors had paraded before the courthouse demanding that they be released, so emotions and tensions were high. Another undetermined number of their supporters had also been arrested for protesting outside the courthouse, and were in the same jail.

The release of all of them was the objective of the prison raid. After marching the prisoners to the town square, the armed men occupied some the buildings. The stories of what happened from here on in differ, sometimes dramatically. The local movie theater was set afire. The insurgents engaged in a rather senseless, almost childish shooting spree at empty autos, then set them afire. Some of the released prisoners were used as human shields, as their captors continued their acts of destruction. In spite of all of this action, by 8 am, workers from the countryside, unaware of what had happened during the night, reported to work and, as they entered their workplaces, they were taken hostage. Local soldiers who rushed to the scene were also taken hostage and some were murdered and their bodies mutilated.

Finally, troops from Tashkent arrived but cautiously stayed off in the distance, surveying the area, deciding what should be their next move. In a bizarre incident, some of the insurgents ranted against the government, pointed to all the dead bodies, and accused the government of the murder of innocent civilians. President Karimov arrived and negotiations began. Observers noted that, on the part of the insurgents, there was none of the usual chanting of religious or political slogans, just a barrage of mostly incoherent complaints and demands. The authorities, in an attempt to avoid further bloodshed, offered them safe passage to the Kyrgyz border. About 5 pm an announcement was made that the buildings were to be stormed and residents were advised to leave the area.

After the troops stormed and entered the buildings, it was clear that many of the insurgents had quietly slipped away; some of them probably joined the crowd of onlookers undetected. Those who remained put up strong resistance, and an exchange of gunfire erupted. In the end, about one hundred insurgents were captured and a large quantity of firearms seized. The freed prisoners voluntarily returned to the prison, and the remaining insurgents disappeared. A group of Uzbek refugees attempting to cross into Kyrgyzstan reported that many young men bearing arms, but acting peacefully, joined them.

Estimating the death toll is not easy. Some Human Rights organizations, privy to estimates given by a number of sources would put the death rate at about 1,000. They claim that the government has purposely hidden this information from the people on the grounds that it would give far more credibility to the potential insurgency power, perhaps frightening many to cooperate with it. Rumors spread that the government had secretly buried hundreds. But the estimate offered by religious leaders is consistent with that of the government. If this is so, then perhaps as many as 300 people were killed during this operation and 250 wounded. One woman later told the BBC that suddenly heavy armored vehicles rumbled into the city square, and at least one helicopter appeared overhead. Then, she said, "Fire rained down on the crowd, with a lot of people killed instantly where they stood. The military began firing. The crowd lay on the ground and pandemonium broke out."

World Reaction
Within a very short time, the European Union foreign ministers, 25 in number, issued a statement threatening to reconsider their ties with Uzbekistan unless the Uzbek government permitted an independent investigation of the incident no later than June 31 2005, just a few weeks later. They also demanded that a European Union human rights official visit Uzbekistan to make an assessment of the situation. President Islam Karimov angrily turned down the EU request on both counts. The EU responded quickly. "The Council urges the Uzbek authorities to reconsider their position by the end of June 2005," and cautioned that the EU would "keep under review the case for a partial suspension of cooperation mechanisms between the EU and Uzbekistan". They made it clear that they might temporally cut diplomatic ties or even impose a travel ban for government officials. United States officials sent cautionary notes to Tashkent. Ironically, the two major units employed to crush the insurgents in Andijon, were trained in Louisiana in 2004. The members of the Uzbek special counter-terrorist units, the "Bars", were trained in the States, and officials from Uzbek security have received conflict management and tactical command instructions in New Mexico in 2003.

Karimov Responds
Equally tough rhetoric emanated from Tashkent. The Tashkent Haqiqati newspaper editorialized that the United States, looking down on Uzbekistan with an "evil eye," was simply interested in exploiting its natural resources. The newspaper also

suspected that "their real plans are becoming inextricably inter-woven with the evil intentions of religious fanatics." They ex-panded their charges by hinting that the Americans were in col-lusion with their neighbor, Kyrgyzstan, because more than one thousand of their citizens sought asylum there. It also reiterated the long-standing determination on the part of the government never to allow religious radicalism to establish a "medieval Ca-liphate." The editor explained that the government's quick action during the event prevented a much wider disaster: "the fatalities would have been 10 or 100 times higher."

The paper also came down heavy on the BBC, which had been a much respected news service in Uzbek, accusing it of bla-tant lies in their reports. Anger was also vented over western me-dia reports about the likelihood of a "green revolution", referring to the color green as a symbol of Islam, swamping Uzbekistan and the rest of the region. A contrary assessment was given by the former editor in chief of Izvestia, Vitaly Tretiakov, who made his own visit to the area. His conclusion was that "there were no shots at all against the peaceful demonstrators. 95% of the accu-sations against the Uzbek government were absurd and ground-less." His argument harked back to comments Uzbek President Islam Karimov made on May 25, 2005. In an interview that would set the tone for much of the official Uzbek response to Western criticisms of his handling of unrest in Andijon, Karimov angrily rejected calls for an independent international investiga-tion. The president asked rhetorically, "Is Uzbekistan an inde-pendent, sovereign state?" He then retorted, "They want us to be obedient to them, making us feel like we're the accused." Kari-mov went on to ask, "Why should we have to give you answers as though we're the accused?" He closed with a phrase that would later provide the title for a book expounding the presi-dent's views on Uzbekistan's place in a post-Andijon world: "The Uzbek people will never be dependent on anyone."

Karimov's remarks on May 25 came on the eve of a visit to China, which feted him even as he was trading barbs with West-ern nations over Andijon. In a lengthy article in Toronto's "The Globe and Mail" on March 4, 2006, Geoffrey York noted that Beijing's "red-carpet welcome to Uzbekistan strongman Islam Karimov" and the $600 million oil deal Karimov signed on his post-Andijon trip to China are part of a Chinese approach to foreign relations based on the idea that "the autocracies of the developing world can stand up to Washington's pressure by forming their own profitable alliances and trade." York cited financially tinged ties between China and Sudan, North Korea, Zimbabwe, and Iran as other examples of Beijing's "model of moral neutrality."

Karimov hinted at a few boycotts of his own. Uzbekistan, a Caspian Sea basin nation lies in an area of potential gas and oil production. Both Bermuda and Switzerland receive oil and gas supplies from Kazakhstan. Zbigniew Brzezinski had long urged that the U.S. develop close relations with the Ukraine, Azerbaijan and Uzbekistan. "The hydrocarbons of the Caspian Sea are an instrument to....eliminate all possibilities of post-Soviet imperial reintegration". In other words, economically viable Caspian Sea nations would lessen the chances of a spreading Russian influence in the region. But, Washington was then and remains tone deaf to the obvious sounds coming from Central Asia.

Russian President Vladimir Putin, who can't believe his good fortune as a result of America's debacle diplomacy with Central Asia, seized on the theme of sovereign strength and outside interference in his state-of-the-nation address on May 10, 2006. According to the official English transcript published on the Kremlin's website (http://www.kremlin.ru/eng), Putin argued, "We must be able to respond to attempts from any quarters to put foreign policy pressure on Russia, including with the aim of strengthening one's own position at our expense. We also need to make clear that the stronger our armed forces are, the lesser the temptation for anyone to put such pressure on us, no matter under what pretext this is done." Obviously it was no coincidence that on May 12th, 2006 Putin met in Sochi with Karimov, who is quickly becoming Putin's soul mate. A la Bush, it appears that they looked into each others' eyes and saw beautiful souls, men who could trust each other. Karimov could not have been more delighted than to confide to journalists while the meeting was in progress that "Russia has defended and will defend its interest without looking over its shoulder at anyone or anything. This gives us confidence."

The post-Cold War era, which began with high hopes of a better world, has, in fact, become more complicated. "Non-interference" now means what it always did: "let me rule the way I want and I will let you rule the way you want." Nothing has changed. It should also be noted, however, that since the Uzbek crackdown on the perpetrators of the prison break-in very little has been heard from the Hizb ut-Tahrir (HT), a Wahhabi mirror image terrorist organization. Some observers say that the group was stunned at the ferocity of the counter attack, and pulled back. And, no doubt, when Karimov sent in his troops against those who broke into the prison, he had in mind a few historical events that buttressed his heavy-handed response.

Andijon had seen Muslim extremism long before 2005. The first Muslim riots in Andijon took place in 1898 against the Czar's army, and Andijon has a history of Muslim persecution of Armenians and Jews, and HT uses this long-standing prejudice to attack Karimov. It makes virulent campaigns against the Uzbek government, the United States and the Jewish community, labeling Karimov as a "Jewish stooge ". Most of the Jewish New Yorkers from Bukhara, who emigrated at the beginning of the 90s, strongly support Karimov. Rafael Nektalov, editor in chief of the Bukharan Times, agrees and adds that Uzbek Jews, 12,000 of them, appreciate the totally non-racist view they have experienced, especially in an area where race and clan are glorified. Even Muslims there seem to find occasion to clash with fellow Muslims. In the late 1980s, Turkish Meskhets were massacred in the city. Violent demonstrations are more common in Andijon than in most parts of the country. Those who defend Karimov point out that the religious group responsible for the prison break-in is reflective of the alliance between Islamist radicals and the Ferghana valley "Mafia types." The Valley is brimming with separatists who would like to use the enormous amounts of money they collect in the drug trade to set up their own little kingdom.

Andijon, an old Source of Trouble

A quick review of the events of the night of May 13 may not excuse Karimov's knee-jerk reaction to the Andijon event, but it may explain why, given Andijon's history, the president acted forcefully. Post-event analysis shows that as many as one hundred heavily armed men, carrying automatic and telescopic sight rifles and Makarov handguns assaulted the prison and killed 52 prison officers. This was followed up by an attack on the weapons arsenal of a local Russian military base where 159 Kalashnikov rifles and 300 fragmentation grenades were stolen. There were reports that the insurgents had in their possession large mounts of cash. One carried $30,000. This report may have been fabricated, but one thing is certain, and that is, in order to carry out such a large operation, which included armored personnel carriers, an awful lot of money had to come from somewhere to fund it.

The drugs from Afghanistan pass through Kyrgyzstan by way of Uzbekistan's Ferghana valley and through Andijon on its way to Tashkent. The troubled Chinese oil-rich Xing Kiang region which lies only 200 km away is plagued with Wahhabi-type Islamic fundamentalists. They are natural allies of the men who made the assault on the prison. Beijing is very disturbed that much of its troubles emanate from religious fundamentalists based in the Andijon area of Uzbekistan. So the further we explore, the thicker the plot of the Andijon story. In considering what should be the West's position vis-à-vis Uzbekistan we need to add these facts into the political and diplomatic equation. We need to do this and do it soon because we have a lot to learn from the CA experience with Islamic terrorism. They are determined to stamp it out before it engulfs the entire region, drawing both Russia and China, who both suffer from the same elements, into the fray. Most international chess games contain enough inner contradictions for no one nation to be singled out. What we do know is that when terrorism succeeds in one nation it increases exponentially everywhere.

All the nations neighboring Uzbekistan, including Afghanistan, have agreed that Islamic militants were behind the Andijon uprising. In fact, on June 2, 2005, the U.S. issued a travel advisory on Uzbekistan. Family members and non-essential staff of the American Embassy in Tashkent were permitted to leave for security reasons. Diplomatic decency would dictate that Washington hold fire at a time when sensitive bilateral negotiations were going on with Tashkent over American military's access to the Karshi-Khanabad airbase in Uzbekistan. There are times when Foggy Bottom is just that.

The events in Andijon have further destabilized the Ferghana Valley, a hotbed of Wahhabism and simmering nationality questions. It accounts for a quarter of the entire region's population and is shared uneasily between Uzbekistan, Kyrgyzstan and Tajikistan. If the Uzbek Government is overthrown and passes power to an Uzbek oligarch living in exile in the U.S. we would have another Iraq in the making. I hope that this is not the State Department's game plan. But it does appear that U.S. policy is repeating the same mistake it made in the 1990s with the Taliban, i.e. attempting to replace existing governments. Central Asian social structures and their political forms may appear archaic, but if we interfere with Central Asian politics then we will introduce to Central Asia the same political fragmentation and anarchy as is occurring in Iraq today. And, there are already disturbing signs that for lack of substantive support Kyrgyzstan is tottering on the edge of anarchy, in spite of Russian efforts to be a peacemaker between the northern and southern clan interests.

The Tulip Revolution[6] has turned out to be anything but peaceful, and the Central Asian commentators, rightly or wrongly, place the blame on United States connivance. When will we learn? While we receive world-wide condemnation for Guantanamo prison, we wring our hands at every news report of an arrest in Uzbekistan. On April 19, 2006 Radio Free Europe announced that a Tashkent court had found eight Uzbek men guilty of illegal religious activity. Three were sentenced to two to three years in a labor camp. The other five were sentenced to milder corrective labor measures and released. Andrea Berg, who attended the trial on behalf of the international watchdog group Human Rights Watch, said the judge dismissed the men's claims of maltreatment as an attempt to avoid responsibility "for their illegal activities." The men were arrested in December on charges of Wahhabism and membership of Hizb ut-Tahrir, a banned religious group.

Before we criticize that we can reflect on the fact that we have many foreign nationals in Guantanamo who have been there a long time without trial and without access to legal assistance. By our own standards-in-practice, the Uzbeks are certainly matching or bettering our treatment of prisoners, not just in Guantanamo, but have we forgotten Ghraib prison in Baghdad, and the many detainees we have tucked away in other countries so that we can avoid using the American justice system? And do we not practice under international agreements the legal process of extradition? On August 29, 2006 Kyrgyzstan justified its extradition of four Uzbek refugees and one asylum seeker to Uzbekistan. Prosecutor-General Kambaraly Kongantiev said they are all guilty of taking part in the Andijon unrest, which Uzbekistan says led to the deaths of 187 people. He described Zhahongir Maqsudov, Yaqub Toshboev, Odilzhon Rahimov, Rasulzhon Pirmatov, and Fayoz Tojihalilov as "criminals and killers." The five were sent back to Uzbekistan on August 9 amid widespread international criticism. Isn't that extradition? We practice it all the time.

Central Asians have always listened attentively and obediently to the clan leadership, so listening to central authority and being obedient to it is nothing new, nothing that violates rights they never had in the first place. The kind of justice we practice at home is a benefit of federalism, but federalism presupposes modern communication, respect, dealing with each other as equals. This they never had, but they are getting a taste of it now and, if we assist them before an ersatz Islam convinces them that they would be better off being part of a world-wide, mullah-led Caliphate, their taste and appetite for democracy will blossom. Sitting back at our luxurious sidelines and commenting on their actions as if we were watching a gladiatorial fight in Roman times does not help generate democracy in Central Asia. We need their help right now, and if we are not wise and judicious they will fail, and if they do we lose, and lose badly because the terrorists together with nations who already wish us harm will control five-plus full fledged governments and have unlimited power and capacity to make America a war-ravaged land. The matter is urgent.

K. Gajendra Singh, an advisor to the Indian government, is saddened by the unenlightened policies of the United States, Saudi Arabia and Pakistan, claiming that they are (except for Saudi Arabia) unwittingly aiding and abetting the cause of Wahhabism in CA. We did that in Afghanistan and we are doing it again. B. Rahman, a writer for Asia Times, member of India's cabinet and currently director, Institute for Topical Studies, has a few observations. He worries about in the very serious threat of Wahhabism around the world. He feels that Bangladesh also is not taking the terrorist problem seriously. Rahman points out that Bangladesh authorities should monitor far more closely than they now do, the large number of Saudi-funded madrasas that have sprung up to spread Wahhabism among the Muslims of Bangladesh and Southeast Asia.

What is happening in Central Asia today is of great importance to the West in its own struggle with religious extremism, so it behooves us to employ a lot of study and wisdom before launching out to attack the leadership of the region. Perhaps it would be valid to speculate on what, given the present heightened fear of violence in both Britain and the United States, might be the reaction of these governments to an Andijon-like event in their homelands.

Chapter Three

WAHHABISM IN AMERICA

Freedom House's[7] Center for Religious Freedom's publication, "Saudi Publications on Hate Ideology Fill American Mosque," gives frightening evidence of Wahhabi influence among American Muslims in the United States. In one mosque a textbook for 8th grade students explains why Jews and Christians were cursed by Allah. Quoting Surat Al-Maida, Verse 60, the lesson explains that Jews and Christians have sinned by accepting polytheism and therefore incurred Allah's wrath. "To punish them, Allah has turned them into apes and pigs." This kind of literature is being spread around the United States by one of our allies!! Wahhabism's intimate relationship with the Saudi government presents American officials with a unique dilemma, in that it is the only foreign government that directly uses religion as a cover for its political activities in the U.S.[8] One such mosque is located three miles from where the World Trade Center once stood. The researchers who collated all this material were American Muslims. They collected several hundred documents, dating back over the last 40 years. The documents are mostly in Arabic, so Freedom House arranged for two translators to work on them. The researchers visited 15 prominent mosques in their quest for literature.

It is clear the Wahhabi propaganda is not as effective as they would wish because, while the publications urge that Muslims should not take citizenship here in the United States, millions of Muslims have eagerly sought citizenship. However, dangerous elements can and do evolve from small disciplined groups and, although the documents may not have dramatic and apocalyptic impact on American Muslims, there is no doubt that they do sow seeds of discontent and feelings of isolation among a significant minority. After all, the documents create a dualistic worldview. First, that the universe of the believer and the "infidel" are completely irreconcilable and, secondly, that when Muslims are in the land of the infidel they must behave as if they're behind enemy lines. They must not befriend, help, support, hire or work for, or imitate infidels. They must get the education or the money that they came here for and use it for jihad or convert others to Islam and then get out.

Those Muslims who refuse to adopt such attitudes and actions are considered apostates and the penalty for apostasy in the kingdom of Saudi Arabia can be death. The documents instill contempt for America, even while enjoying its freedoms and largesse. Those documents analyzed in the study were all connected to the Saudi government and printed, for the most part, in Saudi Arabia. The cultural, religious, education ministries, official libraries and printing houses of the government, publish them.

Muslim newcomers to America are told that Wahhabism is the only true religion. A Freedom House report says, "In a book published by the Saudi Ministry of Islamic Affairs, and collected from the Al Farouq Mosque in Brooklyn, Saudi Arabia's official religious leader, the late Bin Baz, authorizes Muslims to kill converts to Islam who violate sexual mores on adultery and homosexuality." Another document insisted that Muslims who convert to another religion "should be killed because they have denied the Koran." Still another: "If a person says I believe in Allah alone and confirms the truth of everything from Mohammed, except in his forbidding fornication, he becomes a disbeliever. For that, it would be lawful for Muslims to spill his blood and to take his money." Perhaps there is no law in America to prevent such literature from being distributed, but surely there ought to be.

Saudi spokesmen are quick, publicly, to condemn "extremism and hateful expression among people anywhere in the world," while at the same moment pouring such literature into every niche and corner of the United States. In old-fashioned morality, that used to be called hypocrisy. The Saudi textbooks and documents spread throughout American mosques preach a hatred for Jews, treat the forged Protocols of the Elders of Zion as historical fact, and avow that the Muslim's duty is to eliminate the state of Israel.

Muslims who promote tolerance are condemned as infidels. A fatwa in one pamphlet criticizes a European Muslim preacher who teaches that it is not right to condemn Jews and Christians as infidels. "He who casts doubts about their infidelity leaves no doubt about his." Since, under Saudi law, "apostates" from Islam can be sentenced to death, this is an implied death threat against the tolerant Muslim imam, as well as an incitement to promote vigilante "justice." This ideology teaches that if Muslims live in a Western nation, that nation, its peoples and ruler is the enemy. Common sense would tell us that such folks should not receive citizenship or permission to live in the United States but, on this subject, common sense in our government bureaucracy is difficult to find.

Of course, Saudi Arabia, like any nation, is a complex society—what is said of one part cannot necessarily be applied to every part, but certainly the unholy alliance of the House of Saud and the religious extremism of Wahhabism is something that must be discussed publicly in the United States since we are their prime target of opportunity. Singapore's main newspaper[9] published an interview with Sheik Mohammed Hisham Kabbani, the Lebanese-American chairman of the Islamic Supreme Council of America, based in Washington, DC: Back in 1990, arriving for his first Friday prayers in an American mosque in Jersey City, he was shocked to hear Wahhabism being preached. "What I heard there, I had never heard in my native Lebanon. I asked myself: Is Wahhabism active in America? So I started my research. Whichever mosque I went to, it was Wahhabi, Wahhabi, Wahhabi, Wahhabi."

Wahhabi got here First

Interestingly enough, it was the lack of an Islamic establishment in the U. S. that has given the Wahhabi such a dominant position in American Islamic centers. They got here first, so to speak, in the 1980s. So, unlike the Muslim communities in Europe whose origins go back generations, the Wahhabi had

America all to themselves, and, from their headquarters, the Council on American Islamic Relations, they have taken full advantage of their precedence. There was an almost total lack of traditional Islamic scholars in this country to offset, comment on, and disagree with the dark and violent messages coming out of the Wahhabi-infested American mosques. Ironically, while not identifying themselves as Wahhabi, they have managed to influence American Western foreign policy favorably toward the Saudi regime, while at the same time spreading anti-American and anti-Western and anti-moderate Islam messages from the freedom of press guarantees of the United States. They are rejoicing at their unique Islamic position in the heart of the richest and most powerful nation in the world. They can hardly believer their good fortune. They manage to raise funds, while at the same time calling openly for the destruction of both moderate Islam and the U. S. government. The American leaders of the minority moderate Islamic community claim that most Muslim chaplaincies in prisons, the military, and colleges are Wahhabi.

Saudi Funds Promote Wahhabism

Reza F. Safa, author of Inside Islam, estimates that since 1973, the Saudi government has spent $87 billion to promote Wahhabism in the United States, Africa, Southeast Asia and Europe. Interestingly enough the United States is the only nation in the world where the Islamic religious establishment is dominated by the Wahhabi. The Saudis have financed Islamic Centers in Los Angeles; San Francisco; Fresno; Chicago; New York; Washington; Tucson; Raleigh, N.C. and Toledo, Ohio as well as in Austria, Great Britain, France, Spain, Italy, Germany, Russia, Turkey, and even in some Muslim countries such as Morocco, Indonesia, Malaysia and Djibuti. Saudi largess usually comes with strings attached, i.e., the preaching of Islam a la Wahhabism. In 2002, The Center for Monitoring the Impact of Peace (CMIP) did a survey of Saudi Arabian (Wahhabi) textbooks. The Report analyzes 93 school textbooks taught in grades 1-10. In these Wahhabi texts, Islam is presented as the only true religion while all other religions are said to be false. Islam leads its followers to Paradise; they read all other religions send their believers to Hell. The books also make the point that the West is the source of all the misfortunes of the Muslim world, from the evil of democracy to Christian missionaries, to humanitarian and medical aid, all of which is subversive to Arabic religion and culture. The Jews are also blamed for all the evils of history, including both World Wars and the French and Bolshevik revolutions. In Wahhabi textbooks, Israel is not described as an independent nation and its name cannot be found on any textbook map. The Saudi textbooks, even grammar books, praise Jihad, and martyrdom. An estimated 30,000 Muslim children attend Wahhabi day schools in America.

An Egyptian-American newspaper publisher, Seif Ashmawi, writes "Radical Islamic groups have now taken over leadership of the 'mainstream' Islamic institutions in the United States and anyone who pretends otherwise is deliberately engaging in self-deception." Ashmawi probably knew that the Saudis have funded more than 80 percent of the Wahhabi-influenced mosques built in the United States within the last 20 years. Outside the mosque, it is also known that the majority of Muslim Student Associations at U.S. colleges are dominated by Islamic and anti-American thinking and planning.

Susan Katz Keating, writing in *FrontPage* Magazine quotes some textbook passages, as: "Muslims will fight and kill Jews. The cowardly Jews will seek refuge behind trees" that will then shout out, "Oh Muslim, Oh servant of God, here is a Jew hiding behind me. Come here and kill him." Students are taught "it is better to shun and even to dislike Christians, Jews and Shiite Muslims" and it is fine to harm or steal from a non-Muslim. In an article appearing in a June 2002 article in the Washington Times, Cal Thomas wrote that Saudi money supplied to the National Islamic Prison Foundation is used to convert inmates not only to Wahhabism, but also to its anti-Americanism. A *Wall Street Journal* article, datelined February 5, 2003 agrees that Wahhabism is impacting on the prison population. It quoted a New York-based Wahhabi imam, Warith Deen Umar, who helped run New York's growing Islamic prison program by recruiting and training dozens of chaplains and ministering to thousands of inmates himself, as saying: "The 9/11 hijackers should be honored as martyrs. The U.S. risks further terrorism attacks because it oppresses Muslims around the world. Without justice, there will be warfare, and it can come to this country too."

The October 20, 2002 issue of the New York Times quoted Faheem Shuaibe, imam at a large black mosque in Oakland, Calif., as saying that more than 200 African-American imams have been trained so far in Saudi Arabia. He added that: "This was a very deliberate recruitment process by the Saudis - trying to find black Muslims who had a real potential for Islamic learning and also for submission to their agenda. They taught Islam with the intent to expand their influence." The same is true of their attempts to convert non-blacks. The New York Times stresses that the brand of Islam being taught and exported is Wahhabism. The American Wahhabi are dreaming big dreams, including replacing the American Constitution with the Koran. The presence of Wahhabism in America is a serious threat to our security and to our way of life. Our government officials need to face up to the fact that Wahhabism's sponsor, the Saudi religious establishment, is the principal ideological and financial sponsor of Islamic extremism worldwide. According to a Council on Foreign Relations Report, Saudi Arabia is the largest source of financing for al-Qaeda. The report blamed both the U.S. and Saudi governments for not being tough enough.

Karen Hughes

One of President Bush's closest confidantes, Karen Hughes, on September 2nd, 2005 addressed the annual conference of the Islamic Society of North America, an organization whose primary purpose is the propagation of Saudi-sponsored Wahhabi Islam in the United States, a group which has praised suicide bombers, and whose president on his website continues to lavish praise on Osama bin Laden. A Senate committee asked the tax authorities for ISNA's paperwork on January 14, 2004, as part of its investigation into groups that "finance terrorism and perpetuate violence." This was the first major public address in Karen Hughes' role spearheading outreach to the Muslim world. Asked whether the woman who was instrumental in Bush winning the White House knew the true nature of the group she spoke to in Chicago, State Department spokesman Noel Clay responded, "Karen Hughes has been briefed on the organization." Clay also stated that "They do not support terrorism."

But, in a January 2000 press release, ISNA declared, "In order to honor the Shaheeds and the Mujahideen of Chechnya, ISNA has decided to dedicate Shawwal 1, 1420, the day of Eid al Fitr as 'Solidarity with Chechnya Day' throughout North America." "Shaheeds" is the term used by jihadists for suicide bombers. An Administration that has declared war on terrorism honors its principal supporter in the United States at a Washington dinner! Ms. Hughes thanked the group for making a donation to Katrina victims.

The Islamic Society of North America is a spin-off from the Saudi-funded Muslim Students Association (MSA) of over 20 years ago. Not surprisingly, The Islamic Development Bank (IDB), a Saudi-dominated institution, donated 1.03 million Saudi riyals for the expansion and renovation of an ISNA elementary school in Ontario. A month earlier the Department of the Treasury invited ISNA "to be a part of the Treasury Department's standing advisory group on charities and the best practices developed by the Treasury Department to assist U.S.-based charities in reducing the likelihood that charitable funds will be diverted for violent ends." WTHR, an NBC affiliate in Indianapolis, on June 8, 2004 reported that ISNA had received a U.S. government subsidy; two grants, from the Faith Based Community Initiative totaling about $70,000 "to help train religious leaders on how to apply for federal money for social programs."

On April 13, 2004, an official of the Treasury Department, Juan Zarate, attended an ISNA event and in his opening remarks he said: "I have been fortunate enough to speak and work with ISNA in the past, and value our deepening relationship." So, a Saudi-funded organization that advocates jihad counsels the White House on U.S. domestic issues? How interesting. In August 2004, the *St. Louis Post-Dispatch* reported that the State Department assisted ISNA in planning a 10-person delegation to the Sudan for August of that year. In an article entitled, "Money Goes to Controversial Muslim Group," on September 15, 2005, Sherrie Gossett wrote for Accuracy in Media that the Bush administration had sent $50,000 to the Islamic Society of North America. Although he did not mention ISNA, Senator Charles E.

Grassley, republican, and Senator Max Baucus of Montana, Democrat, warned, in a letter to the IRS, dated December 23, 2003, that:" Many of these groups…enjoy tax exempt status…making it easier to hide and move their funds to other groups who threaten our national security. This support for the machinery of terrorism…violates the law and tax regulations." The $50,000 grant was made almost two years later! No one in this White House that proclaims itself as dedicated to searching out and destroying terrorists wherever they hide is listening. Remarkable.

Mohammed El-sanousi, director of community outreach and communications for ISNA, told Ms Gossett his organization received grants in 2003 and 2004 from the Substance Abuse and Mental Health Services Administration of the Department of Health and Human Services. The money did not save anyone from substance abuse or improve mental health, however. Instead, it went for "educational" purposes. "We used the grants to train Muslim community leaders in how to apply for grants to do social services," El-sanousi explained.

Saudi government agencies [10] have generously funded the spread of Wahhabism in the United States: $250,000, in 1999, from the official Saudi financial institution, the Islamic Development Bank in Jedyah, an official Saudi financial institution, for the purchase of land in Washington, D.C. A Wahhabi-owned building was to be constructed on that site. The same bank donated U.S. $295,000 to the Masjid Bilal Islamic Center, for the construction of the Bilal Islamic Primary and Secondary School in California, in 1999.[11] Hassan Akbar, an American Muslim presently charged with a fatal attack on his fellow soldiers in Kuwait during the Iraq intervention, was affiliated with this institution.

Four million dollars was given for the construction of a mosque in Los Angeles, named for Ibn Taymiyah, the forerunner and inspirer of Wahhabism.[12] Six million dollars was donated for a mosque in Cincinnati, Ohio. The same website reported (in 2000) "In the United States, the Kingdom has contributed to the establishment of the Islamic Center in Washington DC, the Omer Bin Al-Khattab Mosque in western Los Angeles, the Los Angeles Islamic Center, and the Fresno Mosque in California, the Islamic

Center in Denver, Colorado, the Islamic center in Harrison, New York City, and the Islamic Center in Northern Virginia."[13]

In an article entitled: Sowing seeds of hatred, written by Larry Cohler, Daily News staff writer, in 2003, he writes:

"Textbooks widely used in New York's Islamic schools contain passages that are blatantly anti-Semitic, condemning Jews as a people, repeating old canards about the Jews wanting to kill Christ and faking their Holy Scriptures to mock God." At the Muslim Center Elementary School on Geranium Ave. in Flushing, Queens, a textbook for grades 6 through 8 teaches that Jews "subscribe to a belief in racial superiority... Their religion even teaches them to call down curses upon the worship places of non-Jews."

The textbooks in question are widely cited by Islamic educators as among the most popular in use. They accuse Catholics of worshiping statues. Eugene Fisher, associate director for inter-religious affairs for the National Conference of Catholic Bishops in Washington, commented, "We don't worship statues. That's teaching their children misunderstandings about Christianity that will lead them to grow up thinking all that stuff in the Koran about idolaters refers to us, their neighbors." There are no reliable breakdowns on how many local schools use the six books reviewed by *Must Repent*.

Muslims who convert out of Islam, of course, are apostates too, and, under Saudi law, they can be put to death. An Urdu-language publication published by the Saudi Ministry of Religious Affairs and found at the American King Fahd Mosque, quotes Sheik Bin Uthaimin: "Our doctrine states that if you accept any religion other than Islam, like Judaism or Christianity, that are not acceptable, you become an unbeliever. If you do not repent, you are an apostate and you should be killed..."[14]

Religious Edicts for the Immigrant Muslim

In a pamphlet displayed at the Islamic Center of Washington DC, on 12/12/03, whose back cover carried greetings from the Saudi Government in Riyadh, the following question was posed and answered: Question: Is it permissible for a Muslim to become naturalized as an American Citizen, specifically, if he is a refugee with no country? Answer: It is forbidden for a Muslim to become a citizen of a country governed by infidels because this is a means of acquiescing to their infidelity...which makes it obligatory for every Muslim who lives in the land of polytheism, to immigrate back to the land of Islam.

In literature found at the King Fahd mosque in California, an elegant building of white marble etched with gold, adorned by a blue minaret that is named after its benefactor, the King of Saudi Arabia, the following selection was found: "Be dissociated from the infidels, hate them for their religion, leave them, never rely on them for support, do not admire them, and always oppose them in every way according to Islamic law."

Congressional Testimony

In testimony before the Senate Subcommittee on Terrorism, Technology and Homeland Security on Thursday, June 26, 2003, Stephen Schwartz, a journalist who directs the Islam and Democracy program at the Foundation for the Defense of Democracies, pointed out that, "The Muslim community only became a significant element in our country's life in the 1980s...The Wahhabi ideological structure in Saudi Arabia perceived this as an opportunity to fill a gap — to gain dominance over an Islamic community in the West with immense potential for political and social influence." The plan was to use the Muslim community in the U.S. to pressure the U.S. government and media in the formulation of policy favorable to Saudi Arabia, just as they have observed other large minorities doing in the regular give and take of American politics. A bit of recruitment was also not far from their mind.

Adam Gadahn, thought to be the "American jihadi" who appeared in a mask on a videotape just before the 2004 elections threatening that America's street would "run with blood," had converted to Islam and became radicalized after spending hours studying Islam with seven or eight other young men at the Islamic Society of Orange County in California. The mosque chairman is quoted telling the *Washington Post* that mosque leaders could not tell precisely what Gadhan and his group were reading, but that, "'They were very rigid, cruel in talking to people...' They criticized [the chair] for wearing Western clothes, for not wearing a beard, for trying to reach out to the local Jewish communities." And, seizing on the Chairman's nickname, Danny, they circulated fliers around the mosque calling him Danny the Jew.

Wahhabi-Saudi policy has always been simple: On the one hand, maintain a policy of alliance with Western military powers, especially the U.S., so that in case of any external emergency (Saddam, for example) there would always be a strong Western military backup sufficient to assure their continued control over the Arabian Peninsula. On the other hand, their money guarantees Wahhabi control over mosques, the appointment of imams, training of imams, content of preaching, and of hate literature distributed in mosques and mosque bookstores. Similar influence extends to Islamic elementary and secondary schools (academies), college campus activity, and the endowment of academic chairs and programs in Middle East studies. How much money, in total, is involved in this effort? Mary Jacoby and Graham Brink in the St. Petersburg Times write that there are in the U.S. Wahhabi supported mosques. If we assume a relatively low average expenditure of $5 million per mosque, we arrive at a sizeable figure. There is clearly a problem of Wahhabi/Saudi extremist influence in American Islam. While this ideological affinity between the Wahhabi and modern day radical Islam is real, it is also true that vast amounts of money available to the Saudis made Wahhabism the chief enabler and dominant influence of the Islamist phenomenon. It is time to face the problem and find ways to enable traditional, mainstream American Muslims to take back their communities, while at the same time employing law enforcement to interdict the growth of Wahhabism and its Saudi financial support. If we fail to do this, Wahhabi extremism will continue to endanger the world, Muslims and non-Muslims alike. Our airways and TV programs are now replete with stories from all around the world telling of a new terror cell discovered in yet another nation.

Remarkably, Saudi commentators, themselves, have observed the relationship between the large number of Saudis involved on September 11 and among the al-Qaeda prisoners in Guantanamo Bay, and the culture of religious rage and violence that is part of Saudi religious education. A study presented to a Saudi forum of 60 intellectuals, researchers, clerics and public figures, convened by then Saudi Crown Prince Abdullah in December 2003 as part of a "National Dialogue" series, found "grave defects" in the religious curricula of the state's boys' schools, particularly with regard to "others," that is, non-Muslims and non-Wahhabi Muslims. The Saudi researchers concluded that this approach "encourages violence toward others, and misguides the pupils into believing that in order to safeguard their own religion, they must violently repress and even physically eliminate the 'other,'" according to their study. The Saudi forum concluded with recommendations for reforming the religious curriculum.

The Saudi government is currently waging a multi-million dollar public relations campaign in the United States to offset the image created by the very literature they themselves place in American mosques. With the same dexterity with which they have always handled the United States, they also claim that textbook reform would have to evolve slowly over many years. They are in no hurry; there is no emergency. It is no wonder that government officials who have little more contact with Saudi officials than at meetings and cocktail parties are kept off balance. The spread of Islamic extremism, such as Wahhabism, is the most serious ideological challenge of our times. Senator Jon Kyle, chairman of the Judiciary Committee's Subcommittee on Terrorism, who held hearings on Wahhabism, said:

"A growing body of accepted evidence and expert research demonstrates that the Wahhabi ideology that dominates, finances, and animates many groups here in the United States, indeed is antithetical to the values of tolerance, individualism and freedom as we conceive these things."

And, from Freedom House documentation: "Our doctrine states that if you accept any religion other than Islam, like Judaism or Christianity, which are not acceptable, you become an unbeliever. If you do not repent, you are an apostate and you should be killed because you have denied the Koran."

The Saudis, in flooding American mosques with hate literature, are violating the religious freedom and tolerance provisions of Article 18 of the Universal Declaration of Human Rights. Freedom House endorsed the recommendation made by the U.S. Commission on International Religious Freedom for an official study of Saudi export of hate ideology around the world. Such a study should include the fact that American public libraries and schools rely on Wahhabi Islamic centers and institutions for their own acquisitions and course curriculum.

Some in Congress recommend that government should insist on the removal of these publications, and seek private or public funding to fill the need for educational materials in American mosques with textbooks and tracts that emphasize religious toleration and other basic human rights. There has been little or no action taken on this proposal so far. Here the question gets a bit sticky. There is, after all, the first Amendment and the rights guaranteed by it. On this question, former CIA Director, James Woolsey, gave his opinion.[15] Woolsey explains the difficulty in combating such literature under present law. He has pointed out that in the Smith Act case back in the 1950s after Congress declared the American Communist Party illegal, the Supreme Court intervened, saying that Congress does not have the power to do that. But Woolsey does not believe that this is a First Amendment issue. "If an imam wants to stand up in a mosque, or a preacher in a pulpit, or a Catholic father in a cathedral and say something hateful, he or she may do so in this country, and may it ever be so. What we have here, however, is a government sponsoring dissemination of this type of material. It's an interesting question."

Hiding True Identity

Both the Saudi government and its partner, the Wahhabi are careful not to identify their ideology as Wahhabism, because they well understand how much the Wahhabi are despised, even by a majority of Muslims, for their extremism. However, hiding behind their façade as the guardians of Islam, the Wahhabi dominate the American Islamic scene. Some parishioners abandon mosque services out of fear that such hate messages will severely compromise the moral rectitude of their children. Unfortunately, there is no established Islamic institution in the United States that has been able to effectively counteract this ideological onslaught. As a result, many young Muslims exposed to the hate literature not only become alienated from American life and thinking, but also from the thinking and practice of moderate Islam.

At a Freedom House Conference in February 2004, Ms. Mirahamadi said: "Wahhabism...is a crude manipulation of sacred texts that coerces Muslims...an ideology of power deliberately drafted to gain control...In contrast, mainstream Islam has been flourishing for hundreds of years in every corner of the world through a process of assimilation of local culture and tradition and peaceful coexistence with its non-Muslim neighbors". The contrived Islamic ideology of Wahhabism is a tragedy for such young persons, for they are destined for perpetual alienation, and the by-product of perpetual alienation in any society is the equivalent of non-participation in civic affairs and, worse, a determination to destroy that civil society.

Some argue that the Government should shut down groups who advocate the overthrow of the American government. But, as we stand today that .would violate First Amendment rights. Anyone, American or otherwise, can stand up in any public place or institution and call for the overthrow of the American government and be protected by the First Amendment. The question that could possibly arise in this area, as Mr. Woolsey pointed out, is the question of whether or not the public dissemination of material calling for the overthrow of the government constitutes an overt act. He certainly is concerned: Woolsey told Congress: "Wahhabi extremism today is the soil in which al-Qaeda and its sister terrorist organizations are growing."

CAIR

Of the many groups that we need to pay attention to, CAIR (Council on American-Islamic Relations) leads the list. It is financed by the government of Saudi Arabia. CAIR has close ties with terrorist groups.CAIR has not shied away from opposing the U.S. government in the war on terrorism, calling into question the U.S.A.-Patriot Act and homeland security measures. It has also denounced the federal government about often-unspecified offenses against Muslims.

Stephen Schwartz has written about CAIR many times. In November 2001, he wrote for the Weekly Standard that "CAIR is, without a doubt, the most obnoxious front for terrorist apologetics to be found in the United States. Since September 11, it has relentlessly sought, on the pretext of promoting 'sensitivity,' to dictate how Islam may be discussed in American media." It is so patently obvious that anyone who knows exactly how to work the plethora of freedoms allowed to Americans and visitors alike in this nation can get away with a lot.

A statement from the Center for Democracy and Human Rights in Saudi Arabia, here in Washington, D.C. could not have been more succinct: "anybody who thinks that a real religious reform in Saudi Arabia is going to happen is beating a dead donkey. It's not going to happen. The only legitimacy the Saudi government has is religion, Wahhabism."

Chapter Four

SAUDI AND WAHHABI FUNDING OF TERRORISM

According to a report submitted to the president of the U.N. Security Council in December 2002, "One must question the real ability and willingness of the [Saudi] Kingdom to exercise any control over the use of religious money in, and outside, the country."

Before September 11, the United Nations Security Council passed resolutions 1267, 1333, and 1363 calling for sanctions against Afghanistan, the Taliban, al-Qaeda, Osama bin Laden and their associates. Later, the UN adopted resolutions 1373 and 1390, agreeing that member states should prevent and suppress the financing of terrorist acts by freezing assets of any organization suspected of terrorist activities. The UN 1267 Sanctions Committee maintains a list of suspects. The effort, in the context of the huge amounts of money sent to terrorist groups by enabling State entities, is of little moment since such freezing of assets has netted less than $200 million so far. The efforts on the part of the UN provide a sort of idealistic cover for what really is UN member inaction, with a fair number of States having private agendas fund terrorist groups in order gain some goal of importance to the individual State. However, these UN Security Council resolutions have formed the legal basis for freezing terrorist assets, so any State wishing to do so can without legal problems.

In order to ensure that the standards of these new laws and regulations are meaningful, the U.S. has worked with the Financial Action Task Force on Money Laundering, which is the world's principal watchdog of regulatory standards and practices on anti-money laundering and counter-terrorist finance. The United States' efforts have enjoyed a measure of success. In October 2001 FATF convened an extraordinary plenary in Washington, DC and issued its Eight Special Recommendations on Terrorist Financing. FATF's "Special 8" represents the best of financial and regulatory standards and practices by which to measure success in creating effective counter-terrorist financing regimes, as all UN members are legally required to do under UN Security Council Resolution 1373. FATF also carries a measure of "teeth" via its Non-Cooperating Countries and Territories program. It is able to blacklist nations that are non-compliant with promises made to the UN. Nigeria and the Philippines, for example, in December 2002 and February 2003, strengthened their respective anti-money laundering laws to avoid imposition of FATF countermeasures. Some national authorities make formal banking channels more transparent and accountable, more accessible to the expatriate workers who otherwise are forced to rely on the alternative remittance sector. Of course, terrorists are ingenious in their ability to evade detection and to work their way around existing methods of transparency, so the task is always ongoing. Investigating terrorist financing is like the peeling of an onion in order to get to its core. Layer after layer after layer must be dealt with and, in the process, a lot of tears. Terrorists raise money from a very wide variety of sources, a world-wide network of legitimate businesses, cooperative banks(they look the other way when money pours in), charitable organizations, nongovernmental organizations, mosques, and, especially states that use terrorist services in order advance their own agendas, which range from the desire of Syria to be the dominant power in the Middle East to the Saudi monarchy which wishes to remain in power in spite of the changing political and economic climate there. For example, Government, individuals and charities in Saudi Arabia have been the most important source of funding terrorist organizations, with the hope that it will keep them from undermining the Saudi royal family. But, in order to avoid detection, states and individuals make use of a variety of financial institutions, one of which, for example, as an example is Hawala.

Hawala[16]

Hawala is a money-handling system originating in South Asia and used around the world to conduct legitimate business. It is also used for money laundering. It can operate outside traditional banking and financial companies, and, in the open, legitimately, even advertising their services. The key to its success is its ability to transfer money without actually moving it. Let us say, for example. That sender A from Canada wishes to send money to his mother in Iran. He goes to a bank and asks how much it will cost to purchase a bank draft for 5,000 dollars. He discovers that it is an expensive transaction so he hears about hawala and investigates. He meets a hawaladar (who handles the hawala transaction) and for a small commission takes care of everything, even ensuring next day delivery of the money. The system is based on trust and there is no public accounting of the transaction. Dubai is a well known center for hawala activity for it has a large number of Pakistani and Indian guest workers. Its main attraction for this activity is the fact that it permits unregulated finance.

Money laundering has three phases: placement, layering and integration.

—Placement: money from criminal activities is introduced into the financial system.

—Layering, the launderer makes the illicit funds appear to come from a legitimate source.

—Integration. The launderer invests in either legitimate business or in other illicit activities.

And then there is always the physical transportation of cash, a method frequently used by al-Qaeda. This is an important method of laundering money because physical form of precious metals and gemstones can later be converted into cash in one way or another. Nations who express the frustration that they really do not have the technical capabilities can receive assistance from the United States and learn techniques that are necessary tools in analyzing financial transfers. FATF also works with the United Nations Committee on Counter-Terrorism and the International Monetary Fund and the World Bank.

In spite of all this, many of America's closest allies complain that the United States does not provide enough detailed information, causing them to provide less than ideal cooperation at their end of the banking system. The U.S., on the other hand, has hinted that perhaps the E.U., for example, does not follow up on matters as well as they should, are not as cooperative as they could be. For example, while it prohibits fund-raising for the military wing of Hamas—Izzedine al-Qassam Brigades—it permits fund raising by Hamas supporters for so-called humanitarian purposes, and does not forbid Hezbollah from fundraising. Of course, the E.U. does have a built-in problem, the Schengen Area group consisting of thirteen of the fifteen EU member countries that abolished border controls among themselves. Free movement across international borders can be a bit problem in the days of Islamic terrorism.

The Schengen Area Group

In 1985. France, Germany, Belgium, Luxembourg and the Netherlands decided in to create a territory without internal borders called the "Schengen area". The name was taken from the name of the town in Luxembourg where the first agreements were signed. The group was expanded to 13 countries in 1997, following the signing of the Treaty of Amsterdam, which incorporated into EU law on 1 May 1999 the decisions taken since 1985 by Schengen group members. Common rules regarding visas, asylum rights and border checks allowed the free movement of persons within the signatory states. Because it was clear to the signatories that such freedom of movement invited dangers of terrorist activity and organized crime, they also set up coordination between the police, customs and the judiciary. To aid in this effort an information system known as the Schengen Information System (SIS) was set up to exchange data on people's identities and the tracking of stolen or lost property.. Twenty six nations now comprise the Schengen group, although several of those governments have not fully implemented their membership. It is anticipated that by mid—2007 this will have been accomplished. Nevertheless, in spite of this activity and expertise, the International Monetary Fund believes that the aggregate size of money laundering in the world could be somewhere between two and five percent of the world's gross domestic product, or about one trillion dollars a year.

The Saudi Factor in Funding Terrorism
 The lure of big money combined with a the stultifying ennui of a life of poverty, a life with no possibility of realizable goals and honorable ambitions, makes Islamic youth very vulnerable to the siren song coming from the Saudi Arabian treasury, a bottomless pit of money. Saudi money has been used for a long time now in developing Middle East terrorists groups. By their training, these terrorists are prepared to induce their own children, young men and young women, to strap themselves with explosives and cause great destruction and loss of life to innocent civilians, whether in Israel, or Indonesia, Malaysia, the Philippines, London or Madrid. The brain washing is so complete that the young develop a false consciousness that their self-destruction will somehow or other, at some time or other, lead to the economic and political freedoms they so desperately seek. In the meantime, they absorb a virulent and criminal mindset that becomes a significant part of their psyche and culture. The taking of life becomes routine, eroding in their consciousness the value of human life. Such is the self-destructive character of this syndrome that even the families of these young terrorists are sucked into the whirlpool, bizarrely making videos of their children as they prepare to commit suicide, and honoring them for the destruction of themselves and many innocents. The psychological fallout of such a culture of death will last for decades, long after the economic and political goals have failed or have been attained. We need only listen to their families' plaintive voices trying their best to be brave and accepting the "necessity" of such tactics in order to attain victory, to feel both sympathy for the misled and outrage at those who lure them with money and false promises. Saudi rulers, encouraged and abetted by the Wahhabi religious establishment, share massive responsibility. They are corrupting Muslim youth, allowing Saudi money to tempt them into a false jihad and spreading carnage in many parts of the world. Muslim youth become collateral damage in whatever it is that motivates a Royal family to be involved in such an enterprise. More than any other single item, Saud money has induced

many thousands of Islamic youth to become proxy fodder in a greater battle being waged for exactly what productive end is difficult to assess. There is an African saying: When two elephants fight, it's the grass that gets hurt. When that battle subsides, as all battles must, and whatever the outcome, the suicide bombers and the terrorist organizations will be cast aside and disowned by their supporters and enablers, for no one will want to be identified with all this destruction. History will record this, in the end, as little more than the cynical manipulation of the rich and powerful. These well-meaning ordinary young men and women, in the course of heeding the call to a false jihad, will have become mercenaries hired then fired once the goals of their manipulators have been fulfilled.

This is the saddest of the many sad aspects of international terrorism, and history will never absolve those who pick up the tab. How obscene it is for them to sit in luxurious splendor, sipping rich wines while the young and idealistic mercenaries they have hired so cheaply self-destruct. It is said that the love of money is the root of all evil. Money certainly has unleashed a wild and very dangerous movement that roams the international landscape and sows destruction wherever it passes. The enormity of the task facing the West in combating terrorism only begins to show its face as one follows the money trail. In Tirana, Albania, authorities are attempting to find the whereabouts of Yasin al Qadi, a Saudi businessman accused of laundering money for Osama bin Laden's terrorist activities. The Albanians, in October 2004, seized 22 apartment units he owns in Albania, and have frozen a number of his bank accounts. He left Albania in 2003. Al Qadi runs the Saudi-based Muwafaq Foundation, which U.S. officials believe moved millions of dollars from affluent Saudis to bin Laden. Albania was involved in the UN listing of Al Qadi as a terrorist. The United Nations requests of all nations that they freeze assets and enact an arms ban on anyone on their terrorist list. Ironically, al-Qaeda has sued the Albanian government for seizing his properties. The Washington Post described him as "a Saudi millionaire who ... continues to direct his international business empire from Switzerland and Saudi Arabia."

On July 31, 2003 there was congressional testimony that revealed, "In Afghanistan, Albania, Bosnia, and Chechnya, [there is] direct support for Islamic resistance by Saudi charities such as Khalid bin Mahfouz's and Yasin al Qadi's Muwafaq or Blessed Relief and Benevolence International, as well as providing direct support to Hamas for terrorist activities." The Palestinian organization, Hamas, has been a key focus of Saudi financing. President Bush announced the asset-freezing of five Hamas fundraisers: CBSP, ASP, Interpal, Palestinian Association in Austria, and the Sanabil Association for Relief and Development. Hamas high level operatives were also named: Sheikh Yassin, Imad al Alami, Usama Hamdan, Khalid Mishaal, Musa Abu Marzouk and Abdel Aziz Rantisi.

Saudi Arabian funding of terrorist organizations goes back to the 1950s and 1960s, giving assistance and sanctuary to, among others, Egypt's Muslim Brotherhood and allied groups in the Sudan, Jordan, and Syria. Not only did some members of these groups receive regular financial assistance but also some were invited to teach at various levels of Saudi educational institutions, including universities. When Egypt's president, Abdul Nasser, executed the Muslim Brotherhood leader, Sayyid Qutb, in 1966, his brother, Mohammed Qutb, was invited to lecture at King Abdul Aziz University in Jeddah. He was joined in the 1970s by one of the heads of the Muslim Brotherhood from Jordan, Abdullah Azzam, the godfather of Islamic terrorism.[17] In 1979, both taught Osama bin Laden, a student at the university. (See chapter on "Papal Succession of Islamic Terrorism"). Furthermore, there developed a connection between the Wahhabi and the Muslim Brotherhood refugees.

They were able to continue their activities in the early 1970s because they were recipients of Saudi government dollar largesse, at the urging of the Wahhabi. Abdullah Azzam headed the office of the Muslim World League in Peshawar, Pakistan, becoming bin Laden's mentor. He was joined by bin Laden, who with Saudi funding also set up the Mujahideen Services Center for Muslim volunteers who traveled to Peshawar to train for the struggle against the Soviet Army in Afghanistan. After Moscow's defeat in Afghanistan, Azzam's office became a headquarters for al-Qaeda, and bin Laden's brother-in-law, Mohammed Jamal Khalifa, took over the Philippine branch of the International Islamic Relief Organization (IIRO), a Muslim World League offshoot, and significant Saudi player in bankrolling terrorism. The twisted tale gets even more interesting as Mohammed Zawahiri, brother of bin Laden's assistant, and chief Qaeda strategist, Ayman Zawahiri, is hired by the Saudis to work for IIRO in Albania. The Muslim Brotherhood and the Wahhabi were now fully in business together organizing terrorist activities worldwide. In May 2003, in a series of articles appearing in the very influential Egyptian weekly, Ruz al-Yousef, a top editor, Wael al-Abrashi, reflected on all of this. He addresses the question of Wahhabism Saudi funding: "Wahhabism leads, as we have seen, to the birth of extremist, closed, and fanatical streams...The extremist religious groups[18] have moved from the stage of Takfir to the stage of 'annihilation and destruction', in accordance with the strategy of Al-Qaeda, which Saudi authorities must admit is a local Saudi organization that drew other organizations into it, and not the other way around. All the organizations emerged from under the robe of Wahhabism."

Ilicit Transactions Group

The Ilicit Transactions Group, a CIA unit that tracks the terrorists and the money launderers that keep Islamic terrorism in business, have been keeping an eye on Osama bin Laden's money transactions for the National Security Council. According to William Wechsler, who heads this unique arm of government, the source of bin Laden's money was undoubtedly Saudi Arabia. Starting in the late 1980s, money raised by Saudi Arabian 'charities' funded the purchase of sophisticated weapons and the training of militant training camps in about 20 countries. Jihad had now gone big time, with real money. The beneficiaries shared in the $70 billion Saudi donation to the cause of Islamic terrorism. In a very general way, U.S. intelligence officials knew what was going on, but it is said that the word got out to government officials to be silent when it comes to Saudi Arabia's role in funding terrorism.

Not after the East African embassy bombings, not after 9/11, not now, has the United States government made any strategic decisions to deal with the source of the threats and problem emanating out of Saudi Arabia. The silence is deafening. If fighting terrorism is the new war, and nations should unite in defeating it, then why the cloak of secrecy about its main funding source? When did the American public ever hear a top official of the United States government even mention the words, Wahhabi or Wahhabism on national television? In spite of the fact that the State Department and intelligence services have been aware of Saudi investment in terrorism since the 1980s, why is it that in a series of National Intelligence Estimates in the 1990s dealing with potential dangers to the United States little is said of al-Qaeda? It is all very intriguing, but also disturbing. Since the 1980s, according to the Saudi periodical, Aim al-Yaqeen, the Saudi money spending frenzy has resulted in the construction of 1,500 mosques, 210 Islamic centers, 202 colleges, and nearly 2,000 schools spread across the globe.

Perhaps the United States government has been slow to act because it all seems so bizarre. Perhaps we are stunned by the enormity of it all. Perhaps the Royal family really believes it is making a better world. Is it that a disruption of oil supplies from Saudi Arabia would cause such a catastrophe that the West simply has no choice but to sit and be silent? Perhaps it is.

Wahhabi clerics saw to it that their followers would dominate Islam by the sheer force of numbers in imams and mosques and access to Saudi money almost on demand. The Muslim World League (IIRO) funded 575 mosques in Indonesia alone, all of which are dominated by Wahhabi clerics who preach disdain and sometimes more for all who will not acknowledge the Wahhabi vision of the world. It could be that that which the Saudis have wrought is not at all what they intended, that the intertwining network of terrorist activity now has a life of its own, uncontrollable by the Saudi princes who created it. It is hard to imagine that they could have intended a worldwide clash of enormous proportions. But, intend it or not, such a situation is becoming a reality.

Of course it is much more complicated than that when one considers that in Afghanistan, the Saudis and the Americans poured an estimated $3.5 billion to support the mujahideen to remove the Soviet presence there. The present web, to some extent, is of our own making, and perhaps that accounts for our inability to come to terms with it. The proliferation of Saudi funded mosques strategically placed around the world has provided, in the name of religion, centers of recruitment and ideological training for all these young men now emerging with back packs stuffed with explosives. This is a work of terrorist art that has been created by the genius of bin Laden and his backers. True, the House of Saud, in doing all of this, was protecting the exposed flank of its corruption, but the price to the rest of the world is only now becoming obvious. One can imagine the dilemma facing the world leaders who either slept though all of this activity or simply wished it would all go away. Bin Laden persuaded the religious communities developed as a result of this massive mosque construction to take up the cause of the establishment of the worldwide Caliphate, and some of them are responding.

The Collection Basket

Zakat, the Islamic equivalent of the Sunday collection in Christian churches, has been a major source of funding for Islamic terrorism. But that is not surprising since, in radical Islam, the state is the mosque and the mosque is the state. Ironically, while religious groups have been concerned about the secularization of society, the real problem has become the conversion of the secular society into religious fanaticism. Who would ever have predicted such an event? The concern among moderate Muslims today is not that their sons and daughters will become secularized, but that they will be converted to fundamentalist religion. Just when we breathed a sigh of relief that the women and children of Afghanistan have been given the opportunity to live without fear, another reality is seeping into our collective consciousness telling us that in the very act of helping bin laden liberate Afghanistan, America and its allies helped forge a network that is now spreading its fundamentalist doctrine across the globe.

A report released by the U.N. in 2003 warned that al-Qaeda "has already taken the decision to use chemical and bio-weapons in their forthcoming attacks." It is clear that we need to do our best to cut off the flow of terrorist financing as one part of an overall strategy to prevent the deployment of such weapons against innocent civilians. During the Afghan war, the man who ran the Muslim World League office in Peshawar, Pakistan, was bin Laden's mentor, Abdullah Azzam. Another official there was Wael Julaidan, a Saudi fundraiser who would join bin Laden in founding al-Qaeda in 1988. Born in Saudi Arabia in January 1958, Julaidan fought alongside bin Laden against the Soviets in Afghanistan in the 1980s. Documents seized in raids after 9/11 reveal just how close those ties were. One such document contained minutes of a meeting held in Bosnia between bin Laden and others. Notes found beneath a Muslim World League letterhead suggested that offices be opened in Pakistan, so that terrorist activities could be planned from there. A Saudi Red Crescent letterhead contained a plea from bin Laden to Wa'el Hamza Julaidan citing "an extreme need for weapons." The United States and Saudi Arabia have frozen the assets of Saudi national Wael Hamza Julaidan for his association with Osama Bin Laden. Julaidan, who was involved in Saudi charitable activities in Afghanistan, Bosnia and Kosovo, has run the Rabita Trust Islamic charity since February 2000. Just days after 9/11 Rabita Trust was added to the list of terrorist financiers and its assets were frozen. Julaidan's name was included in a civil suit filed recently in Washington by more than 1,000 relatives of people killed in last year's attacks.

As early as 1994, the French complained to the Saudi government that Saudi funds were supporting Algerian terrorists. President Clinton complained that Saudi funding of Hamas suicide bombers was not helpful in solving the problems between Israel and Palestine. Investigations of reports that there was an al-Qaeda plot to murder the pope in the Philippines and bomb a dozen U.S. airliners led directly to the local IIRO office. A CIA report read: "Even high-ranking members of the collecting or monitoring agencies in Saudi Arabia, Kuwait, and Pakistan--such as the Saudi High Commission—are involved in illicit activities, including support for terrorists." Other forms of assistance include safe houses, the provision of false identification papers, passports, arms and whatever else the good terrorist needed to carry out his mission. The Muslim World League alone manned 30 branches worldwide, while the IIRO had offices in more than 90 countries, plus six militant training camps in Afghanistan. And, of course, no one is surprised to discover that both the Muslim World League and the IIRO are supervised by the Grand

Mufti of Saudi Arabia, the nation's top cleric. Both organizations are allowed, not only substantial government funding, but also the open use of Saudi embassies abroad. The Muslim World League's current secretary general, Abdullah Al-Turki, is the brother of Prince Turki, the present Saudi Ambassador to the United States. The IIRO's Canadian chief brazenly testified in a 1999 court case, "I work for the government of Saudi Arabia." Bob Baer, former CIA operative claims in his book, Sleeping With the Devil: How Washington Sold Our Soul for Saudi Crude, that Saudi money corrupted Washington officials with money, in exchange for silence about their dealings with terrorists. He calls it "Washington's 401(k) Plan." His list of donees includes ambassadors, CIA station chiefs and even a cabinet secretary or two. How is all this money moved without too much attention?

Follow the Money

The Saudi offensive to spread Wahhabism in such an aggressive manner began when the kingdom, after imposing an oil embargo in 1973, received an incredible financial windfall. Now was the time for spreading the Wahhabi word, for the Wahhabi word served their political and financial interests. As Wahhabi followers were violently suppressed in places like Egypt and Algeria, the Saudis quickly co-opted them by providing sanctuary and financial assistance in whatever country they were operating. Alex Alexiev, a former CIA consultant on ethnic and religious conflict, says of the Saudi funding program, it is "the largest worldwide propaganda campaign ever mounted." Thus, the economic and logistical dependence of many of these extremists on the Saudis, and the ongoing radicalization of Wahhabism itself, created a highly synergistic relationship between the Wahhabi supporters and their Saudi paymasters, in spite of the fact that Osama bin Laden resented the Saudi regime. Money talks, even among the 'purists.'

Hamas funding

The Hamas-Saudi connection is very clear. Hamas emerged in 1987 from the Gaza branch of Muslim Brotherhood, which has been a key Saudi and Wahhabi ally for decades. Bin Laden made the fate of Sheikh Yasin, Hamas spiritual leader, an issue for his al-Qaeda followers as well. In his 1996 "Declaration of War," he listed Sheikh Yasin's release from prison as one of his demands or grievances. Reporter Timothy Starks, writing in The *New York Sun*, June 13, 2003 reported that:

"At a news conference called here to claim that the Saudi Arabian government was cracking down on terrorism, a top Saudi Arabian official [Al-Jubeir] yesterday refused to condemn the terrorist group Hamas…" The reporter pressed: "Why not say, 'We condemn Hamas for this act of terrorism?'"

There was no reply. The evasiveness of the clever Saudi government spokesperson, Al-Jubeir, suggests a close relationship between the Wahhabi and Hamas. President Clinton, on a visit to Saudi Arabia complained that Saudi money was helping support Hamas, which in turn, was sending suicide bombers onto buses and into schools and cafes in Israel, destroying innocent lives. In Palestine, Hamas challenged both Arafat and his successor, arguing that they betrayed the national rights of the Palestinian people. A critic of the Saudi government, Ali Al-Ahmed, who runs the Saudi Institute in Washington, said there is no doubt of the Saudi link to Hamas. He was not surprised that Al-Jubeir did not condemn the group. "He can't. He'd be fried back home. He wouldn't be the spokesman any longer." When Sheikh Yasin was released from an Israeli prison in 1998, he went to Saudi Arabia for medical treatment and Crown Prince Abdullah, now King Abdullah, made a high-profile visit to his hospital bedside.

One of the strongest pieces of Saudi/Hamas complicity is a handwritten letter written in Arabic by the current Palestinian Prime Minister, Mahmud Abbas (Abu Mazen), on December 30, 2000, to Prince Salman, governor of Riyadh and a full brother of King Fahd. Abbas complained that Saudi donations in the Gaza Strip went to al-Jamiya al-Islamiya (the Islamic Society), which Abbas explained, "belongs to Hamas." He wanted the funds for the militant organization, Fatah. It is all really very clear. Hamas' resorting to terrorism is not likely to produce a permanent politically stable force in the society, but it is popular among the masses, because Wahhabi funding enables them to bring much-needed social services to Palestinians. For this, the Palestinians are very grateful. But, without outside funding Hamas would not be attractive. With Wahhabi and Iranian support they are faring better than their ideological cousins, the Lebanese Hezbollah, who, in the elections of June 2005, lost face and have virtually abandoned the idea of an Islamic state within Lebanon. However, as their resistance to Israel in the summer of 2006 has shown, they are a force to be reckoned with.

Shortly after 9/11 a Saudi book, entitled, The Foundations of the Legality of the Destruction That Befell America, appeared, justifying the murder of thousands of Americans. The Introduction to the book was written by a prominent Saudi religious leader, Sheikh Hamud bin Uqla al-Shuaibi. Saudi connections to terrorism continue to appear.

Chapter Five

WAHHABI VERSION
OF DEMOCRACY

The Washington-based Saudi Institute director, Ali Al-Ahmed, testified before the United States Congress on Thursday October 6, 2004 at an International Relations hearing on religious freedom.[19] In a U.S. State Department report, Saudi Arabia was added to the list of Countries of Particular Concern (CPC) due to the lack of religious freedom in Saudi Arabia. Al Ahmed's opening words reflect the feelings of millions of Saudis from around the globe who are so grateful for having support from outside nations in their quest for freedom from oppression.

Let me first express my thanks for the work done by the U.S. State Department office of Religious Freedom...The United States commitment to the protection of religious freedoms of people around the world...is a great testament to the founders of this great nation. As a Saudi whose brother is in prison because of my speaking out here in America, I must say "thank you America for giving your treasure and effort to protect the freedoms of others."

Saudi Arabia, Mr. Ahmed pointed out, does not allow religious freedom to its Muslim citizens, even to those who are Wahhabi. It practices a rigid form of control on the interpretation of Islam in every sphere of life. The books of non-Wahhabi scholars, especially those of Christians and Jews, are banned, and government control over religion and its understanding of Islam is the root cause of extremism in the country. The Islamic faith, he said, has been used as a political tool against reformers, and critics. He points out that Saudi Arabia is a glaring example of religious apartheid. The religious institutions, judges, religious curriculums, and all religious instructions in the media must conform to the Wahhabi understanding of Islam, adhered to by less than 40% of the population. Religious apartheid, he said, is the order of the day in Saudi Arabia. Christian and Jewish symbols are banned from public display.

A Brief Profile of Saudi Apartheid

Names that are not suitable to the official religious institution are banned. In 1992 a new directive was issued banning any name derived from the Koran, even though many of them have been used since the founding of Islam. Descendents of the Prophet Mohammed are banned from using their titles in identification cards or official documents. There is a ban on importing religious books that are not accepted by the official religious institution. Fines, lashes or prison can be imposed if one is found with such a book. Libraries of Saudi universities do not contain Shia books, but anti-Shia books are printed by government institutions and distributed free. Religious songs applauding the Prophet Mohammed, Shia religious songs, known as Noha or Aza, used during commemorations are also banned. The government recognizes only two holidays, Eid Al Fitr (after Ramadan) and Eid Aladha (After Hajj). Prophet Mohammed birthday celebrations are banned. The government controls Internet access, and frequently blocks web sites, citing moral, political and religious reasons. This has been referred to as "Cyber Jihad." Although Shia is a minority in the country, over 95% of prisoners are Shia. However, if these prisoners agree to become Sunnis, charges against them are reduced.

Imprisoned clerics are asked to stop religious activities and seek other forms of work. Passports are seized without reference to any judicial reason or process. Sheikh Hassan Al-Maliki, a noted Sunni Hanbali Muslim, asked that a national dialogue be held to discuss religious freedom. He was immediately fired from his job at the Saudi ministry of education, and his passport was seized. He was under virtual house arrest for over two years. Professor Mohammed Al-Hassan, formerly of King Saud University, a Washington State University graduate, testified that he was removed from his job, banned from travel, and interrogated by Saudi security for weeks for publicly expressing his distaste at the religious hatred his 12 year-old daughter had experienced in her school. All his children were expelled. He pointed out that non-Wahhabi fear appearing in court for any reason whatsoever because of the possibility that they may be condemned as heretics.

The only acceptable interpretation of Sharia law allowed is that of the Wahhabi, even though they comprise a minority of the population. Ali Al-Ahmed noted that he and his colleagues at the Saudi Institute were the first to call for a review of Saudi religious textbooks used in the United States because they promoted extremism and religious hatred. But as of until 2004 the Saudi textbooks have not been revised. Ahmed called on the legislators to demand an end to the spread of such religious hatred and fanaticism in the United States by a foreign government. It is in the interests of the security of the United States, he said, that our government cleanses the cancer of religious hatred from Wahhabi mosques in the United States. The Saudis themselves must be amazed that they can get away with all of this. Facing this reality in all its dimensions is an urgent requirement of United States foreign and domestic policy.

The majority of Muslims around the world support Ahmed's call. This is evident from a study made among the world's Muslims by Ronald Inglehart and Pippa Norris. They discovered that a majority of the world's Muslims endorse the adoption of modernity and democracy. The authors compared opinion in eleven Muslim-majority societies with several Western countries and found that in all but one of the Muslim countries (Pakistan) public support for democracy was equal to or even greater than in Western countries. Where Muslim and Western attitudes diverged was not on matters of democracy, but in such areas as gay rights and full gender equality.

There is a certain sad simplicity about the Wahhabi approach to democracy, an approach that has built into it its own destruction. Wahhabism declares Western-style democracy an evil, thus going a long way toward closing the door on the subject, and inviting its inevitable destruction. They show every sign of understanding this but they assume that their money will keep the wolves away from their doors during their lifetime. Self-illusion usually is its own punishment. After all, for the Family of Saud to critically examine the main pillar of its support, Wahhabism, is to invite the possibility that such an examination would result in a demand for doing away with the House of Saud itself. This, understandably, the Saud Family has never been willing to face. Perhaps someone like Nelson Mandela, on assignment with the United Nations, could be a special envoy to the Saudi government, and help it, diplomatically, to understand. A Mandela could offer them a face-saving way out, a secret plan for Saudi-Western cooperation, done outside the glare of the media, a strategic plan aimed at saving the present Monarchy with diminished power, a form of Constitutional Monarchy, state-supported. In the long run and certainly for the history books, the Saud Family could one day be remembered for having begun the process of liberating the people of Saudi Arabia. From what we can gather in the body language and eloquence of the Saudi Family, there is hope that their experience in the world and their education would assist them in allowing a reasonable and face-saving plan to play itself out.

Wahhabi Democracy is Theocracy

The Wahhabi insist that democracy derives from the absolute majesty and sovereignty of God. That is not such a bad thing to believe. After all, when Jesus was arrested, Pilate, not satisfied with a response Jesus made, warned him that he had the authority to decide his fate. Jesus did not deny that. He simply replied that any authority Pilate had came from God. So, the Christian concept of democracy is not that a person does not have authority, but that, ultimately, any authority exercised by a man is derived from God. This being the case then, the man exercising authority should be acting godly in a manner, i.e., morally. This, perhaps, is a concept too sophisticated for the Wahhabi mentality. For the Wahhabi, God works not through humans but through the literalness of the law, with no room for compromise, no room for compassion, no room for human weakness (at least for fe-

males), no room for forgiveness. They have painted their humanity into a corner and they do not know how to get out. Perhaps
quiet diplomacy mixed with a lot of understanding and compassion can lead them out from their self-imposed ideological
prison. They are not unique. Perhaps a reading of how we were
in the Middle Ages when we burned Joan of Arc at the stake
would help us, not to agree with what is done, surely, but to put
the situation in an historical context. The Catholic bishops of that
time asked Joan how she dared listen to her own voices rather
than theirs, and she replied that she was obliged to listen to
God's voice in her own soul. The bishops retaliated. They set her
afire. That proved, in their twisted version of Christianity, how
righteous they were. In our probe into Wahhabism, we need to
remind ourselves that we are not speaking about extremism as if
it were exclusively a characteristic of Islam. Extremists everywhere are guilty of self-righteousness salted with suffocating
policies. They know everything.

In the late 15th century, in the name of the Catholic King and
Queen, Ferdinand and Isabella, of Spain, Tomas de Torquemada,
Queen Isabella's confessor, supervised the workings of the Spanish Inquisition. In the name of Christianity he murdered thousands, of Jews, Muslims, and dissident Christians. He claimed he
was acting in the name of Christianity. Of course, he was not.
Hitler's destruction of six million Jews took place in a Christian
nation, as did Stalin's rule of murder and oppression. Perhaps the
lessons we learn from our own history[20] we can patiently, behind
closed doors, pass on to our Muslim brothers and sisters trapped
in a web of their own making. Some of the brightest Muslim
scholars in America are committed to encouraging religious tolerance among hard-line Islamic groups. But it is not an easy task.
Students who chide them for not being sufficiently radical, reportedly, harass their professors. The Catholic Church, both in
America and abroad can also play a part, mindful of its role in
the Crusades, and also having bloodily dispatched countless dis-
senting Catholics and non-Catholics in the Middle Ages. By
more frequent and wider discussions with Islamic imams and
scholars, the Church can encourage Islam to make its own case,
using its own religious and legal traditions, for religious tolerance. We also need to review briefly the different histories and

pathways that each religion took and the human elements in their respective backgrounds in terms of Church/State relations. For example, since al-Qaeda from the start was rooted in the Wahhabi/Saudi establishment, it is a reflection of their concept of Mosque/State relations, i.e., a theocratic state.

The Christian political ethos has always made a distinction between church and state, even if, at times, the lines were blurred. Going back to Jesus' admonition to "render unto Caesar what is Caesar's, and render unto God what is God's," it has always been a basic part of Christian doctrine that the church and the state represent equal but separate entities, each having its own function.

Conservatives are generally concerned about any government limitation on their liberties, but it is also true that governments also feel sometimes that there is Church interference in civil affairs. There is really nothing wrong with this. In the field of philosophy this sort of situation is called "creative tension."

In addition, Christianity also had about 300 years to develop its theology before it joined in a union with state power. Once the Christian Roman Empire became an institution, many Christian doctrines were already firmly established and accepted. Islam, however, had a different beginning. Mohammed was leader of all the people in all areas of life. For him and his followers it was very natural to think and believe that mosque and state were two sides of one coin. Mohammed was the spiritual and political leader, and the principal judge. He embraced in his person the executive, legislative and judicial functions.

This has always been the Islamic ideal (although not its consistent practice). Some insisted that only a person from Mohammed's family could legitimately succeed him. At the time, they were supporting Ali, one of the two who were eligible. He was not chosen, and since that time his supporters became disaffected from the rest of the community. Even today they represent the largest minority sect in Islam, the Shiites. It does not behoove the West to make financial assistance, good inter-governmental relations and foreign policy decisions dependent on the separation of mosque and state. That is not nrcessarily our business.

Questionable Doctrine

Since there are only about eighty-odd Koranic verses that are regulative, the thousands of Sharia regulations can obviously be examined both for theological accuracy and to what extent mores and even prejudices may have infiltrated the teachings. We have had a history of that in Christian theological debates and in-house challenges. So, it is not surprising that 17th and 18th century Sunni and Shia jurists could have differed so widely on the same teachings. It simply informs us that, as in all other religions, different interpretations of non-essential doctrine are the norm. Islamic scholar Taj Hashmi, Simon Fraser University, Vancouver, Canada, writes: "From its absurdity to abysmal vulgarity, unscientific crudeness, the Hadis literature[21] is full of contradictions, lies and concoctions to justify anything that suits the caprice of unrefined kings and nobles, debauched husbands and womanizers, polygamists, rapists and child abusers, dictators, ruthless murderers and slave owners." That is perhaps too harsh a judgment, but it does resonate in our Christian handling of morality over the centuries.

To the extent that these questionable Hadises impact on relations between Muslims and non-Muslims, the world awaits an answer to the all-important question: Can fundamentalist Islam, in its own meetings and councils, arrive at the conclusion that it can live happily and peacefully with both moderate Muslims and non-Muslims, or are they so torn apart by past grievances that our generation will not see such a change? We pray for the best, as Muslims everywhere pass through one of the most difficult ideological and spiritual periods in their history. We need to exercise compassion and understanding. Most importantly, slanderous Islam bashing by those carrying the weight of built-in prejudice against Islam, combined with their abysmal ignorance of Islamic religion, history and culture, is counter-productive. It took the Catholic Church centuries to come to the conclusion so well expressed at Vatican II. "The Church, by reason of her role and competence, is not identified with any political community nor bound by ties to any political system." If both the West and Islam could say this in our decade, it would be a very important development and turn the Christian-Islamic dialogue on its head, thereby helping to produce a new Pax Romana. There is no doubt whatsoever that, excepting the fact of occasional backsliding, historical democratization is on the march. Nations arrive at its practice at different paces and within different cultural, political and religious milieus.

The jury is still out on Central Asia, but certainly political events and changes of leadership of late 2004 and 2005 demonstrate genuine examples of "people-power" (one definition of democracy). Whether or not events in Iraq will become a democratic stimulus, under the domino theory, is yet to be seen. It would likely not go any further than a secular state with strong Islamic overtures. One would hope that it would. In the case of the Saudis, the art of regime change has to be very sophisticated. We have here, not just the state but also the mosque, and each needs the other to ward off eventual retribution when the inevitable comes. And, what might not strike Westerners as overly important is that the two most sacred Muslim shrines are located in Saudi Arabia, in the cities of Mecca and Medina. How does a state move against the very religious power that keeps it in existence and increasingly represents a larger and larger segment of the Islamic world? The solutions are not easy.

The Middle Class

Regime change usually follows a particular pattern. History has taught us that when the division between the very powerless and the very powerful begins to narrow, i.e. when a Middle Class emerges, democratic ideas are not far behind. Among other reasons, the Middle Class becomes the owners of the nation's business and a serious repository of collective wealth. And, as we know, money and commerce 'talk.' In Saudi Arabia a solid and potentially influential Middle Class already exists that desires to equal or surpass the freedoms enjoyed by their counterparts in Europe and the United States. It is beginning to resent the lack of meaningful civil rights in the Kingdom. In the past, such resentment sometimes leads to a complete erosion of a system. An opportunity to see where the Saudi Middle Class would go, if free to speak out, was missed when several newspapers in Saudi Arabia began to publish analytical articles on the nature of the regime. The editor of one such newspaper, Watan[22], was fired, aborting that particular line of research. But, more will come, and, each time it happens, the regime will be progressively less able to contain it.

The Broader View

We are focusing on Saudi Arabia, but in order to achieve a lasting peace in the region, we need to have a comprehensive view. The governments of neighboring Arab countries share the Wahhabi ethos. Prior to the elections in Iraq even our friend, King Abdullah of Jordan, cautioned that elections could well bring into power an anti-American Shiite government. Shiites spell trouble for the region's authoritarian regimes, for the simple reason that all of the Arab countries have Sunni governments and they need to be careful not to appear to their Sunni base that they are anything other than anti-Shiite. The Wahhabi clergy, Sunnis, from its powerful financial base in the House of Saud, has for decades worked assiduously to gather an army of followers who are committed to jihad, who will give their lives to destroy as much a segment of Western democracy and Shiite autocracy as is possible. The Caliphate cannot come, they maintain, unless democratic forces in the West and their growing influence in the Middle East, including Iraq, is ended. Anything can happen, but at the moment at least, this is not a likely scenario. The Sunnis are not only a minority in sheer numbers in Iraq, but also and more importantly they have lost power, a Saddam-based power, to crush Shiites.

It has become, under Wahhabi influence, an article of faith that an Islamist empire, the Caliphate, be established by destroying democratic societies, since they are based on Judeo-Christian values of tolerance and pluralism. Of course, the American memory of Iranians holding Americans hostage in 1979 has negatively influenced our perception of Shiites. And, unquestionably, Shiite governance in Iran is far from being a model. However, snap judgments must not be made about any Arab government or Islamic government. The Shiites have not rejected the concept of secularism contained within an Islamic worldview, simply because the Wahhabi have rejected it.

In Iraq we have had the opportunity, now that people are free to express their opinions openly, to listen to and observe what a wise and most powerful Shiite cleric has to say on the Islamic state. Ayatollah Sistani rejects the theory of the unification of a theocracy that calls for government by clerics according to the rules laid down in Islamic law. He favors an Islamic state, but not a theocracy. That is the key distinction to be made and we need to support Sistani to the extent that he contributes to moderate Islam. He does say that no law in a Muslim nation should conflict with Islamic principles, and he does ask that Islam be recognized in law as the religion of the majority of Iraqis, but that would simply be in line with their ancient history, and not something to be concerned about. Actually, a majority of Shiite religious scholars follow the principles of quietism, which holds that clerics shouldn't get involved in day-to-day matters of politics. Religious leaders, they say, should remain independent of politics. Their task is to call for government accountability and the protection of religion. But that is not much different than the many references presidents have made in regard to America being a nation founded on Christian principles and guided by its religious leaders. At the same time, Jefferson declared that it is not in the best interest of a nation that a priest ever has secular power in the new Republic. The immense and forceful struggle now existing between Western democracy and Wahhabi-dominated extremism is all about secular and theocratic power, and where they are invested and how they should be used.

The Wahhabi can be 'credited' with reviving the desires and power of the Ottoman Empire. Sitting, as it were, on the goldmine of the holy cities of Mecca and Medina, the Wahhabi have had the greatest opportunity of any Muslim state to influence the thinking of Muslims world-wide. Indian, Chinese and Thai pilgrims to the holy cities have returned to their respective homes and have become involved in the dream of the first local Muslim-controlled governments and then, linking with each other, realizing the cherished dream of the Caliphate. Saudi Arabia is the eye of the terrorist storm and is, at the same time, the heart of Islam.

Muslims Wary

One attempt to create a Wahhabi state occurred in Egypt when the Muslim Brotherhood tried to seize political power. The reaction of the Egyptian establishment was swift and severe, with all the organs of the state uniting to crush their influence. The fires of Caliphate-building were stoked by Abul Ala Maududi's influence, through his writing and preaching, and resulting in the development of the Jamiati Islamic organization. The dream of a proliferation of Islamic states being set up after many Muslim nations achieve independence beginning in 1945, however, did not materialize. On the contrary, national states in the European model based on Western legal codes emerged. The real end to the Ottoman culture came with the secularization of Turkey after World War I, along the lines of European models of government. The transition to a secular state was not an easy one and its repercussions are still being felt in Turkish society today. Nevertheless, the secularization of Islam heralded a real break with the Ottoman tradition and heritage. Ottomans tried for centuries to deal with political and radical Islam.

When Kemal Ataturk founded modern Turkey in 1923, he ended the Shariat and Caliphate, as they would, in his opinion, prevent Turkey's integration into the modern, Western world. He did not deny people learning about or practicing Islam, but he did ban madrasas that were filled with people who were teaching different forms of Islam. He created a state ministry that coordinated the teaching of Islam in a traditional way. Turkey first concentrated on creating an economically prosperous state and then introduced a multi-party system and democratic elections. Since then Turkey has gone through several cycles of increased openness to Islamic groups, followed by the banning of religious activities, and even military coups. It has been a roller coaster ride, and is still in the process of finding itself.

Over the ensuing eight decades, the tension between the secular establishment and Islamists has not entirely disappeared, but the end result is that today in Turkey there is no radical Islamic movement with any significant following. The dream of another Ottoman Empire[23] began to recede, as one-party states, and government ownership of industry in centrally planned economies became the dominant trend. The dream then switched to the Pakistani model, a real chance for living in a modern Islamic democracy. However, when the Pakistani experiment was unable to overcome ethnic warfare, militarism, government corruption, economic mismanagement, military takeovers, and an equitable distribution of wealth, Muslims worldwide began to have second thoughts about the feasibility of forming democratic Islamic states. Perhaps, they thought, it could not work. A more radical approach to the formation of government, they felt, was needed. Thus, aided and abetted by the Wahhabi and their success in controlling the organs of power in Saudi Arabia, the Ottoman dream emerged once again. Always in the background is the desire of another successful Islamic empire. It is woven into the consciousness, both in the Muslim states and in the scattered but linked Diaspora. It is the European absorption of many Muslims that causes concern among Europeans today. Bernard Lewis, author, caused an uproar in Europe by telling the conservative Hamburg-based daily Die Welt that Europe would be Islamic by the end of this century "at the very latest." It has prompted many discussions in Germany as to the wisdom of allowing Islamic Turkey into the European Union.

Chapter Six

PRINCE NAYEF BIN ABDUL-AZIZ

Our long and familiar relationship with Saudi Arabia and the flowing gowns of its kings and princes sweeping majestically through the halls of Congress and the White House has obscured the police state that keeps the Saud family in power. The illusion of a friendly and jolly ally is maintained even as the House of Saud has successfully hidden from public view the mechanisms of a brutal police state. If the King and the princes are such 'nice guys,' then who runs this police state? The man who has been in charge of the Ministry of Interior for the last 27 years is Prince Nayef bin Abdul-Aziz, arguably the most powerful man in Saudi Arabia. At 69 years of age he heads five major oversight committees and controls four other ministries. His brothers, Prince Sultan and now King Abdullah must be aware that should dissatisfaction with the state of affairs in the Kingdom come to a boiling point, Nayef will bear the brunt of public-vented anger and frustration.

But, there are in Saudi Arabia, as in all nations, conflicting opinions on how to deal with the world. King Abdullah is in favor of the gradual reformation of the Kingdom's political and foreign policy positions, seeking a pragmatic rapprochement with the West, while Prince Nayef shows every indication of siding with the anti-American Wahhabi religious establishment that aligns itself with extreme Islamic militant groups. Abdullah cuts a higher profile abroad -- but at home Nayef casts a shadow. He controls the Commission for the Promotion of Virtue and Prevention of Vice (CPVPV). The CPVVP made the news in March

2002 when they used batons to beat schoolgirls for trying to flee from a burning dormitory without dressing first in their Islamic attire. Several girls died in the fire. Nayef denied that the religious police did anything wrong. Prince, now King, Abdullah favors the doctrine of Taqarub, which works at bringing together in public forums Muslims and non-Muslims. Taqarub represents peaceful coexistence with nonbelievers, Shiites, secularists, feminists, and so on. It also minimizes the importance of jihad, allowing Saudis to live in peace with Christians, Jews and even Shiite Iranians. Taqarubis are open to the world. Abdullah favors more public debate, democratic institutions and the scaling back of clerical power, but he does not go so far as to alienate the religious establishment. Nothing sinister here; he is simply a good politician.

In May of 2003 he encouraged a "national dialogue with Saudi liberals." The dialogue produced the National Reform Document, suggesting ways in which the Kingdom could make advances in creating democratic institutions, including direct elections and increased participation by women in public matters, while at the same time respecting Islamic law. It also produced a program called, Partners in the Homeland, calling for more freedom for the oppressed Shiite community, and yet the Saudi religious establishment is viscerally and vocally hostile to Shiism, which constitutes 10 to 15 percent of the population. At the moment the Shiites do not enjoy even the most basic rights of religious freedom. On subjects ranging from Saudi participation in the World Trade Organization, the Ministerial Committee on Morality or in matters of foreign policy, Nayef's presence is an omnipresence.

Dr. Fouad bin Abdul Salaam bin Mohammed Al Farsi is the information minister, but just to make certain that Abdul Salaam does not get out of hand, a Supreme Council on Information, headed by Nayef, has "supreme" control of relations with the media, what is to be said and not said. As head of the Interior Ministry he controls the policing of the population through the security services, the borders and coasts through the Borders and Coast Guards, and the tribes through the so-called Mujahideen Forces. His personal guards and operatives belong to the Special Police Forces and the Anti-terrorist Squad. Enhancing his power is the fact that all individual civil services within the country's provinces report directly to his ministry even if they are attached to other ministries. With all this power, the courts are Nayef's play things. His total control of the media enables him to create a reality that suits the whims and fancies and credibility of the corrupt House of Saud. In the infamous March 1980 Decree no. 78, Nayef arranged to monitor the activities of all newsmen in the nation. He has not shied away from publicity in raising money for Palestinian causes, one example being a telethon in April of 2002. In November 2002 he absolved the Saudi hijackers of responsibility for the September 11, 2001 terrorist attacks. On April 28, 1998, Prince Nayef gave an interview to the Arabic Service of the BBC. He was asked if the Government was considering allowing women to drive, to participate in voting, etc. His response was: "Females in the Kingdom of Saudi Arabia enjoy full respect, and advance at the same pace as males. Whatever benefits women and at the same time does not contradict Islamic Sharia and is accepted by our society, will be realized." Saudi women may not be too pleased with this response, but Nayef knows how to finesse intrusive questions.

This assumed authority to excommunicate dissident Muslims, or Muslims of different traditions, such as the Sufis or the Shiites, is very intimidating to the average Saudi, for excommunication can also imply the possibility of bodily harm and violence. It is made very clear in government-supported documents that interfaith dialogue is sinful and that the wall of resentment between the Muslim and the unbelievers must be maintained.[24] Hatred for the infidel is a given in Wahhabi theology. Any imams who reach out to other faiths for mutual understanding are considered heretics and their prayers are said to be of no value. An Urdu-language publication published by the Saudi Ministry of Religious Affairs quotes Sheik Bin Uthaimin: "Our doctrine states that if you accept any religion other than Islam, like Judaism or Christianity, which are not acceptable, you become an unbeliever. If you do not repent, you are an apostate and you should be killed because you have denied the Koran."[25]

On the surface, then Prince, now King Abdullah represented his country at international conferences, the White House, and other capitals around the world. But the home front has always been left to Prince Nayef. Indeed, Nayef takes care of the day-to-day running of the nation, and controls the atmosphere and circumstances in which Islam's greatest pilgrimage, the all-important hajj, the pilgrimage to Mecca, takes place. He chairs the Supreme Committee on the Hajj. The official minister of the hajj, Dr. Iyad bin Ameen Madani, has been on the job since 1999 but defers to Nayef. The Saudis are very interested in getting into the World Trade Organization. This comes under the portfolio of the minister of commerce, Osama bin Jafar bin Ibrahim Faqih. But, once again, it is Prince Nayef, this time wearing the hat of the head of the Ministerial Oversight Committee on the WTO, who holds the press conference on the subject and makes the decisions on behalf of the government. The ubiquitous Nayef shows up at ministerial conferences revolving around foreign policy. He even took on the United States. The then Prince Saud had backed a possible invasion of Iraq by American armed forces, but Nayef had his own agenda, and publicly announced in October of 2001 his opposition to such a move, leaving Prince Saud, the foreign minister looking a bit silly.

The Western media has become increasingly stronger in its anti-Saudi reporting, much to the displeasure of Prince Nayef. He ascribes all such attacks to Jewish lobbies and insists that the Kingdom will not be swayed from its internal and external policies. As for the suggestion that Saudi Arabian sources funded 9/11, Prince Nayef scoffed at the idea and resurrected the view that the Jews were behind the attacks. The English edition of the Saudi newsweekly *Ain Al-Yaqeen* of November 29, 2002, read:

"Prince Nayef bin Abdul Aziz said that he greatly suspected that these terrorist organizations have relations with foreign intelligence that worked against Arab and Muslims, topped by Israeli intelligence. They wanted to attack us at our bases and tenets, notably our religion and the Palestinian issue."

It was impossible, Nayef said, that nineteen youths including seventeen Saudis could possibly have carried out such a massive operation, or that al-Qaeda could have carried it out on its own. " We can say that these people are either agents or ignorant since their action was against Islam and Muslims. By this action the world turned against Islam, Muslims and Arabs." Nayef takes pride in not having been tainted by Western propaganda. It is his badge of courage. However, he is no fool. He knows that the day of reckoning is coming and he is determined to beat it. His greatest fear is that members of his own security guard may turn against him. His main threat is not from the United States but from Osama bin Laden, so he pays his dues and respect to that revolutionary figure, staving off what others consider inevitable. His monetary support for the Palestinians has been high profile. The website of his Saudi Committee for Support of the Al-Quds Intifada carries exhaustive reports on Saudi financial and media support for the Palestinians. Nayef is also general supervisor of the Joint Saudi Committee for the Relief of Kosovo and Chechnya, which funds Muslim activities and conducts training courses in these two countries. Many of the jihadist Arabs in Taliban-run Afghanistan had previously fought in Chechnya.

As interior minister, Prince Nayef is responsible for controlling the clergy within the kingdom. Although he has had the occasional extremist cleric arrested, he stands aside while many others preach jihad. One example from a long list is Ibn Jebreen, a respected sheikh from the Najd region, the heartland of Wahhabism. It was from here that the Saud family would conquer the rest of the regions now making up the country. In modern Saudi Arabia Najd is called the Central Region, comprising 3 provinces. The sheikh has the reputation of lustily preaching jihad, notably in support of the Muslim brothers in Chechnya. By his logic, anytime Muslims are under attack it is incumbent on other Muslims to go to their aid. Given that a majority of Saudis cheered the 9/11 attacks, we can expect that many Saudis regularly head north to help their fellow Muslims in clashes with the Coalition forces in Iraq. News reports often carry information that it is not unusual for Saudi nationals to be involved in fighting with the Iraqi or Coalition forces. Nayef is not subtle in his warnings to clerics who do not follow the party line. He said there are more than 50,000 imams at the Kingdom's mosques that follow the official line of thinking. "If they deviate from this line and persist doing so, they will have to find other jobs." Referring to a meeting he had with officials of the Commission for the Promotion of Virtue and Prevention of Vice, Prince Nayef said the meeting was fruitful. He said the commission must employ efficient and learned people to carry out their mission.

"During the meeting the grand mufti gave a speech on the commission's responsibilities, and urged its officials to shed rigidity and avoid mistakes," he added.

Further evidence of Prince Nayef's riding the jihadist wave is the case of Sheikh Salman bin Fahd Al-Oadah. Arrested by the Interior Ministry in 1994 for his radical preaching, Al-Oadah was released in 1999 without cause or comment. Since then, he has launched a website, Islam today.net, from his home in Buraydah, in the Najd.

Nayef is Shocked

On December 30, 2004, Nayef got the shock of his life, and one can sympathize with him. That night three huge explosions shook Riyadh, followed by bursts of gunfire in northern and eastern Riyadh. Three car bomb blasts were designed by al-Qaeda to murder Nayef's son, bin Abdelaziz, deputy minister and director of the ministry's security unit, a first attempt by Osama bin Laden's organization to assassinate a member of the Saudi royal family. The first blast occurred at 20:35 local time in a traffic tunnel through which Prince Mohammed's convoy was driving on its way to a conference with Saudi security and intelligence chiefs. Al-Qaeda operatives detonated the car bomb in the lane opposite that of the prince's car. The fact that Al-Qaeda had such highly secret information on the time and place of the conference, together with the fact that the young Prince would be present, was highly significant. al-Qaeda has its own operatives inside the 'tent.' The would-be assassins even prepared a back-up plan in the event that Mohammed survived the tunnel blast. A second car bomb was detonated at the reinforced gates of the high-rise interior ministry building, while gunmen rained automatic fire on the entrance and parking lot. Half an hour later, and not far away, a third car blew up at the Saudi Special Forces recruiting center, the suspected safe-house for the young Prince. It was a major setback for Nayef, who for an entire year worked diligently to maintain a dialogue with the Saudi al-Qaeda cell through his connections in the clergy. Saudi al-Qaeda leader, Saud bin Hamoud al-Uteibi, is suspected of being behind the assassination attempt, for he did not trust Nayef and accused him of planting agents inside the terror cell. Chaos could have engulfed the region if the assassination attempt succeeded. That the price of oil would have rocketed can be gathered from the fact that as news reports trickled in a sharp 4% rise took place immediately. The Saudis have become more aggressive against selected al-Qaeda targets since. The problem is no one really knows who is inside the Saudi Family tent and who is outside. The most likely scenario is that the Family itself does not know for certain. Sic transit Gloria.

Chapter Seven

THE WAHHABI
IN HISTORICAL PERSPECTIVE

Wahhabism was established by Mohammed ibn 'Abd al-Wahhab. He was born in Huraimila in Najd in 1111 (1699 A.D.) and died in 1206 (1791 A.D.). For many years he engaged in commerce in Iraq, Iran, India and Damascus. In Baghdad he married an affluent woman whose property he inherited when she died. Moving to Iran, he began to teach there. On returning to his native city, he wrote Kitab at-tawhid ("Book of Unity"), which is the main text for Wahhabi doctrines. His followers call themselves "Unitarians." Non-Muslims and opponents generally use the term 'Wahhabi'. In 1744, Abd al-Wahhab was exiled from his native city, Uyayna, because of his controversial preaching and the teachings in his book published in Egypt. It served to spread his ideas throughout the Arabian Peninsula and beyond. He considered this movement an effort to purify Islam by returning all Muslims to what he believed were the original principles of Islam, and to reject what he regarded as corruptions introduced by Bida (innovation) and Shirk (idolatry).

His followers became known as Wahhabi or Najdis. They increased in number, and he declared that only the people over whom he ruled should succeed him. At first, his father, Abd al-Wahhab, opposed Ibn's teachings, but later, in 1150, proclaimed Wahhabism the one true religion of Islam.[26] His controversial teachings gained him many enemies so he fled for protection to Mohammed Ibn Saud, (d.1765) ruler of the town and area of Ad-

Dar'iyah. Protection was granted, and this became the basis for an alliance that remains today among the followers of both men.

The Saudi sheik was impressed with al-Wahhab and adopted as his mission in life to wage holy war, jihad, against all other forms of Islam. He set out to conquer his neighbors in 1763. By 1811, the Wahhabi and the Saud family ruled all Arabia, except Yemen, from their capital at Riyadh. The wedding of Ibn Saud's son to Abdul Wahhab's daughter strengthened their alliance. Ibn Saud spread the ideology of Wahhab among other tribes in the Arabian peninsula that were prepared to base their power not on politics but on religion, the most potent force among the ordinary people.

The fortunes of the Wahhabi brand of Islam became a political force to be reckoned with when it decided to take on any further advance of the Ottoman Turks down along the Arabian Peninsula. The confrontation was fierce and bloody, with the Wahhabi killing Muslims and non-Muslims. Islamic Jurists of the time branded the Wahhabi the contemporary equivalents of the Kharijites, a particularly extreme form of Islam that threatened to murder both contenders to the Mohammed succession. The Ottoman sultan, with help from the Egyptians, limited Saud/Wahhabi expansion for a time, but they reassembled their power and from 1821 to 1833 gained control over the Persian Gulf coast of Arabia. A third triumph came for the Wahhabi movement, when Ibn Saud advanced from his capture of Riyadh in 1902 to the reconstitution in 1932 of his ancestral domain, under the name, Saudi Arabia. The Saudi/Wahhab venture came to fruition and still stands to this day. The Basic Law adopted in 1992 declared that Saudi Arabia is a monarchy ruled by the sons and grandsons of King Abdul Aziz Al-Saud. The formation of political parties is forbidden.

Theological Basis

Wahhabi theology and jurisprudence is based respectively on the religious teachings of Ibn Taymiyah, a reformer who advocated a return to a fundamentalist interpretation of Koranic principles, and on the legal school of Ahmad ibn Hanbal, Muslim theologian, founder of Hanbali, the strictest of the 4 Islamic schools of law. Ibn Taymiah was Hanbal's disciple. They stress literal belief in the Koran and Hadith and the establishment of a Muslim state based solely on Islamic law. Their influence is pervasive. From an early age, 7-15, young men are indoctrinated in the Wahhabi worldview. At the ages of 15-25 most young adults are invited to take part in military training, preparing themselves for jihad, a very appealing siren song to young men whose imagination is fired up by legendary military heroes. Other young men are designated as teachers, but they must teach extreme fundamentalism. For all, the goal of total conquest of Muslim nations is always in the forefront of their minds.

Given the fact that in many parts of the Islamic world the term 'Wahhabi" is used pejoratively; the Saudis prefer to call themselves Unitarians, believers in one indivisible deity. The followers of both the Deobandi[27] movement and the Wahhabi movement reject the value of profane human knowledge. Both have spawned many fundamentalist groups in the Muslim world, including the Taliban, Hamas, Hezbollah. So, when we talk of "the Wahhabi" we are speaking of millions who have never been to Saudi Arabia, just as when we 'Catholic' we are referring million who have never been to Rome. The violence inflicted because of Deobandi and Wahhabi religious ideology has been substantial. Abu Abd al-Rahman al-Najdi, an al-Qaeda spokesman, in early October 2003, issued a statement:

"We call openly on our brothers, all the mujahideen in Iraq, to kill the Sunni clerics who befriend the Americans, because those clerics are infidel apostates, to kill every satanic Shiite Ayatollah who befriends the Americans -- first among them the satanic Ayatollah Mohammed Bahr al-Ulum and those like him. Likewise we demand from the Shiite youth that they return to the book of God and the Sunnah[28] of Mohammed."

Among the thousands of discussions of Islamic fundamentalism since September 11, one statement sums up the religious connection: "Not all Muslims are suicide bombers, but all Muslim suicide bombers are Wahhabi." There is a complete list of terrorists and groups identified under Executive Order 13224, signed by President Bush on September 23, 2001.[29] The Wahhabi ascendancy to the dominating religious role in Saudi Arabia came to its apex in the 1970s when wealthy Saudis were happy to build Wahhabi schools and mosques, not only in Islamabad and Riyadh but overseas as well, in their historic quid-pro-quo relationship. Changing the status quo will be difficult. Getting Riyadh to divorce itself from radical Wahhabism would be like the Soviet Union in its heyday, renouncing communism. Is there a Saudi "Gorbachev" out there? Perhaps, but as yet he has not made his presence felt. The Wahhabi portray themselves as the custodians of Islam. As proof of this they point to the fact that they guard and are entrusted with the world's two most famous Islamic shrines; one at Medina and the other at Mecca. The obvious conclusion, they say, is that Wahhabism constitutes the right version of Islam.

Worldwide Network

The ideological onslaught of Wahhabism is massive and worldwide, beginning with the heart of Islam, Mecca. Millions of pilgrims receive packets of Wahhabi literature in their home language (over 100 languages), in order to reinforce the image. Since Wahhabism is the basis for an entire political/religious system, it is not surprising that, in spite of their hard line approach to others, the Wahhabi are more interested in survival than in the purity of their religious fanaticism.

They are not always winners in Arab lands. Expressing a more aggressive policy toward Wahhabi propaganda in Kuwait, the former Kuwaiti oil minister Ali al-Baghli wrote in the Kuwait daily Al Qabas on February 2, 2005: "What is needed is to cut off the snake's head, namely the masters of terror and all those who propagate terror in mosques and the media." The Associated Press confirmed that Kuwaiti authorities have blocked Islamic websites that incite violence, have seized radical books from mosques, and have purged textbooks of extremism. Several Muslims arrested in Turkey for fomenting subversive activities grew up in Germany and attended Islamic schools there. Bernard Lewis writes that, "The Islam which is taught in German schools is the complete Wahhabi version." In Spain, where the very large Islamic Center of Madrid has been directly financed by Saudi Arabia, Wahhabism is on the rise. As long ago as 2002, the Spanish secret services were worried about the radicalization of the local Muslim community. So, it came as no surprise after the March 11, 2004 train bombings in Madrid, that a connection was made between a Madrid mosque and the men arrested for the bombing.

In France, which has the largest Muslim community in Europe, between 5 million and 8 million people, the link between radical mosques and terrorism is strong. Louis Caprioli, former head of the counterterrorism unit of the DST, the French equivalent of the FBI, had this to say: "Behind every Muslim terrorist is a radical imam." The DST finally arrested imam Binchellali on January 6, 2003, along with his wife, another son, and a Vénissieux pharmacist on the grounds that they were planning a major chemical attack in France. French authorities learned, in March 2005, (as reported in the daily Le Parisien) that a group of detained Islamists confirmed that Binchellali had installed a chemical lab in his apartment and was on his way to manufacturing bombs containing the deadly poison ricin.

Three young French Muslims died fighting the Coalition in Iraq, and three more were arrested by American troops in Falluja. All six had attended the same mosque in Paris, where the imam called for young men to join the jihad. The mother of one of them told a reporter her son had been brainwashed and manipulated by an Islamist guru. Finally, the government of the Netherlands has been on alert since the murder of Theo Van Gogh, on November 2, 2004, by an Islamist following the release of Van Gogh's documentary critical of Islam. The government issued a report on "Saudi Influences in the Netherlands: Links between the Salafist Mission, Radicalization Processes, and Islamic Terrorism" (available in English on the website of the Dutch Interior Ministry). It speaks of "sermons and prayers that showed overt jihadist features, in which, for example, Allah was asked to 'deal with the enemies of Islam,' namely Bush, Sharon, and the 'enemies of Islam in Chechnya and Kashmir.'" In Saudi Arabia if democratic reforms do not come at the hands of the Family of Saud, then, when it does come, it could arrive in the form of revenge on the Wahhabi and the House of Saud.

As for the Saudi and Wahhabi establishments, their determination to maintain the status quo is leading them to international isolation. History is replete with such failed political and ideological enterprises. They must know as (their frantic efforts to hide the true nature of their activity prove) they are hurtling toward a dead end. They fear what is probably true, i.e., if they destroy their religious base they destroy whatever credibility and source of power they have left. They live in a milieu of uneasiness, but are destined to go down with the ship. Their inability to change determines their ultimate end. In Iraq, the extremists' nightmare scenario is that the Americans and the Iraqi Shiites will, by example, force Riyadh to enact broad reforms and bring the Saudi Shiites into the political community. That, of course, would end the reign of the Family of Saud. The West needs to be mindful of such fears, even within the Family of Saud. A specific policy of assisting and cajoling the Saudis to make a 180 degree turn would help them as well as the rest of us. In the final analysis, we are all brothers and sisters.

There is no question that many hard-line Saudi clerics share precisely the same fears. Even before the United States attacked Afghanistan, Saudi clerics preached the doctrine of a Jewish-American conspiracy to destroy Islam. The Saudi religious establishment fears the possibility (as time passes, even the likelihood) that the Americans and the Shiites will join forces to rid the world of Wahhabism. They encourage, abet, and pay suicide bombers for attacks on American soldiers and Shiite mosques. "The friend of my enemy is my enemy."

The citizens of Najaf had no doubt who was responsible for all the sufferings and damage in that great city: "Wahhabi," cried one group. "Baathists," cried another. Washington is very sensitive to the fact that if it continues business-as-usual with the Saudis, it will become painted with the Wahhabi brush. Sunni radical, Nasir al-Umar, urges the Saudi government to fire Shiite employees from any position of responsibility. Most commentators interpret him as urging the Saudi government to engage in some form of ethnic cleansing in the Shiite dominated eastern province. For al-Ulmar, the war in Iraq demonstrated "the strength of the bond between America and the Shiite heretics," to destroy the Sunni community. Iran was not excluded from the long reach of the Wahhabi. Beginning in 1979, after the revolutionary Shiite clergy in Iran overthrew the monarchy and panicked the Saudi royal family, Wahhabi "missionaries" were given a free hand and countless millions to spread their anti-Shiite faith all over the world. It was their way of protesting Shiite success in Iran.

The Saudi royal family belatedly recognized in 2004 that Wahhabism was sowing the seeds of the kingdom's destruction. More than 1,000 imams were summoned to a meeting in Riyadh and told they could no longer use the words jihad (holy war) and jihadis (holy warriors) in their Friday prayers under penalty of detention and rehabilitation. Because of the long-honored pact with Wahhabism, the Saudi royal family feels protected against the kind of democratic tidal wave that swept over Iraq in 2005, where 6 million citizens who could have been murdered for voting, voted. And then, of course, in the convoluted politics of the Middle East, there is always Osama bin Laden. He will keep "the troops" in line, even if he hates the Royal Family.

Salafism

Wahhabism did not spread in the modern Muslim world under its own banner, but under that of Salafism. It is important to note that the term "Wahhabism" is considered derogatory to the followers of Abd al-Wahhab since Wahhabi prefer to see themselves as the representatives of Islamic orthodoxy. This was a very crafty political move. Salafism has even done its best to interpret contemporary forms of democracy and socialism in terms of the teachings of Mohammed. It has been accused of opportunism, but perhaps that is too harsh, since it was doing nothing more than abandoning rigid apologetics that isolated it from the world as it was developing. It also gave them an opportunity for their own survival to pretend that it was Islam that developed democratic institutions, liberated women and contributed greatly to the developing world. Thus, the Wahhabi, while remaining rigid, felt safe enough to identify them with the more acceptable Salafi. The Wahhabi were so successful in this metamorphosis, that in the 1970s a new term emerged: Salafabism.

The Wahhabi are determined to create a new golden age of Islam, a modern Islamic utopia. In the face of historical reality, 'on the ground,' very few Muslims really believe this is going to happen. Nevertheless, it remains true that in rejecting an Islamic School label, the Wahhabi have successfully given their religious movement and doctrines a universality that otherwise it would not have. Once again, as a reality check, we need to remind ourselves that fundamentalist Christians think along the same lines. The fact that Islamic fundamentalism is afraid of the consequences of modernity says far more about the fundamentalists than it does of modernity. When faithfulness to a written text comes in the context of self-righteousness and a studied ignorance of world realities, it becomes as dangerous as the proverbial cornered animal. Its inner logic becomes so twisted that it loses all theological or philosophical meaning. Salafabism has made a determination not to identify itself with a legitimate culture but rather to identify itself with a vague, all-pervasive counter-culture. Salafabism is, in reality, the total domination of Salafism by Wahhabism, but it remains convenient for the Wahhabi not to reveal this.

Ahmed Shah Massoud

Nations sometimes make deals with groups and movements and governments that they later regret having made. An example was America's support of the Taliban in an effort to dislodge the Soviets from Afghanistan. Of course in the long run it all turned out well for the Afghan people, but that is not the point. Let us take a brief look at a man who could have removed, if he had been supported by the United States, the source of many U.S. woes. He is, perhaps, the archetypical opponent of Wahhabi inspired and Wahhabi financed international terrorism. He was the Afghan anti-Taliban resistance leader. His name is Ahmed Shah Massoud. Massoud was born in 1952, about 60 miles north of Kabul, and by 1978 he had already dedicated his life to the removal of the Soviet-backed Communist rule of Afghanistan. He developed his habitat, Panjshir Valley, into his well-fortified base of operations against the Soviet military in Afghanistan. Like the present-day attempt to kill or capture bin Laden, the Soviets tried mightily to eliminate or capture him, but he survived, later achieving the high status of the Lion of the Panjshir. He was part of the U.S.-backed Afghan Islamic resistance, the Mujahideen, although from his home base.

In 1992 Massoud captured Kabul and helped to establish the first Mujahideen Islamic government. His moderation and foresight did not prevail and Afghanistan came under the control of the Wahhabi Taliban. Massoud repeatedly warned the international community that a dangerous alliance was developing between the extremist Islamic Taliban militia, and al-Qaeda. He appealed to the United States, but Washington decided not to support him. In spite of this, his forces provided the critical bridgehead in the U.S. campaign against terror in Afghanistan. His struggle against the Taliban and Al-Qaeda resulted in his assassination on September 9, 2001 suspiciously close to the 9/11 attacks on the United States. Massoud was a remarkable liberation strategist and fighter. In Afghanistan, he is officially recognized as a national hero.

Arab nations Vulnerable

With the exception of Turkey, there is not a single stable democracy in the Islamic world. Therefore, one is not surprised to observe that Muslims living under repressive regimes turn to Islamists for moral and military support. The Middle East fragile civil society is described by Human Rights Watch in its report of 2003: "Throughout the region, political parties…and other entities came under attack from the state…because laws did not permit them to exist legally. In Iran and Saudi Arabia, conservative clerical establishments remained entrenched and powerful…"

On July 2, 2002, in a depressing report on Arab societies, the United Nations Development Program released the Arab Human Development Report 2002. It reports the general lack of civil freedoms and the repression of women. Arabs wrote the report. The Middle East Quarterly, reported: "with uncommon candor and a battery of statistics, a sorry story of two decades of failed planning and developmental decline. One inescapable conclusion emerges… the Arab world is in decline, even relative to the developing world." The fact that the report was written by Arabs made its arguments more palatable to Arab intellectuals and policy makers. However, such political soil is ripe for Wahhabi influence and domination, for money talks and the Wahhabi, thanks to the House of Saud, have plenty to spread around.

PART TWO:

TERRORISM AND ITS ENABLERS

Chapter Eight

THE 'PAPAL SUCCESSION' OF ISLAMIC TERRORISTS

There are many names that can be mentioned when discussing the founders of terrorism, but some stand out. We shall highlight them and describe their individual contributions. As with the successors of St. Peter, there is a chain connecting each of the major founders, and here we profile them. Other important but lesser lights will be either footnoted or briefly mentioned; for example, the founder of the Muslim Brotherhood, Hasasin al Banna. In the mid 1970s he, along with Sayyid Mawdudi and Sayyid Qutb became the spiritual fathers of the emerging revival of Islam in the former Muslim Central Asian republics of the Soviet Union.

"Papal" Succession

The man we discuss first is Sayyid Abdul'l-A'la Mawdudi. Mawdudi leads us to Sayyid Qutb; Qutb leads us to Abdullah Azzam; Azzam leads us to Osama bin Laden, Osama bin Laden leads us to Ayman al-Zawahiri. Zawahiri leads us to Zarqawi in Iraq. We know where Zarqawi, the butcher of Baghdad, led us. We now watch his successor, Abu Hamza al Masri. He appears, in the Fall of 2006 to be on the same path. This knowledge is invaluable for making informed decisions about the future of anti-terrorism methods.

Sayyid Abu -A'la Mawdudi

Sayyid Abdul'l-A'la Mawdudi (1903-1979) was born in the city of Aurangabad in South India. Beside being a significant Muslim personality on his own, for our purposes he leads us along the chain to Sayyhid Qutb, who, inspired by Mawdudi, developed, more than any other modern Muslim, a strain of Islam that advocates the use of violence in the quest for Islamic purity. Not only is violence in that quest legitimate, but may even be required of religious Muslims. Mawdudi studied at the Fatihpuri mosque seminary in New Delhi in the early 1920s. He moved to Hyderabad where, while leading the Muslim community, he contemplated and agonized over the serious decline of Muslim influence in India. He came to the conclusion that the ecumenical practices among Muslims and Hindus were the underlying cause of their moral decay. His solution: Islam must be purged of all alien elements, and all social and political ties with Hindus must be severed. Contact with non-Muslims, in his view, was polluting the pure religious way of life inherited from the Prophet. He believed in active resistance to any action he considered to be an aberration of Islamic doctrine. He justified his warlike attitude on a passage from the Koran, s.2:190-193, and on the hadith, "I have been ordered to fight people (al-nas) until they say 'There is no God but God.'"

Maududi became a journalist at the age of 17. In just a few short years he moved from the editorship of small newspapers to that of large and influential Islamic newspapers, including Muslim (1921-23), and later of al-Jam'iyat (1925-28), both of which were organs of the Jam'iyat-i 'Ulama-i Hind, an organization of Muslim religious scholars. He soon became recognized as an outstanding Islamic scholar by producing his first major work, al-Jihad fi al-Islam, a treatise on the Islamic law of war and peace. He attacked nationalism as incompatible with Islamic teaching, claiming that it would lead to the destruction of Muslim identity. At this point he had become very famous in the world of Islam.

His fame brought him invitations to lecture in many cities During 1956-74 he lectured in Cairo, Damascus, Amman, Makka, Medina, Jeddah, Kuwait, Rabat, Istanbul, London, New York, and Toronto. He was invited to take a prominent part in ten major Islamic international conferences, and devoted himself to visiting Islam's holy places in Saudi Arabia, Jordan, Syria and Egypt. In 1952, he became a co-founder of the Islamic University of Medina, and remains today the most widely read Islamic scholar. His works have been translated into Arabic, English, Turkish, Persian, Hindi, French, German, Swahili, Tamil, and Bingali. In April 1979, suffering from kidney and heart problems, he left for the United States and was hospitalized in Buffalo, New York. After several operations, he died on September 22, 1979 at the age of 76. His funeral was held in Buffalo but he was buried in an unmarked grave at his home in Lahore. He died honored by this fellow Muslims worldwide.

For Maududi, Jihad, including war, is a major tool in bringing about the Caliphate. He wrote: "(Islam) wants and requires the entire inhabited world... in order that the human race can enjoy the concept and practical program of human happiness." To attain this blessed state the people must employ all forces and means necessary for bringing about a universal all-embracing revolution.

Sayyid Qutb-The Father of Militant Islam

Sayyid Qutb, 1906-1966, an Egyptian and a member of the Muslim Brotherhood, was a prominent Islamist, a chief architect of contemporary Islamic resurgence, a thinker strongly influenced by Maududi's revolutionary radicalism. Qutb, perhaps more than any other radical Islamist, influenced the thinking of Muslim Arab youths since the 1960s. He was born in 1906. His private time he dedicated to studying literary criticism, a practice that preoccupied him for the rest of his life. His free time he spent in the company of other scholars and poets. However, his book, jahiliyya ("pagan ignorance and rebellion against God"), inspired a host of today's revivalists to engage in Islamic Jihad. In 1941, he founded Jama'at-I Islami. Between 1948 and 1950 he lived in the United State in order to study American educational institutions, but was unable to adjust to its culture. Qutb described American churches as entertainment centers and sexual playgrounds. He left America determined to play a role in ridding the world of such a culture. Upon his return home in 1951 he joined the fundamentalist Muslim Brotherhood, and his life took a very radical turn. The Muslim Brotherhood is a social and political movement which was started in Egypt in 1928 by Hasan al-Banna for the purpose of establishing a pan-Islamic state, transcending all current political and geographic divisions.

In his writings "Signposts on the Road," and "A Muslim's Nationality and his Beliefs," he confronted modernity and challenged its presuppositions, especially the idea of Western democracy. Democracy, for Qutb, was the road that led to cultural and political destruction. His followers throughout the Arab world today uphold his message and the Wahhabi fund their programs. Qutb, together with a group of army officers, self-styled 'Free Officers', and sympathetic members of the Muslim Brotherhood, plotted to remove King Farouk of Egypt from power. The group included such figures as then colonels Gamal Abd al-Nasser (who assumed power as a result of the group's actions) and Anwar Sadat, who called Qutb the inspirer of the Free Officers' revolution.

During the period 1948-66, Qutb was put behind bars on four different occasions, in different prisons. Later, he was sentenced to 15 years imprisonment with hard labor in Jarah prison near Cairo. After serving 10 years of his sentence his health deteriorated and he was released through the good offices of the Iraqi President, Abdul Salam Arif. Later, he spent more time in jail for his association with the Muslim Brotherhood, was released in 1964, and rearrested in 1965 after members of the Brotherhood attempted to assassinate Nasser. As far as the Egyptian authorities were concerned, Qutb's fingerprints were all over the plot. He was hanged on August 29 1966. Ironically, the specific charge against him was that he denounced the existing order in Muslim societies. In the end, the purist was not considered a pure Muslim. His best-known work is Milestones [Ma'alim fi'l Tariq].

In total, he authored more than one hundred works on Islam, and his writings have been translated into forty languages. No one escaped his criticism, especially those who simply 'pretended' to be Muslims, and more especially those who were charged with the duty of implementing the Sharia, including Nasser and the Saudi royal family. He declared that the leaders of most Islamic countries were corrupt, ignorant, and irreligious.

He compared them to the Jahili Arabs, i.e., the pre-Mohammed Arabs who lived pagan lives. "They should be over-thrown," he declared. His words haunt the Saudi monarchy, mo-tivating it to support Wahhabi terrorist organizations with a view to keeping them away from its doorstep. In militant Islam his ap-peal is universal. He inspired the reclusive and shy Taliban leader, Mullah Omar, whose goal was limited to establishing Sharia law in one nation under the guidance of the Mullahs. He also has greatly inspired and motivated the media-wise al-Qaeda leader, bin Laden, who aspires to a global jihad without the re-strictions that the Mullahs might bring to the table. It was not un-til the creation of the Afghan mujahideen in the 1980s that the disparate elements, mullah and foot soldier, dreamers and doers, came together to create a fighting force. Peshawar, Pakistan, was where the terrorists gathered, the place where sweet Pakistani "milk tea" and where Wahhabism and its relatives were served a la carte. (Abdullah Azzam, the Jihad Godfather. Azzam is dis-cussed in great detail in Chapter 13 because of his connection with the city of Peshawar, so we move on to the most famous Is-lamic terrorist)

Osama bin Laden[30]

The Spiritual Leader of Al-Qaeda, Osama bin Laden, born in Riyadh, Saudi Arabia, 1957, one of 20 sons, is of Saudi Yemeni origins. His family is a prominent pillar of the Saudi Arabian rul-ing class, with close personal, financial and political ties to that country's royal family. King Faisal appointed his father Saudi Arabia's minister of public works. Not being a shy man, bin Laden senior promptly awarded his own construction company lucrative contracts to rebuild Islam's holiest mosques in Mecca and Medina. An already rich man became super rich. In the process, the bin Laden family company became, in 1996, the world's largest private construction company. Osama bin Laden's father died in 1968, leaving him a personal fortune of $200-300 million. To Abdullah Azzam's good fortune bin Laden used it to bankroll Azzam's military action against the Soviet occupation of Afghanistan.

Bin Laden's al-Qaeda gradually developed

During the Taliban regime al-Qaeda operated out of Afghanistan and maintained its training camps there. Their autonomous underground cells can now be found in the United States, the United Kingdom, Italy, France, Spain, Germany, Albania, Uganda, and elsewhere. It's impossible to say precisely how many members it has because al-Qaeda is decentralized. Estimates range from several hundred to several thousand members. Sheikh Omar Abdel Rahman, the militant cleric convicted in the 1993 plot, once led an Egyptian group now affiliated with al-Qaeda; two of his sons are senior al-Qaeda officials. Many of his operatives live in the United States. In February 2003, FBI Director Robert Mueller stated that several hundred Islamist radicals with links to al-Qaeda are living in America, some of them organized into cells that are plotting future attacks. In January 2003, British officials said that documents in their possession led them to conclude that al-Qaeda had successfully built a small "dirty bomb."[31]

Bin Laden first took an interest in Iraq when that country invaded Kuwait in 1990. He feared that the secular Iraqi Baathist party might invade Saudi Arabia, so he offered to send his mujahideen militias to Saudi Arabia to defend the homeland against a possible Saddam military thrust. The Saudi government declined, opting to invite the Americans instead. Bin Laden became a "terrorist" in U.S. eyes when he fell out with the Saudi royal family over its decision to allow more than 540,000 US troops to be stationed on Saudi Arabian soil. His initial anger turned to rage and his rage turned to plans for attacking American interest wherever he could. He declared that Saudi Arabia was an American puppet and that it was the duty of every Muslim to drive the U.S. out of the Gulf States. Like the proverbial City, Osama never sleeps.

If American policy makers had hindsight as part of their foresight, they would certainly have done things differently. The CIA, Pakistan, and Britain armed the Afghan contra fighters, including the tens of thousands of mercenaries recruited and paid for by bin Laden. Tom Carew, a former British SAS soldier who fought with the mujahideen, told the August 13, 2000 British Observer, "The Americans were keen to teach the Afghans the techniques of urban terrorism — car bombing and so on — so that they could strike at the Russians in major towns ... Many of them are now using their knowledge and expertise to wage war on everything they hate."

In cooperation with other terrorist networks bin Laden maintained training camps in the Sudan, and Yemen, where he trained fighters for Islamist armies as far apart from each other as Chechnya and western China. The men he trained in Afghanistan are believed to have created cells in some 50 countries, thus widening the base of potential threats against the U.S. Milt Bearden, the CIA's station chief in Pakistan from 1986 to 1989, admitted to the January 24, 2000, New Yorker that while he never personally met bin Laden, "Did I know that he was out there? Yes, I did ...[Guys like] bin Laden were bringing $20-$25 million a month from other Saudis and Gulf Arabs to underwrite the war. And that is a lot of money. It's an extra $200-$300 million a year. And this is what bin Laden did."

Twin Towers

Was bin Laden behind the September 11 attacks? Perhaps. Investigators found financial records, and communications among al-Qaeda members, linking bin Laden to September 11. Moreover, bin Laden and other al-Qaeda operatives appear to have claimed responsibility for the attacks. In a videotape recorded in Afghanistan in November 2001, bin Laden said of the strikes on the World Trade Center. "We had notification since the previous Thursday that the event would take place that day," he said. "We calculated in advance the number of casualties." In another tape released in April 2002, bin Laden and one of his top deputies were shown kneeling to praise their "great victory" on September 11.

In any case, bin Laden has learned from 9/11 that infrastructural damage on a large scale can destabilize international stock markets. This, he reasons correctly, can strengthen his own position in his adversarial engagement with the United States and its Western allies. Bin Laden was asked in an interview why he had issued a call for Muslims to take arms against America in particular. His answer: "The call to wage war against America was made because America has spear-headed the crusade against the Islamic nation, sending tens of thousands to their death." He was then asked what he had to say about the fact that the West considered him a terrorist. His answer: "Terrorizing oppressors and criminals and thieves and robbers is necessary for the safety of people and for the protection of their property." His message to Israel was particularly severe. "The enmity between us and the Jews goes far back in time and is deep rooted. There is no question that war between the two of us is inevitable"

Certainly bin Laden wants to wound the U.S. but he is too realistic to believe that he can destroy it. Also, he does continue to keep the Family of Saud on pins and needles. Although the current policy of the princes of the Arabian Peninsula is to pour out money for terrorists in the hope that al-Qaeda and its allies will go away and pick on someone else, that is unlikely to happen. Bin laden has his eyes on the Family of Saud and, suitcases of money or not, they know he is there and untamed. The last known sighting of bin Laden was on November 10, 2002 in Jalalabad, capital of Eastern Afghanistan's Nanzaher Province. He was seen standing in front of Babarak Khan's row of guesthouses, surrounded by a host of security folks. "We saw Osama while standing here in front of our guest house with many Cars and six armored vehicles at 9 p.m. on that Tuesday." He emerged from one of several hundred that made up his convoy sporting a Kalishnakov machine gun. He was visibly nervous as he held the hand of Maulvi Abdul Kabir, the Taliban governor of Jalalabad, a custom for Muslim men who are spiritually close. He is a survivor.

Ayman al-Zawahiri

Pursuing Ayman al-Zawahiri, al-Qaeda's CEO and number-two man with a 25 million dollar price tag for his capture could be a full-time occupation. He had unlikely beginnings as a member of one of Egypt's most respected families, a graduate of an exclusive preparatory school, a learned scholar, an accomplished eye surgeon and poet. His grandfather was the grand imam of Al Azhar in Cairo, one of the most important mosques in the Arab world and a center of Islamic thought. A great-uncle was the first secretary-general of the Arab League. Al Zawahiri is the "mastermind" behind al-Qaeda attacks, and a principal founder of the Egyptian Islamic Jihad, as well as the chief ideologue of al-Qaeda. He is "credited" with being the operational brains behind the 11 September attacks on the World Trade Center. Foden, author of a book on the 1998 US embassy bombings in Kenya and Tanzania, revealed that Dr Zawahiri controls most of al-Qaeda's finance operations. He faces a death sentence in Egypt for his involvement in the 1981 assassination of President Anwar Sadat.

Zawahiri has written several books to morally justify indiscriminate murder under the pretext of jihad, one of which is, *Knights Under the Prophet's Banner*, written in an Afghan cave while avoiding the U.S. bombers overhead. Certainly, from a material point of view, he gave up a lot. He went from attending to the rich and famous in his once flourishing medical clinic, and being a frequenter of trendy art galleries, to sharing a cave with bin Laden in Afghanistan. In 1998, he was the second of five signatories to bin Laden's notorious 1998 "fatwa" calling for attacks against US civilians. His monitored satellite telephone conversations were used as proof that bin Laden was behind 9/11. He is also listed on the US Government's indictment sheet for his role in the 1998 U.S. embassy bombings in East Africa.

Bin Laden first met Zawahiri in Peshawar in the mid-1980s, but it wasn't Zawahiri's first trip to that city of terrorists. He had already spent half a year there in 1980 working with the Islamic Red Crescent in a hospital for wounded mujahideen. His appointment by a number of militant groups as press spokesperson catapulted his identity and reputation among Arabs. He has become a superstar among terrorists and many observers believe that he directs al-Qaeda, while bin Laden, a greater-than-life internationally known superstar, keeps the dollars coming in from Saudi Arabia and elsewhere. His command of English is also important for his ability to communicate directly with British and American readers or audiences. Hiding somewhere in the mountains of Afghanistan, the gray-bearded Ayman al-Zawahiri shares the same vision and has been working side by side with bin Laden for ten years. In spite of his education and sophistication, he set his course at the age of 15 when he became a member of Egypt's Muslim Brotherhood.

The Russian Connection

Zawahiri is suspected of connections with Russian intelligence circles. In the early morning hours of 1 December 1996, al-Zawahiri, disguised as Mr. Amin and using fake Sudanese passports tried, together with two associates and a Chechen guide, to cross the Chechen border in an attempt to establish a base in that territory. He was arrested at the border with his advanced communications equipment and a large sum of money in different denominations. According to Jane's Intelligence Review, October 3, 2001, he also had "a visa application for Taiwan; a bank card from Hong Kong; details of a bank account in Guangdong, China, a receipt for a computer modem bought in Dubai, a copy of a Malaysian company's registration certificate that listed Dr. Zawahiri under an alias, as a director, and details of an account in a bank in St. Louis, Mo." When asked about the purpose of his visit, he replied that he wanted to inquire of the price for leather, medicine and other goods. His real intention: To set up a training camp in Chechnya for his Egyptian jihad movement. Two Wall Street Journal reporters, Alan Cullison and Andrew Higgins, purchased Zawahiri's discarded laptop computer. This enabled them to follow his actions and plans going back for a long period of time. They downloaded hundreds of files regarding the organization, including his private correspondence and mode of operation. They described the event:[32] Traveling in a minivan with two confederates, he came equipped with $6,400 in cash, a fake identity as a businessman, a laptop computer, a satellite phone, a fax machine and a small library of medical textbooks.

The Russians, who have very serious problems in Chechnya at the hands of the Wahhabi, kept Zawahiri in detention for six months. Anyone who is familiar with the KGB system should know that Zawahiri's release would never have happened unless a deal was made with the Russians. This had to be the case, since the death penalty or life imprisonment would have been the natural result of aiding and abetting the very Wahhabi who were and are killing Russian soldiers and civilians in Chechnya. KGB detainees in Soviet days were never released from KGB custody without a written agreement to cooperate with them in the future, an agreement which, if not adhered to, would result in the most serious consequences, including assassination. It is inconceivable that Zawahiri would simply have been released unless he made them an offer they could not refuse.[33]

A University Responds

An explosive attack on al-Zawahiri came from Al-Azhar University in Cairo.[34] The University accuses him of wanting to use Egypt as "an Islamic base through which they exercise control over the Arab and Muslim world." He is accused of wanting to create a Caliphate like the one the Taliban leader, Mullah Omar, created in Afghanistan. The University takes the gloves off. They accuse him of murdering tourists, killing a child[35] and terrorizing anyone who disagrees with him. He has a lot of blood on his hands, they said. al-Zawahiri's movement is "a misguided group outside the book of Allah and his messenger."[36] And, in reference to Zawahiri's call for Islamic fighters to be efficient in their work, others point out that when one of his aides was arrested he had on his person a computer disc listing all the members of the Islamic Jihad worldwide, resulting in the conviction of 108 members of the organization. We do not know where Zawahiri is but like the Heisenberg principle[37] we always know where he was by tracking the trail of his destruction, murder and mayhem.

Musab al-Zarqawi

The now-famous beheader of Baghdad, Musab al-Zarqawi, was born in October 1966, in Jordan. The son of Palestinian refugees, Zarqawi grew up in Zarqa and at the age of 17 he dropped out of school. In 1989, he traveled to Afghanistan to join the US-backed insurgency against the Soviet invasion of Afghanistan, so he became a reporter for an Islamist newsletter. Reportedly, he then traveled to Europe and started the al-Tawhid militant organization, a group dedicated to killing Jews and installing an Islamic regime in Jordan. He was arrested in Jordan in 1992, and spent seven years in a Jordanian prison for conspiring to overthrow the monarchy and establish an Islamic Caliphate. The U.S. government offered a $25 million reward for information leading to his capture. On October 21, 2004, Zarqawi officially announced his allegiance to al-Qaeda. On December 27, 2004. Al-Jazeera broadcast an audiotape of bin Laden calling Zarqawi "the prince of al-Qaeda in Iraq" and asked "all our organization brethren to listen to him and obey him in his good deeds." On 15 October 2004, the U.S. State Department added Zarqawi and the Jama'at al-Tawhid wal Jihad group to its list of Foreign Terrorist Organizations and ordered a freeze on any assets that the group might have in the United States. He fled Jordan and traveled to Peshawar, Pakistan, near the Afghan border. In Afghanistan, Zarqawi established a militant training camp that competed with al-Qaeda for recruits and specialized in poisons and explosives.

In May 2004 a videotape was released showing a group of five men beheading American-Israeli dual citizen Nick Berg, a civilian who had been abducted and taken hostage in Iraq weeks earlier. The speaker on the tape, wielding the knife that killed Nick Berg, identified himself as Zarqawi and claimed responsibility for planning the operation. He stated that the murder was in retaliation for U.S. abuses at the Abu Ghraib prison. CIA analysis of the voice concluded that it was indeed Zarqawi's. Bin Laden said that he was "pleased" with al-Zarqawi's "gallant operations" against the Americans. After killing Baghdad's Shiite Governor Ali-al-Haidari, Zarqawi posted a statement on Al-Qaeda's website, "We tell every traitor and supporter of the Jews and Christians that this is your fate. Zarqawi was killed in Iraq in July 2006. We can now observe his successor, Abu Ayyub al Masri." The 'Papal Succession' goes on.

Chapter Nine

ISLAMIC TERRORISM

Terrorism and violence is not the same thing, even though they can be mixed together in a particular incident. There are four key elements in an act of terrorism:

—It is premeditated—planned in advance, rather than an impulsive act of rage.

—It is political—not criminal, like the violence that groups such as the mafia use to get money, but designed to change the existing political order.

—It is aimed at civilians—not at military targets or combat-ready troops.

—It is carried out by subnational groups—not by the army of a country.

Terrorism as Theater

One thing we average citizens observe about terrorism versus simple violence is that in the case of simple violence the perpetrator would rather not be identified. In fact, the first thing he does is run away from the scene and hide. However, an act of terrorism is the ultimate theater. It begs for recognition and free advertising. When Hamas kills civilians in Israel, it does not hide underground. On the contrary, a press conference is called to say "We did it." What event in history has received more world-wide media coverage than the bombing of the World Trade Center? It might not be an exaggeration to say that billions of television viewers saws the event and its aftermath, giving instant notoriety and advertising to al-Qaeda and its leader, Osama bin Laden, a man who thrives on media coverage. Terrorists love audiences, and that bombing was the ultimate audience generator.

Religion and Terrorism

We all know the expression: Religion is the last refuge of scoundrels. Perhaps you may have thought of that each time you saw Saddam Hussein kneeling down and praying in one or other of Iraq's mosques. Regrettably, religiously inspired or pseudo religiously inspired terrorist groups are the fastest growing form of terrorism. When religion becomes ideology it can be the most dangerous form of terror. What could be more terrifying than for a religious teacher to tell his students that if they want to go to heaven all they need to do is strap a bomb around their waist and explode it in a restaurant in order to kill men, women and other children? It is horrifying but it goes on every day somewhere around the world.

Even heads of state have been killed by suicide bombers. The Tamil Tigers of Sri Lanka killed two heads of state, Indian Prime Minister Rajiv Gandhi, in 1991, and Sri Lankan President Ranasinghe Premadasa, in 1993. Other groups that engage in suicide bombings are Hezbollah, the Palestinian Islamist group Hamas, and al-Qaeda (two famous cases were the bombings of the U.S. embassies in Kenya and Tanzania in 1998.) Women are also used in suicide bombings, especially pregnant ones. Often they are dressed to either give the appearance of being pregnant or are actually pregnant, giving them easier access to areas where the bombs are to be detonated. Women have carried out about one-third of the Tamil Tiger suicide attacks and two-thirds of the PKK's. Robert A. Pape writes in the New York Times, Tuesday, September 23, 2003:

"Most worrisome, my research shows that the raw number of suicide attacks has been climbing at an alarming rate, even while the rates of other types of terrorism actually declined." The first female Palestinian suicide bombers began to appear in 2002. Many students are vulnerable because they do not understand the subtly nuanced 7th and 8th century verses of the Koran that are related to the totally different social and political realities of the early Islamic state.

Terrorism of the Coward

After religious sponsorship of terrorism comes another despicable form of terrorism, the terrorism of the coward. A coward is a person who is afraid to perpetrate an evil act himself for fear of getting caught. He pays someone else to perform the act. Nation states sometime engage in this activity. Actually, this is the second most common form of terrorism. All you need to be this kind of terrorist is a lot of money. And there are states ready to pay if their own agendas can be advanced. It happens so often that the expression "state-sponsored terrorism" Is now a part of every language's lexicon. In waging the war against terrorism, however, the U.S. government needs to be aware of the extent to which some of its "allies," in spite of public statements to the contrary, are using the anti-terrorist crusade as an excuse to portray indigenous national liberation movements as Islamic terrorist organizations. This gives them a pretext for military and political repression. Perhaps the most obvious example of this is the Russian government's long and bloody war in Chechnya.

The Chechens

The Russian/Chechen quarrel has been going on since 1783. It started when Catherine the Great declared that the Caucasus belonged to her. The Chechens were Catherine's most ferocious opponents. They fought conquest until 1859, fought Russian occupation until 1917, were an autonomous region and then an autonomous republic under the Bolsheviks. Stalin deported many to Central Asia. After his death they returned. When President Boris Yeltsin in 1991 declared the Soviet Union finished, the Chechens declared independence.

President Vladimir Putin has exploited similarities in the ideological rhetoric of Chechen separatists and Islamic terrorists to equate the two and thereby seek U.S. and international sanction for military operations. This is the kind of "war against terrorism" that we must not fall into the trap of supporting. Pseudo Muslims desperately select a few verses out of context from the Koran and Islamic theology to use as pretext for terrorist acts.

Among Islamic militants we find Islamic socialism, Arabian nationalism and Iraqi-Syrian Baathism. These elements certainly constitute the fabric of al-Qaeda today. Islamic socialism, Arabian nationalism and Baathism emerged in Egypt, Syria, and Iraq in the early 1950s amid a growing determination to rid the Middle East of national monarchies. The founders of these three kinds of political movements were representatives of local intelligentsia, mostly younger military officers who were inspired by religious and nationalistic ideals. 9/11 and its exposure of the vulnerability of the United States and the West in general has encouraged a proliferation of terrorist groupings that want a piece of the action, that want to settle long-standing scores with the West.

For us to understand the growth of Islamic terrorism in spite of the strong Islamic teaching against it, we need to examine all the clues we can find. What we do know and what needs to be explained is that a very rich young bin Laden, son of one of the leading financial families in Saudi Arabia, gave up what would have been a life of luxury, comfort and social acceptance to become the world's most famous (infamous?) terrorist leader. Bin Laden was motivated by the so-called "Father of terrorism", Sayyid Qutb, whose life and death inspired the serious and radical decisions bin Laden made about the direction his life was to take. We need to know more about such men. Observing and reading what they did and said may bring us closer to an understanding of what, for a Westerner, is not understandable, i.e. the indiscriminate killing and maiming of the innocent in the name of religion. We want to know this, not just out of curiosity, although that is a normal human trait, but more importantly to understand how it is that so many Muslims now believe, contrary to the tenets of their own faith, that a jihad of war and blood, destruction and self-detonation is the raison d'etre and moral imperative of their young lives.

JIHAD

Many Muslim scholars are saddened at the thought that jihad, which means "internal struggle for a just cause," has been co-opted by extremists, and used by them to negatively depict all of Islam. Khalid Ahmed, an editor at The Friday Times, a weekly in Lahore, Pakistan, points out that "jihad is precisely the term being used to captivate youth here. The moderates are going to have to start dealing with that." In its literal sense jihad in Arabic simply means a struggle or striving to one's utmost to further a worthy cause. When the word jihad became a part of Islamic terminology, the concept of reward or worship came to be associated with it. One who struggles for a just cause out of love of Allah performs an act of worship, and has attached to it a reward from God. "Strive for the cause of God as you ought to strive."(The Koran :(22:78). In its literal sense jihad in Arabic simply means struggle — striving to one's utmost to further a worthy cause. As we say in English, "We must struggle against this prejudice". Jihad in the sense of an armed struggle (qital) is always subject to the Koranic condition of its being carried out in the path of God (jihad fi sabilillah). Struggle merely for the sake of acquiring material gain is completely forbidden by Islam. The only war which can be termed jihad is that which takes place solely for the sake of God's laws.

Verses in the book of Hadith[38] reflect the same meaning of jihad as found in the Koran, i.e., a struggle engaged in solely for material gain does not relate to God's understanding of jihad. An extension of this concept is that jihad is a defensive war, not a pre-planned aggressive act. The Koran is very specific about this. An unilateral aggression, i.e. when Muslims are attacked without provocation, simply because of the evil designs of an enemy, justifies a counter attack. As the Koran explains: "To those against whom war is made, permission is given (to fight) because they are wronged." (22:39) Unprovoked aggression justifies self defense. Except for that case, the Koran advises believers to avoid occasions of conflict. (7:199). Negotiation is preferable to laying down the gauntlet. Mohammed not only preached such a message, he also practiced it.

Certain verses in the Koran do, however, convey the command to do battle (qital) (22:39). If attacked and there is no diplomatic possibility of avoiding such an attack then the Koran is clear: "Fight for the sake of God those that fight against you, but do not be aggressive." (2:190). Defensive war is permitted in Islam, a war is one in which aggression is committed by some other party. Some like to quote the Koranic verse which reads: "Fight against them until fitna is no more," (2:193) as justification for war, this is a misinterpretation. Here, fitna signifies a political system which has gone to extremes in religious persecution.

Interestingly enough it was Islam that acted as a precursor in the fight against imperial rule and religious persecution, the kind of imperial rule that allowed for no freedom of speech, the kind of imperial rule that allowed a Roman emperor to kill and maim at will, even publicly. Not enough attention has been paid to the Islamic fight against this kind of oppression and its role in liberating people from tyranny. Its incredibly "Christian" response to oppression was similar to that of Martin Luther King and Gandhi. Absolutism always and everywhere crushes both spiritual and material progress by its arrogant intolerance of even the slightest deviation from the rules, even when, or, we should say, especially when the rules themselves are a form of humiliation and slavery. Saddam Hussein was simply the latest in a long list of egomaniacal absolutists. The video tape of him sitting at the first meeting he called of government ministers, gleefully watching his henchmen pick out members of the audience for immediate assassination, just at his whim, is the kind of absolutism that Mohammed railed against. He was a liberator at a time when absolutism flourished in both East and West. His fire was not the fire of revenge but of a well-balanced righteousness. Absolute imperialism had to be brought to an end, and this is what he represented. He fought for and then maintained freedom of thought. Considering the [political and sociological tenor of his time, comparing him to Martin Luther King and Gandhi is not out of line. He pointed to the Koran: "Cursed be the people of the trench, who lighted the consuming fire and who sat around it watching the believers whom they were torturing. And they had nothing against them, save that they believed in God, the Mighty, the Praiseworthy." (85:4-5) And, there is the Makkan tradition narrated by Khabbab ibn al Arat: "We claimed to the prophet at that time: when he was resting in the shade of the Kabah wall. We said to him: 'Don't you pray for us to God?' The prophet replied: Those who went before you faced such unbearable trials. One of them would be brought for trial, a pit would be dug for him, and then he would be buried in it in a standing posture, with his head above the edge of the pit. Then a saw would be passed through his head until it split into two parts. Yet even such severe trials did not cause him to waver from his faith. People were scraped with iron combs until their skin came off and the bones of their bodies were exposed.[39] Yet these acts of persecution did not deter them from adhering to their faith."

Was this any different from the opposition to Hitler and Stalin, Papa Doc and Saddam Hussein? Were nations able, justifiably, to sit back and watch fellow human beings tortured, maimed, gassed by the hundreds of thousands, and do nothing? In each of the above examples the Christian conscience prevailed and massive and effective opposition resulted in the end of dictatorial oppression. This was the challenge that Mohammed faced and he did not flinch. He called on all his followers to march for freedom and as a result the Sassanid and Byzantine empires were torn down and a better climate of freedom and humanity ensued.

For Islam as for Christians, religious coercion or persecution is totally against any sense of morality. Our mutual understanding is that God made us free, so free in fact that he would not interfere even with our doing of evil. That He is on the side of the persecuted and the oppressed is a given and that He would allow the persecuted and the oppressed to take up arms for the purpose of obtaining freedom is attested to by the lessons of history. Abdullah bin Umar, a companion of Mohammed, during the infighting that was taking place among Mohammed's followers, kept himself above the battle. Some of the members asked him: "has not God enjoined us to fight till persecution (fitna) ceased?" ibn Umar answered by defining the meaning of 'fitna' "We fought till fitna ceased. Religion became only for god, and now you want to fight so that fitna may return, and religion will no longer be for God."

In other words, we learn that the war against fitna was a war of limited duration, not meant to be engaged in beyond the point of its specific purpose being served. Invoking the Koranic exhortation to do battle against fitna in order to validate acts of war that had quite other aims is highly improper. For the Muslim all rites of worship have certain conditions for their proper performance. For example if prayers are said without ablution or in the opposite direction to the Kaba, they will not be acceptable to God. The same is the case with jihad. One of these conditions is that jihad (in the sense of fighting) should be a state affair. That is, it is not the prerogative of individuals. Islam does not give them the right to wage war in the name of jihad. They can perform peaceful jihad, that is, a struggling to the utmost in the cause of God. This may involve social work, educating people, striving to improve their spiritual life, etc. The Prophet of Islam called jihad the greater jihad. The right to declare war, or jihad bis saif, is vested only in an established government. Another condition is that there must be a reasonable expectation that a war would produce positive results, would advance the will of God in one form or another. If the net result of war is simply bloodshed and economic devastation then it is fasad and not jihad.

Another point is that, just as with the Just War Theory of the Catholic Church, even the jihad of war that was permissible in the past may no longer be permissible. The armed jihad in the past was done by the sword and confined to the battlefield. The rest of the world was not affected by it. Now, with the technology of modern warfare, it is impossible to confine the effects of war to the battlefield. Any armed jihad today will cause widespread destruction with innocent people being killed on a large scale, and the economy destroyed.

The Big Question

There are those who hold the view that jihad has to be waged to establish an Islamic world order. At no place in the Koran and Hadith do we find teachings that justify this kind of jihad. Anyone who expresses such an opinion is simply giving vent to his own personal view, which has no basis in the Koran or Hadith. To those who say that lands previously occupied by Muslims should now be retrieved by war, the response is that according to the Koran political power is no one's monopoly. No individual can be in a position of dominance forever. This law of nature is recognized by the Koran: "We alternate these vicissitudes (victory/defeat) among mankind so that Allah may know the true believers." (3:140) Another verse tells us that power on this earth does not belong to any individual or group. It is the prerogative of God alone. He bestows it as he wills: "You bestow sovereignty on whom You will, and take it away from whom you please." (3:26)

The Arabic word jahadu is derived from jihad or muj ahida, and the addition of fina (for Us) shows that jihad is the spiritual striving to attain nearness to God, and the result of this jihad is stated to be God's guiding those striving in His ways. The word is used precisely in the same sense twice in a previous verse in the same chapter: "And whoever strives hard (jahadu), he strives (yujahidu) only for his own soul," that is, for his own benefit, "for Allah is self-sufficient, above need of the worlds" (29:6). In the same chapter the word is used in the sense of a contention carried on in words: And we have enjoined on man goodness to his parents, and if they contend (jahada) with thee that thou shouldst associate others with Me, of which thou hast no knowledge, do not obey them" (29:8). A struggle for national existence was forced on the Muslims when they reached Medina and had to take up the sword in self-defense. This struggle went also, and rightly, under the name of jihad; but even in the Medina suras the word is used in the wider sense of a struggle carried on by words or deeds of any kind. Jihadism is anti-Islam.

Prophet Mohammed often came across people who were completely unresponsive to his words, while others were stirred, believed and were prepared to listen. In dealing with the former, he occasionally grew impatient and felt frustrated, but believed that if he has placed the true view in simple terms before the people he has fulfilled his mission. He never felt it his duty to see that the people accept the view. His duty is only to tell them which is the right path and which the wrong one and to acquaint them with the consequences of following the one or the other. They are free to choose for themselves. Mohammed never considered that he had the power to compel people to accept Islam, even after he had became ruler over most of Arabia. He never saw Islam as other than a religion that was a gift from God to the world, a blessing from, not a tool for oppression.

Gone Global

The Islamic struggle has inserted itself as global, and wrapped itself in ideology, religion and culture. On the international political scene at least, the Muslim community has been hijacked by its own. We are watching the very sad spectacle of a relatively few but ideologically driven nihilists establishing almost unopposed a militant portrayal of Islam which defines jihad as obliging its young to engage in violence, indiscriminate terrorism and suicide bombings. It is a terrible thing, this major misinterpretation of Islam spreading like wildfire in the Middle East. It is a massive march to self-destruction, far beyond any harm real or fictional Western enemies could possibly inflict. If religion is the last refuge of rogues, it is even more so the last refuge of the modern Islamist terrorist. Catholics, years ago, were told that if they missed Mass on Sunday and died that day without confession, they would go to hell because it was a mortal sin to miss the Sunday liturgy. Catholic wives were told that no matter what the brutality, physical or psychological, they must remain with their husbands because it was God's will. Countless numbers of women were traumatized by that claim. This same mentality is true of militant Islam. According to their canonical interpretation of Islamic law, when a Muslim abandons Islam to embrace another faith he is found guilty of apostasy, and thus liable to punishment by death. If it were literally enforced the Reaper would be very busy indeed.

The young are called to return to ancient traditions, glamorized by armaments and deified by religious incantations which, in fact, will lead them to self-destruction, a world that, in fact, they would hate. They are asked to idealize and romanticize the Islamic interpretation of Ibn Hanbal (7th Century), Ibn Taymiyah (14th Century), and Ibn `Abd al-Wahhab (18th Century), the most prominent fundamentalist Islamic scholars. The whole process has an air of unreality. It is at least doubtful that the answer to poverty, disease and bad government is a hatred for the relatively free and affluent West, while they try to survive in an atmosphere of Middle East dictatorial regimes. It would be far better for these young men and women to call for democracy and a more equitable sharing of Middle East riches than to lash out at those whom the extremists label as the party of the devil (Hizb al-Shaytan) set against the true believers, the party of God (Hezbollah). Such anger, falsely relieving the terrible prospects of continued exposure to brutal and repressive regimes is, in the end, a severe form of social schizophrenia. The Jihadists are calling for the death of Americans and Muslims who do not interpret jihad in a warlike manner under the guise of preaching Islam and enforcing Islamic Sharia. A study of the Prophet Mohammad's reaction to his circumstances provides a very different picture. According to Maulana Mohammad Ali (The Religion of Islam), when the Prophet grew worried that people did not pay attention to his words and did not try to understand them, he was admonished in this way: "If Allah Willed, all who are on the earth would have believed (in Him). Would thou (Mohammed) compel men until they are believers?" (10:99) In contrast, the militant jihadist says: Believe or die!

Of course nothing is quite that simple. We can only go so far in being logical on either side. But, if moderate Islamic teachers fail to engage this mentality in the schools of religion and higher learning, if the theological discourse among Islamic scholars does not include the true meaning of the prophet's theology, then they will all be trapped in an intellectually infantile and sterile view of the world. Literalism and reductionism will build an Islamic world, a terrifying one, with old men who are not adults, who cannot think for themselves, who will be part of an army of automatons. If Islamic clerics remove reason from the future, there will be no meaningful future. How horrible. Youths subject to forced Islamic identity will become alienated from Islam and from the larger world, which, because of modern technology (like the internet), is getting smaller all the time. Forced community breeds loneliness.

Then there are the Palestinians who long ago judged their leadership to be corrupt, but whose frustration to some extent has been mitigated by the social action of terrorist groups. Hezbollah in Lebanon and Hamas in the Palestinian territories, by their attention to the needs of the local populations, enjoy public support and sympathy. In the struggle between Arafat and Hamas and/or the Islamic Jihad, Arafat was the loser. Hamas performed better than the Palestinian Authority. This economic activity provides social cover and immunity, and the immunity is the cover for terrorist activity.

West versus Islam?

The Western press bends over backwards to claim that the war on terrorism is not a battle between the West and Islam. Don't tell that to bin Laden and his followers. Western commentators, of course, are speaking of mainstream Islam, a version of Islam, ancient and sacred that is learned about in academic institutions. That version is losing ground and its advocates are becoming a very silent majority. It is also clear that if the mission of religion in the 21st century is to contribute concretely to the peaceful coexistence of humankind, it is having a problem. Exclusionary theology and fanaticism wrapping themselves in the language and symbols of religion are just as dangerous today as they were in the Middle Ages.

We might say that the war is not between the West and Islam, but that does not reflect what a large segment of Islam is thinking or saying. The Islamic fundamentalists have cornered the political market; the silent majority remains mute for fear that they will be targeted for abuse or even assassination. One would have to be a blind deaf and dumb mute not to see and hear the cacophony of radical Islamic voices shouting above the voice of moderates, demanding the establishment of One Nation, under the Prophet. This one nation would be ruled by the severest Sharia law and guided by the theology of Salafiyya and having its fullest expression in the heart of the Saudi government, the royal family, and the Wahhabi.

In the present jihad atmosphere, falling on deaf ears is the argument that picking up the sword is spiritually, intellectually and politically anti-Islamic. That argument is solid, but seems to be at the moment beside the point. The rational argument: The Koran and the Prophet Mohammed are the daily guides for every Muslim around the world. Under the Prophet's direct guidance and for the first 13 years of Islam's existence he forbade picking up the sword, some say even in self-defense, in the midst of the terrible persecution they suffered in Mecca. They were permitted to defend themselves for the first time in Medina when they were attacked by the Meccans. It was literally kill or be killed. Later, when the Prophet and his followers became militarily dominant in that same Mecca, and many of them were calling for revenge, the Prophet opted for peace. He even went so far as to sign what many of his followers described as a self-imposed humiliation, the Treaty of Hudaibiya,[40] and he later granted a general amnesty to all, including those who mutilated the dead bodies of his close relatives. Mutilation of dead bodies is a mediaeval pre-Islamic

practice, a practice Islam came to fight against. Those who perpetrate such acts in this day and age cannot claim to be Muslims.
In any case Muslims cannot accept them as their co-religionists.
That is, of course, in theory, because many groups are proud to
announce death to non-believers. The new Iraqi Sunni organization al-Jama'a al-Salafiya al-Mujahida offers a radically different
Islamic platform. It bears a symbol of a holy war against the
United States engraved on its flag. It began to take an active role
in jihad in Iraq since the beginning of July 2003.

The word 'Mercy' has been used 173 times in the Koran.
The word Wrath or anger appears only 3 times: (Sura Al-Fatiha
1.07, Al Baqra 2.90, and Al-Imran 3.11) The word wrathful or
angry occurs four times: Al-Mada, Al-Fath, Al-Mujadila and Al-
Murntahina. It is clear as day that God is conceived in Islam as
the personification of compassion, not the personification of
wrath as some theologians claim in their justification of the new
religion of Jihadism.

Folk Islam

"Folk religion" is the large number of superstitions, black
magic and non-rational behavior that characterizes any religion.
In Islam it is called Folk Islam and can be found across the spectrum of Islamic nations. Like moderate and militant groups of
Muslims, its borders overlap the traditional divisions that followed the early disputes over Mohammed's successor. Most
Muslims that practice Folk Islam would also be labeled Sunni
since over 90% of Muslims worldwide are Sunni. But, like the
second largest division called Shiites, the Sunnis also feed the
growing army of militants bent on Jihad. We can also find many
traces of Folk Islam in what has become a growing Folk Christianity among the young (and their parents!) in their addiction to
the occult suggestions of the Harry Potter books, violent cartoons, and occult games. At the same time, all who indulge in either Folk Islam or Folk Christianity would be horrified at the
suggestion that they did not strictly adhere to the biblical caution: "When you come into the land which the Lord your God is
giving you, you shall not learn to follow the abominations of
those nations. There shall not be found among you anyone who...
practices witchcraft, or a soothsayer, or one who interprets

omens, or a sorcerer, or one who conjures spells, or a medium, or a spiritist, or one who calls up the dead. For all who do these things are an abomination to the Lord, and because of these abominations the Lord your God drives them out..." Deuteronomy 18:9-12

A Mixture

Islamic terrorism tied to al-Qaeda grew out of a mix of Islamic socialism, Arabian nationalism and Iraqi-Syrian Baathism. In al-Qaeda today these elements have been fused into an unbreakable whole. Moreover, Islamic socialism, Arabian nationalism and Baathism emerged in Egypt, Syria, and Iraq in the early 1950s amid the disintegration of national monarchies in those countries. The men and women who made up these groups were representatives of local intelligentsia--mostly younger military officers who were inspired by religious and nationalistic ideals.

In Saudi Arabia this same nexus of ideas has also attracted the adversaries of monarchic rule, the same idealists who also believe the United States to be the primary obstacle to reshaping the international economic order in their favor. They sincerely believe that the possession of petroleum resources and the huge revenues accruing from their sale gives them the right and opportunity to define global economic conditions. They also seek to destabilize international stock markets to profit from falling stock prices, believing that such a development would strengthen their own position in any future adversarial engagement with the United States and its Western allies.

Indeed, the domestic adversaries of the Saudi monarchy understand, just as the leaders of the Soviet Union did, that they are unable to wage and win an open war against the United States. And so this new World Dictatorship relies on a "terrorist international"—on al-Qaeda and other Islamic terrorist organizations—just as Soviet communists created a Communist International and supported international terrorism under the guise of promoting "national liberation" movements. This new, contemporary "terrorist international" is the beneficiary of massive financial assistance, as well as support from the intelligence services of Iran, Syria, the Sudan and other cooperating nations. The Syrians and Libyans supported the PLO dissident Abu Nidal. Iran and

Syria supported the Lebanese Hezbollah militia that has waged a guerrilla war against Israel in southern Lebanon, and also is suspected of terrorist attacks both inside Lebanon and abroad. But unlike bin Laden's group, Hezbollah remains focused on home ground, while bin Laden's network roams everywhere looking for targets of opportunity.

In order to allay suspicions in the West and to avoid possible military retaliation, both the Iranian, Syrian and Sudanese governments and the opponents of the Saudi monarchy have taken every precaution to mask their secret communications and connections with Islamic terrorists. It is precisely this secrecy that makes it so difficult to find irrefutable evidence of links between the two. Moreover, much like the Soviet Bolsheviks before them, these advocates of a new World Dictatorship have created a system of schools--in this case the "madrasas"--in order to disseminate their ideology and to prepare rank-and-file terrorists to support and fight for the world vision.

It is worth noting that during the Cold War both the United States and the Soviet Union lent support to activists in various national liberation movements, some of whom emerged as the predecessors of those working in contemporary terrorist organizations. One form that this Cold War-era support took was the transferal of expertise from the U.S. and Soviet state special services to nonprofessionals from the national liberation movements. Though Washington and Moscow later abandoned these movements, some of the recipients of their earlier support have since offered their specialized skills to new masters. The transfer of expertise from state intelligence agencies to representatives of terrorist organizations has continued in camps in Syria, Lebanon, Somalia and elsewhere.

Social, cultural and economic conditions of life for the populations of dismally poor Muslim countries such as Yemen, Afghanistan, and Palestine, meanwhile, continue to generate new recruits for the army of Islamic terrorism. And even some educated young from the rich Muslim countries have been attracted to al-Qaeda and fallen under the ideological influence of its aggressive form of Islamic terrorism. Against this background, the destruction of the al-Qaeda network in Afghanistan and in a number of other countries is likely to be but the first stage in a larger struggle of Democracy against determined terrorist organizations. It behooves the United States, meanwhile, to seek much greater development of its own domestic petroleum resources and heavily invest in alternative fuels. The resultant reductions in revenue for Middle Eastern oil producers will have the benefit of reducing the appetites of those advocating the new World Dictatorship, and will stymie their hopes of using the profits of Middle Eastern oil producers to reshape the world's international economic system.

Chapter Ten

THE KORAN AND VIOLENCE

The Koran (Arabic: القرآن al-qur□ān, literally "the recitation") is the primary and revered religious text of Islam, believed by Muslims to be the literal word of God (Arabic: Allah) as revealed to Mohammed, over a period of twenty-two years(some say twenty three years) by the angel Gabriel. Just as with the Christian Bible, it is considered to be God's final revelation to mankind. Etymologically, in Arabic grammar, Koran derives from the Arabic word, "to read", used primarily as a verbal noun, as in lecture or reading or recital. The Koran is composed of 114 surah (chapters) with a total of 6236 ayat (verses), arranged not in chronological order but in a descending order according to size.

The Koran is substantially a series of revelations God gave to the Prophet Mohammed in Arabic, the first of which was given in the year 610 CE while he was making a private retreat in the Cave of Hira, located at Mt Hira, (also called the Mountain of light-Jabal al-nur) in the outskirts of Mecca. The revelations were given at intervals during a twenty-two year (some say 23 years) period. Both Eastern and Western scholars maintain that the Arabic form used in the Koran is substantively the same as the very Arabic used by Mohammed while he was writing the Koran, a claim not bade by scholars for the present version Aramaic version of the Christian Bible. This preservation of the integrity of the original text however is paralleled by the agreement among scholars that the writing of the text (but not the text itself) has evolved. For example, the original text was written without diacritical points that distinguish some letters from others. These were added later on.

It is the belief of Muslims that the very recitation of the Koran brings spiritual and social blessings (baraka), so that those who read the Koran, even though they do not understand Arabic, receive blessings equal to those given to persons who do understand Arabic. Since Muslims preach that Koranic verses are revealed by God, the act of reciting or reading the Koran is believed to be a means of receiving blessings (baraka) from God. Hence it is not uncommon that Muslims will learn how to read Arabic and the Koran without understanding it. Also, even those who cannot read the Arabic letters of the Koran believe that they can nevertheless benefit from simply attentively listening to sacred words in the original Arabic.

There is argument, however, among scholars as to the full integrity of translations from the original Arabic, with some advising that, depending on the author of the translation, more or less of the original literal meaning can be lost.

The Koran and Islamic Terrorism

Every Religion has multiple theological understandings compounded by and intertwined with political ideologies. For example, we have the Christian pacifist viewpoint that interprets Christ's teaching as meaning that no matter what harm is done to us as an individual we must never strike back. "If a man strikes you on the left cheek, turn to give him your right cheek... If a man steals your cloak, give him your coat." At the other end of the spectrum, Christ tells us that "No greater love hath a man for his brother than that he would give his life for him." The function of religion in both Christianity and Islam is to provide to both groups the best possible understanding of the relevant arguments and questions to evaluate the true claims of Christianity and Islam. Could giving one's life for one's brother include suicide bombing, or inflicting harm on one's enemy? Would a man be justified to kill another man in defense of his wife and children if their lives were threatened? At the moment of crisis the theoretical discussions suddenly becomes an existential action based on the best understanding the person has of truth and justice.

The Supreme Religious Leader of Iran, Ayatollah Seyyed Ali Khamenei, in a speech at Ayatollah Khomeini's Mausoleum, June 4, 2002, supported the Palestinian suicide-homicide martyrdoms that are deliberately carried out on innocent Israelis. He said: "This quest for martyrdom is not based on emotions; it is based on belief in Islam and faith in [the] Judgment Day and faith in life after death. Anywhere Islam exists in its true sense, arrogance faces this threat." For him, if there is no other way to preserve Arabic dignity, martyrdom is justified by the Koran. During World War II a priest in an Axis concentration camp offered to give his life in place of another in the camp that was destined to be murdered. That priest became a hero in the West.

Therefore, if one looks at the entire panorama of history the question of the morality of using the sword against an enemy has always been a very difficult one. Political ideology has very often substituted itself for religious doctrine, has insinuated itself into its fabric. When the Ayatollah Ruhollah Khomeini issued his fatwa against Salman Rushdie, he mirrored actions taken by many Bishops during the Inquisition. Who can recall the burning body of Joan of Arc without cringing at the thought that the love of Jesus Christ as expressed by the Church leadership of that time was not different from Khomeini's condemnation of Rushdie. In the Fall of 2006 Khatami became President of Iran he refused to carry out the still-standing fatwa against Rushdie. All through history we see political ideology interpreting religious theology, usually to the detriment of spirituality. The author attended a meeting of concerned citizens in the Chicago area in which the subject of illegal immigration was the topic among Christian men and women. One man stood up and shouted: "The way to stop illegal immigration is to shoot to kill every Mexican who crosses the border" The hall erupted in cheering and clapping, affirming in no uncertain tones the speaker's remarks. Any observer could, I suppose, come to the conclusion that Christians are, by virtue of their religion, murderers. On could argue, of course, that the people at the meeting are not there as Christians, but as private citizens venting their frustration. But, that reduces itself to the Catholic who reserves his Catholicism to Sunday

Mass followed by donuts and coffee. The ideology has struck again. Ideology inserts itself into every niche and corner of our religious lives. We Christians are, basically, no different in molding our religion to suit our ideology than are the Muslims.

The Koran, the words of Allah as transcribed by Mohammed, to which the Muslim world is dedicated, can be interpreted, as has the bible in the course of history, by the ideological theology of a particular group in a particular place at a particular time in history. That is a fact, and sometimes a sad and perilous fact, because particular ideological theologies serve, not the truth, but the agendas of the practitioners. We must be very discreet and not ascribe to a group what individuals in that group do. We need to understand that in the act of pointing the forefinger of blame at the practices of others, our thumb points directly at ourselves.

The Koran Does Not Condone Killing the Innocent
The stereotypical perception, not unreasonable within this particular historical context of television portraying excited Muslims rejoicing over carnage in New York and Washington, does imprint itself on our minds the concept "Muslim". But, apart from individual terrorist actions, sadly all too frequent, both mainstream Christians and mainstream Muslims desire peace and tranquility. Most Christians and most Muslims condemn radical clerics and militant fringe groups. Bin Laden is not admired for contorting the holy words of peace into actions of gratuitous violence, and neither are those Christians who bomb abortion clinics, endangering, even desiring the death of the employees who work there.

Muslims are not permitted to interpret the meaning of the Koran on their own, and their leaders do not support gratuitous violence. There is support, however, for self-defense, even the use of suicide bombers if a nation, Christian or not, takes up arms against them. The Koran says Muslims can retaliate if attacked but are forbidden to initiate unprovoked violence. The bible has a similar approach, making clear that it is permissible to take "an eye for an eye and a tooth for a tooth." (Leviticus 24:17-21). However, there is no doubt that the New Testament teachings greatly modified that approach.

The Koran also speaks of moderation: "And fight in the way of Allah with those who fight with you, and do not exceed the limits, surely Allah does not love those who exceed the limits." (Chapter 2, verse 193). Three verses later, the Koran explains what those limits are: "And fight with them until there is no persecution, and religion should be only for Allah, but if they desist, then there should be no hostility except against the oppressors." Under Islamic law, the penalty for slaughtering innocent people is beheading. Of the 1.2 billion Muslims scattered throughout the Islamic world a relatively small group, for their own purposes as well as their resentment of the West and its values, is engaged in what has come to be known as Islamic terrorism. Since it has become part of the international vocabulary, 'Islamic terrorism" must be understood in that context. However, it must also be admitted that if a group of Christians, say the IRA, were called Christian terrorists, we Christians would take offense.

Did Mohammed Advocate Violence?

We should no more be surprised that Mohammed advocated the use of force at times than that those who financed the Crusades in the name of Christianity advocated the use of force. In the so-called "Sword Verses" of the Koran Mohammed did explicitly ordered the use of offensive warfare. For example: "Fighting is prescribed for you, and ye dislike it. But it is possible that ye dislike a thing which is good for you, and that ye love a thing which is bad for you. But God knoweth, and ye know not (2:216)." "But when the forbidden months are past, then fight and slay the pagans wherever ye find them, and seize them, beleaguer them, and lie in wait for them in every stratagem (of war); but if they repent, and establish regular prayers and practice regular charity, then open the way for them: for God is Oft-forgiving, Most Merciful (9:5)."

Seeming Contradictions

And yet there are seeming contradictions. In Sura 73:10,11 Mohammed instructs his followers to be patient toward unbelievers: "And have patience with what they say, and leave them with noble (dignity). And leave me (alone to deal with) those in possession of the good things of life, who (yet) deny the truth, and bear with them for a little while."

In Sura 52:45, 47, 48 the prophet preaches much the same advice: "So leave them alone until they encounter that day of theirs, wherein they shall (perforce) swoon (with terror) ... And verily, for those who do wrong, there is another punishment besides this... Now await in patience the command of thy Lord, for verily thou art in Our eyes."

Scholars explain the seeming contradictions of the contrasting verses, i.e. advocating fighting and asking for patience, in terms of the changing circumstances of the Islamic peoples over the years, including being attacked and defamed, for the variety of solutions Mohammed adopted as he tried to work out his master plan against severe opposition. Reuven Firestone wrote in his book, Jihad: The Origin of Holy War in Islam, published by Oxford University Press in 1999: "Muslim scholars came to the conclusion that the scriptural verses regarding war were revealed in direct relation to the historic needs of Mohammed during his prophetic mission. At the beginning of his prophetic career in Mecca when he was weak and his followers few, the divine revelations encouraged avoidance of physical conflict." However, as he began to consolidate his position, Mohammed's situation and circumstances changed. Firestone continues: "After the intense persecutions that caused Mohammed and his followers to emigrate to Medina they were given leave to engage in defensive warfare. The early surahs, especially 'The Spoils of War' (8) and 'The Repentance' (9) are clear and unequivocal about the religious correctness of self-defense in a hostile environment. Repeatedly it says that Islam is worth fighting for, notably in the section 'Believers Permitted to Fight'. One could call these verses the moral Islamic equivalent of the Catholic Church's Just War theory. "To those against whom war is made, permission is given to fight because they are wronged; and verily, God is Most Powerful for their aid. They are those who have been expelled from their homes in defiance of right, for no cause except that they say, 'Our Lord is God'"(22:39). As the Muslim community grew in strength, further revelations broadened the conditions under which war could be waged.

No Personal Interpretation

Muslims are not permitted individual interpretation of the Koran. Only clerics and Islamic scholars can do so, and their conclusion has been and remains that there is no support in the Koran for initiating unprovoked attacks against anyone or any place. When Islamist radicals took responsibility for the deadly London transit attacks July 7, mainstream Muslims reacted with vigor denouncing the attacks. In North America scholars issued a fatwa condemning violence against civilians. Some called on the writings of Mohammed. In Sura 2:190 instruction is given to fight until persecution is stopped: "Fight in the cause of God those who fight you, but do not transgress limits; for God loveth not transgressors." The Muslim American Society encouraged imams to give sermons against "terror, hate and violence." in their mosques. The Koran contains 2 ayas (verses in the Koran) that guide its readers on the question on violence. "People who do not abuse you or deprive you of your land and heritage should be treated with respect and gentleness." "Those who persecute Muslims because of their religion should be attacked and defeated."

Islamic scholars explain some of the language used, for example: surah 8:12 says, "I will instill terror into the hearts of the unbelievers: Smite ye above their necks and smite all their fingertips off them." There is near uniformity in insisting that to some extent this is an emotional statement to rally the troops, so to speak, in time of war. It was reported that during World War II a certain unit of the American military had animal blood sprayed on their faces before entering battle. The comparison may be odious but then anyone who has ever played on a football team can recall the coach's half time pep talk. Someone from another culture who has never seen an American football game and not familiar with the cultural language of that game, on hearing such talk might come to the conclusion that the coach is recommending killing members of the opposite team. Another comparison with Christian teaching may help to put the subject in focus. "A fire has been prepared for the disbelievers, whose fuel is men and stones." 2:24. "Disbelievers will be burned with fire." 2:39, 90. A Christian might well consider this a fair description of hell as it is taught in catechism instruction.

Islam instructs that those who die fighting for Allah's teachings shall be forgiven their sins and will enter Paradise. This accepted notion inspires young Palestinians and Hezbollah to become suicide bombers. A martyr's death is a guarantee of eternal life. Suicide bombers see self-immolation as the ultimate sacrifice for a better Islamic future. We should not use emotionally-charged verses and extrapolate from them meanings which it is obvious do not apply to the vast majority of Muslims going about their daily lives throughout the world. On the other hand, it is true that some radical clerics have gone to the extreme of promising a direct passage to heaven and all its, ironically, earthly delights to those who die attempting to destroy the infidels, i.e., Westerners and those Muslims who have adopted Western ways. And of course, Muslims must also understand Western anxiety, for there is a lot at stake here when you consider that Islam is the world's second-largest religion spread out over 56 countries in Asia and Africa alone.

The Inquisition

It would not be fair to equate the horrors of the Inquisition with Islamic terrorism because the Inquisition was an official arm of both the Church and State while Islamic terrorists are, for the most part, rogue groups that operate extra-state. However, the comparison is beneficial, not for proving a particular point but as food for thought for Christians. While we must resist terrorism in any form or from wherever it emanates, an effective foreign policy and approach to Arab nations must take into account our Christian past, and the humility and sensitivity with which we should approach Arab nations in dialogue.

Religion for Christian people who lived during the Inquisition era was their whole life, their science, their politics, their very identity. In much of the Muslim world today, a world that can only look from the sidelines at progress, affluence, freedom and democracy, Islam is, likewise, their entire life. The person then who attacks their religion is attacking their entire existence, so the voice of the attacker must be quieted by whatever means necessary. A heretic in the Western world today would be no more than an oddity; he is in no way a danger to the system of democracy. However, this is not true in much of Islam. Therefore, a brief glance at Europe during the Middle Ages is appropriate, not for imitation obviously, but simply to understand the milieu in which some Muslims, at this moment in history, must live and survive.

From Rome to Rome
During the Roman Empire the law dictated that heresy was treason on the simple ground that since leadership was, they said, a gift from God to a particular person or family, heresy was by its nature a challenge to law and order, to the legal foundations of the state. Heresy, to the Roman establishment, was divisive, rebellious, arrogant and just plain unlawful; heresy was actions and states of mind punishable by God. This attitude and belief persisted from Roman times through the Middle Ages. The Christians of that time, mostly Catholics, saw the Inquisition as a tool for establishing order and justice. That the Church would be the judge of heresy was natural for a people who saw the government as too remote, capricious and dangerous. Only the Church, they believed, would make a reasoned, compassionate and just judgment as to who was a heretic and who was not.

Began in 1184
The Inquisition began in 1184 during the reign of Pope Lucius III, born Ulbano Allucingoli. He spent most of his pontificate in exile and had a predisposition for being tough on dissenters of any kind. In November 1184 he held a synod at Verona which condemned the Cathars, Paterines, Waldensians and Arnoldists. In sweeping documents he anathematized all of them and sent a list of heresies to Europe's bishops demanding that they play an active role in what eventually became the Inquisition. He did not trust the law and the courts to do a more efficient job since they might, he argued, use the prosecution of infidels for their own nefarious purposes. He ordered the bishops to appoint competent clergy who would examine all those suspected of heresy, using as their guidelines the Roman laws of evidence. They were to "inquire" of the nature of the belief of suspected individuals, thus the term "inquisition." began to be used.

Heretics were the lost sheep of the Church and, following the example of Jesus, who sought out the lost sheep, the Church had a duty, Pope Lucius maintained, to bring those sheep back into the fold. The task of medieval kings, he argued, was to safeguard the realm. The solemn duty of the Church was to save souls. The Inquisition was his instrument of choice. He offered heretics the opportunity to escape punishment by simply expressing loyalty to the Catholic Church and its teachings. Joan of Arc and many others did not take up the Inquisition's offer. However, the Inquisition had the right, if the penitent appeared to be incorrigible, to order his or her death anyway, expressions of loyalty notwithstanding, in order to spare the rest of civil society the danger he or she posed to the Holy Church. Unrepentant "heretics" were excommunicated and handed over to the secular authorities for torture, burning or perhaps being torn apart by the rack. The Carolina, or criminal law of Charles V, the Holy Roman Emperor, issued in 1532, permitted the use of blinding, mutilation, tearing with hot pincers, burning alive, and breaking on the wheel. In Denmark, as late as 1683, blasphemers were beheaded after having their tongues cut out. In France, until the Revolution, beheading was reserved for nobles because it was a quick and relatively painless death. Ordinary folks got no such privilege. If beheading was the preferred method of torture for nobles in the Middle Ages, death by burning at the stake was the preferred method for heretics accused and convicted by the Inquisition. Not that it should make a difference, but it must be admitted that the tortures imposed by the Inquisition were those imposed by the society in general: the wheel, the boiling oil, burning alive, burying alive, flaying alive, and being torn apart by wild horses. While this is true it was not much consolation to those who were tortured and murdered.

Pope Insistent

Pope Clement V (1305-1314) assured the King of England that some Knights Templar, under torture, had confessed to heresy. King Edward II did not believe him and demanded that the Knights Templar no longer be subject to the Inquisition's torture. The King insisted that he would hold a trial for the remainder of the Knights and seek the truth himself. When the court trial concluded, the men were not found guilty. This enraged Pope Clement the Humane (ironically named). He protested and demanded that the king should permit torture, claiming that Church law was higher than English civil law. When King Edward II (1307-1327) protested that torture was opposed to English law, Pope Clement sent the king a note reminding him that he, the pope, had more authority than the King of England, even in England. "We hear that you forbid torture as contrary to the laws of your land... I command you at once to submit those men to torture." This sort of exchange would not happen today in the West because there no longer exists in the West a moral, spiritual and juridical unity between Church and State, a unity that constitutes a closely knit polity. However, it can happen in the Islam of today simply because the kind of closely knit polity that existed in the Middle Ages does, in fact, exist in several Arab Islamist nations, as in Saudi Arabia. The fact that the barbarism of beheading was done in Christian Europe for centuries does not, of course, excuse its continuation among men like the late Zarqawi and other terrorists. Not at all. But it does sober us in the West to realize and recall that we were once "there" ourselves.

PART THREE

THE ENABLERS

Chapter Eleven

THE ENABLERS

A terrorist organization needs:

—A base where its headquarters are located, weapons are stored and manufactured, and its fighters are trained,

—Sources of financing,

—Intelligence information in the volume and of the quality that is available only to government intelligence agencies,

—Means of covering up its traces, such as forged papers, impeccable cover-up stories, legalized safe houses in the country of the enemy, etc.

—Available diplomatic channels that can be used to ship weapons, money, information, instructions and even terrorists themselves.

—Access to mass media controlled by the governments or big businesses in Muslim countries in order to advance its action program and to line up public support.

—Opportunities to spread its ideology through the system of public education in Muslim countries.

Government agencies that have a stake in terrorist activities and are directing such activities provide all of the above to terrorist organizations. Governments have always engaged in terrorism and have been the major perpetrators of politically motivated murder, imprisonment, and mass intimidation in the 20th century. The outstanding examples have been Nazi Germany and the

Union of Soviet Socialist Republics. On a smaller scale, the murderous tactics of state security services and military "death squads" in El Salvador and Guatemala and the sinister practice of mass "disappearances" (desaparecidos) adopted by the junta in Argentina from 1976 to 1982 against the youth of that country would run the totalitarian giants a close second. Virtually all Palestinian and Islamic fundamentalist terrorism has been funded and based outside the target area, notably in Libya, Syria, Iran, and Sudan.

Enablers Hard to Catch

Enablers are able to send money and instructions across international borders without detection. For example, in order to allay suspicions in the West and to avoid possible military retaliation, both the Iranian and former Iraqi governments and the opponents of the Saudi monarchy have taken every precaution to mask their secret communications and connections with Islamic terrorists. This international dimension creates formidable jurisdictional hurdles. Domestic terrorism is the province of local law-enforcement authorities, and the problems of dealing with it are not much different from a legal standpoint than dealing with organized crime. But, where the site of the terrorist crime is overseas, or the suspects have fled to another country, traditional concepts of sovereignty severely limit options. In practice, extradition proceedings depend on the kind of cooperation already established by individual nations in their relationships with one another. For example, evidence derived from plea-bargaining of others is viewed in most nations as too tainted to support a fugitive's extradition. Radically different rules of trial procedure, admissibility of evidence, and defendants' rights often make convictions for crimes committed overseas difficult to sustain in U.S. appellate courts.

The 1985 hijacking of the Italian cruise ship Achille Lauro took place in international waters off Egypt, and the victims, terrorists, crew, and vessel registration were of different nationalities. Aircraft hijackings and sabotage also frequently transcend national boundaries. There are international agreements on how to deal with terrorists. The Tokyo, Hague, and Montreal conventions of 1963, 1970, and 1971, respectively, the 1977 European

Convention on Suppression of Terrorism, and the United Nations conventions of 1973 and 1979 have made aircraft sabotage, hijacking, hostage taking, and other related crimes punishable by any state. These agreements constitute a juridical foundation for prosecution. Their effectiveness depends on international cooperation, not always provided. These juridical difficulties, together with the need to protect intelligence sources and surveillance techniques, have shifted the emphasis of counterterrorism methods from physical deterrence to acquiring detailed intelligence from deep-cover agents and penetration of terrorist networks and support systems. States are adopting a terrorist equivalent of "An ounce of prevention is worth more than a ton of cure."

Extreme Anti-Americanism as an organized force of global terror directed at the United States at first appears to be the work of such organizations as al-Qaeda, Hamas, Islamic Jihad, al-Aksa and a slew of others formed to cause mayhem and destruction around the world either to American interests or those connected with America. Of course, they are organized and they are destructive but, in reality, they are much more than that. They are the agents or, as the author prefer to call them, the mercenaries financially beholden to three categories of governments.

—First, the group of governments that sponsor state terrorism, such as Syria, the Sudan, Libya, Iran, until recently, Iraq, the Palestinian Authority, and representatives of the oil-owning clans of the Persian Gulf, including wealthy Saudi Arabian families.

—Second, a group of nations that, by their silence, behavior, foreign policy decisions, clandestine assistance and positions taken at international conferences, designedly give aid and comfort to terrorist organizations. These governments share a common agenda: the desire to limit the power and influence of the United States around the world and the enhancement of their own political, economic and military ascendancy. In this category are the present-day governments of: Russia, China, and North Korea. The political and, for some, covert financial support of anti-American groups serves as the cornerstone of a long range policy of enhancing their own status of power, influence and economic success on the world stage.

—Third, a group of nations that, while not supporting terrorism, long for the day when American power is greatly diminished. France, and until recently, Germany are among those States. These two nations resent the long military, economic and political arm that America projects on the world stage, making them feel like second class citizens in their own European milieu. Sensing a vulnerability not seen since the Trade Tower attack, they have boldly stepped forward to make their subtle anti-Americanism presence felt at the United Nations and other international forums.

Islamic terrorism is the cheapest, most convenient, sanitized method of accomplishing the goals of group one and group two. Their mercenaries, in the self-deluding assumption that they themselves will acquire significant political leverage in the process are happy to play along with the private agendas of their state sponsors. The third group sits on the sidelines assuming that, by so doing, they will accomplish two goals: keep the terrorists away from their own door and watch as America's role in the wider world diminishes, like the late afternoon setting sun. It is a risky strategy for all concerned but, at the moment, is very appealing.

Until September 11, 2001, modern history knew of only two instances in which open military challenges were leveled at the United States, but the present Islamic terrorism, a vast undocumented array of non-conventional warriors using unconventional weapons is the most dangerous in our history. Opposition to the United States in the Middle East appeared in the 1970s when oil rich countries established full control over their resources and began to dictate prices on the world oil market.[41] As a result, massive numbers of petrodollars flowed into Iraq, Iran, Libya, Saudi Arabia and other countries of the Persian Gulf. Not surprisingly, riches on this scale among men whose ancestors had for centuries lived a nomadic life on the very desert sands which covered seemingly endless deposits of black gold dramatically changed lifestyles and introduced the potential for wielding great power. They began to live already-legendary lives on a sumptuous scale: huge palaces, luxurious automobiles, dozens and even hundreds of wives and concubines.

But, in spite of their huge amounts of money and a plethora of luxuries, the Middle East monarchs and dictators are very uneasy. The American presence in the Middle East, imperfect as it may be, is sowing the seeds of democratic ideas in the region. Saudi citizens are now openly calling for democracy. In Iran, until the 2005 election of Mahmoud Ahmadinejad as president, the young were crying out for democracy, chanting American slogans and holding American flags aloft at demonstrations. For the monarchs and clerical theocrats of the region, the extraordinary scenes in Tiananmen Square of Chinese students building paper and plastic replicas of the Statue of Liberty continue to haunt their subconscious.

The Long Chill

A long chill is running through the body politic of all these monarchic, dictatorial and theocratic power brokers. They understand full well that if they do not remove the American presence in Iraq and the region, the possibility of democratic regimes could lead to the collapse of their lifestyle, their riches, perhaps even their lives at the hands of angry crowds. At the many hectic conferences called by the Arab League, the language of the resolutions passed and discussions held display their fear that unless the USA leaves Iraq, their future looks very bleak indeed. A democratic Iraq, if it happens at all, would signal the beginning of the end of their many years of power. They are not at all concerned, their protestations notwithstanding, about Civil War in Iraq or the emergence of a new Iraqi dictatorship. Their concerns revolve around their own survival. They have, until recently, lacked the understanding that their own security would have been greatly enhanced if they had used the wealth squandered on palaces and private jets on the development of local industry, communications, a banking system, even quasi-democratic governmental institutions, and support for a free market economy. This approach would have produced jobs and the possibility of a minimally decent living for a worker and his family. This might have saved them, but now it is too late.

With time quickly running out, they have no choice other than to implement the strategic plan, the removal of America from their midst. And, if they are able to end the American military presence, they can take one further step that will guarantee them security. They can purchase atomic weaponry to be used as bargaining chips in the discussions with the Americans. Korea has already played this card. Iran is about to play this card, and the Saudis are already shuffling the deck. They are determined to stay one step ahead of democratic ideas now beginning to take hold in the sociological and political milieu. They must expel the United States from the region before it is too late. They have clearly made a strategic decision to do just that. Their mercenaries are relatively cheap to financially sustain. At the same time, they diligently work to keep the United States at bay by promises of helping to destroy the very terrorists they have hired to carry out their plan. If their plan begins to falter, if the terrorists groups, once inside the house, want to take it over, they will even seek United States military assistance! It is a bold plan. With Russia supplying Iran the accoutrements of nuclear power, and North Korea openly defying their South Asian neighbors to do anything about their acquisition of a nuclear arsenal, and the United States hesitating to alienate the Saudi Royal family, they hope that time is on their side.

A Second Look

Mercenaries, however, should take a good look at history. Those who create violence are, in the end, abandoned by those who finance their violence, and even destroyed by them, for fear that these same mercenary terrorists, observing the life style and riches of their patrons, might be tempted to move to claim all of this for themselves. A good example was the relationship of Hamas to Yasser Arafat. They served his dream of power and dominance over Israel for years but, having failed to accomplish his strategic dream, Arafat tried as diplomatically as possible, to distance himself from Hamas in an effort to survive. The problem for Arafat was that Hamas became more powerful than their patron. They had no intention of simply melting away. They have developed horizontally, building a family of organizational infrastructure with political, military, educational, welfare, media and publishing components. Al Jezeera is theirs to use. Serbian television paid a critical role in the years leading up to the Yugoslav wars in promoting nationalist propaganda, comparing contemporary events with the Second World War and the 1389 battle of Kosovo. In the end, Hamas as it is presently configured will have to be either downsized or become part of the establishment. Such is the intrigue of Middle East politics and such is the danger of becoming a mercenary for a regional power.

Western-Islamic estrangement grows as perceptions and misperceptions abound in an unending propaganda war of ideas. Many have a great deal of sympathy for and solidarity with the followers of Islam, all of whom deserve to be treated with dignity and equality in a sometimes unequal world. For others, where classes of people are perceived as being backward or strangely religious, these public perceptions often become private psychological realities causing irreparable damage to innumerable psyches. The law-abiding Muslim often suffers from distorted self-perceptions that devastate his personality and sear his soul. The West, on the other hand, also suffers a psychological quandary. How can it be that on the basis of religious belief we must observe and even experience the horror of massacred innocent men, women, and children at the hands of suicide bombers? What kind of mind, we ask, can conceive and justify such behavior?

Chapter Twelve

RUSSIA'S EURANASIA

The state symbol of Russia is the 15th century Byzantine Empire's two-headed eagle, one head looking East and the other looking West. It symbolizes Russia's past efforts to expand its territory both to the East and the West. Rather than territorial aggrandizement, Russia is looking in the 21st century to strengthen its ties to its neighbors to the East and West and to create alternative foci of power to offset the global leadership position of the United States, a strategy that some call: Eurasianism. Russia's elites are preoccupied with advancing Eurasianism, a counter force to the maritime and commercial Euro-Atlantic world. Russian analyst Yu. V. Tikhonravov makes the point that Russia has both by location and necessity a special role in the Middle East/Asia/Europe as a necessary alternative and balancing force to United States hegemony. Eurasian strategy calls for Russia to develop closer cooperation with China, and the Arab world. This strategy began a long time ago, lost ground during the Soviet political upheavals that led to Glasnost and Perestroika, but has recently returned to center stage in Russian foreign policy, picking up enormous energy and direction under Vladimir Putin and Euvgeny Primakov, Russia's most knowledgeable Muslim-watcher.

The Russians, in their effort to recoup their former imperial power in Central Asia are fully aware that the Muslim party elite there base their power and influence on a mixture of communist and Islamic principles. They openly endorse Islamic ideas, laws and mechanisms of power, but use the traditional party-based structure of power and security bodies in order to remain in power. The Russians are also very aware of the power of the local clergy. Under Soviet administration they winked at the practice of the local elite replacing the regular clergy in the mosques and madrasas by loyal clergymen willing to follow the directives of party committees and the KGB. However, efforts by the Soviets to infiltrate the clergy for purposes of spying on or influencing the local elite, or using the clergy to spy on the people did not meet with success. While there was no way of opposing Soviet power, clergy and people remained quietly loyal to each other. It was the clergy, after all who knew Arabic, could read the Koran and religiously pilgrimaged (made a "hadj") to Saudi Arabia. The Soviets came to understand this and began a program of trying to win the hearts of the clergy, making overtures of their own by lavishly praising them, sending them on prestige missions to Muslim communities worldwide, spreading the word that 59 million Soviet Muslims had freedom of religion and that the Soviets encouraged the viability of Islamic culture. Everyone played a game of survival. Foreign Muslims who visited Soviet Central Asia were carefully screened and the KGB kept them from direct contacts with the Soviet Muslim faithful. The parallel existence of official and underground (the intellectual elite) Islam in Central Asia continued to the mid-1980s. Then the policy of perestroika and glasnost gradually enabled the Muslim community to come out into the open with their own thoughts and plans for the future of Islam in their area. They increased their contacts with Iran, Egypt, Libya and Algeria, each of which encouraged them to move in the direction of a full return to Islam and the reconstruction of society on Islamic principles and the laws of Sharia.

The Central Asian rulers turned to Islamic doctrine in search of a politically correct language to be used in the new perestroika and post-perestroika atmosphere. They gradually declared themselves genuine defenders of Islam, not only in everyday life and in interpersonal relationships, but on every official level. However, they did not identify with Wahhabi radical fundamentalism and they openly disavowed any return to a medieval Islamic society. The general trend among them is more democratic and secular rather than religious and fundamentalist. Their socio-political and economic model is that of Turkey because Turkish culture combines modem Western and traditional Eastern cultures. Unlike the Russian Orthodox Church, which became a non-entity in Russia, Central Asian Islam went underground during the Soviet period, avoiding official places of worship, and meeting in secret communities without official clergy.

Soviets Never Trusted Muslims

Soviet Muslims always resisted the Kremlin authorities but did so very diplomatically. For them, Islam provided its followers with the organizational, ideological and institutional help they needed to preserve their national culture, identity and way of life. The government's anti-Islamic policy actually increased when Gorbachev came to power. In November 1986 Gorbachev met with members of the Central Committee of the Uzbek Communist Party. He expressed so much hostility towards Islam in his instructions to local communists that his speech, except for being published in Pravda, was not reported in any major Soviet newspaper. That did not disturb the Muslim populations. They defended their religion and traditions as a legitimate possession of their national heritage. The Kremlin, however, not understanding the depth of their attachment to Islam, considered Islam a threat to the Soviet system, and considered their repression of Muslims as a struggle against nationalism and chauvinism, calling Muslims political mafia and common criminals.

Times Have Changed

Now, successive Russian and Western leaders have begun to understand the reality of the power of Islam. Until recently the West has accepted stereotypical ideas about Soviet Muslim political passiveness, conservatism, and adherence to tradition. The United States needs to understand these powerful politico-religious forces if it is to craft an intelligent policy toward the region and avoid the mistakes made by Soviet policymakers because they ignored Islamic realities. "Islamophobia" was widespread in Soviet times but the humiliating defeat the Russians suffered in 1979 at the hands of what they had considered primitive Afghans was a wakeup call. The Mujahideen forced the Soviets into unconventional warfare. As we are learning in Iraq, that is a lose-lose situation. They had miscalculated both the strength of indigenous determination, the near impossibility of defeating home-grown resistance and the powerful hold that Islam has on the people. Foreign political and economic systems forcefully implanted are shifting sands with no foundation. The Kremlin leaders learned years ago and the new leadership is learning today that the Central Asian leadership and people consider themselves to be Muslims first. Islam in Central Asia is not simply a religion but a treasured way of life.

The Background

Russian interest in Central Asia took concrete form in the Czarist Russia of the mid-1800s which, during several large-scale military incursions, established a colonial empire in Central Asia. The first governor-general, General Kaufmann, was appointed in 1867. In spite of seven decades of massive post-revolutionary attempts (including education and technological modernization) to integrate Central Asia with the Soviet Weltanschauung, the Muslims remained aloof both from Soviet Politics and Soviet culture. Within a month of the Bolshevik revolution, Lenin assured the Muslims that their religion and customs, their national and cultural institutions "are proclaimed free and inviolable." It was a promise not to be kept. Most of the country's 26,000 mosques and 24,000 religious schools were shut down and turned into warehouses and nightclubs, the teachers either killed or imprisoned. Soviet and Russian inattention to Islam had deep roots. Marx and his mentor, Hegel, dismissed Islam's ability to play a role in modern society. Marx and Hegel believed that "Islam had already exited the world historical arena. It was not just Islam, of course, that the Soviets denounced. All religion was 'the opium of the masses.'" They mistakenly believed that destroying mosques and imprisoning Muslim clergymen would have the same effect on Islam within the Soviet Union that destroying churches and arresting priests had had on Russian Orthodoxy. They were intent on wiping out the Muslim leadership, not understanding that any faithful Muslim man can become a spiritual leader. The Soviets blundered, for there is no hierarchy.

Russians intent on Leadership

The Russians, having understood their shortcomings and not wanting the Muslim republics to be lured away in the future by the United States or Western Europe, began, in the mid-1980s, an intensive study of Islam, a process that would have been very useful to the United States at the time of the Andijon event. We can learn from the Russians the dynamics of political change in Islamic Central Asia. There is so much we have to discover so quickly. How will the strengthening of fundamentalism affect the stability of neo-Bolshevik regimes in Central Asia and the relations between the republics and the Russian authorities in Moscow? What would be the geo-socio-political consequences for the United States and its allies? Would it produce a neo-Caliphate that would become a massive Islamic terrorism with an anti-Western and anti-American posture? It is vitally important to American interests that we not wait to find out after-the-fact.

The Russians and we need to realize that Central Asians are not fodder for cultural and economic domination and integration and are very vulnerable to Pan-Islamic overtures. They are listening to Pan Islamic voices reminding them that Central Asia, as a Russian colony, produced almost all of the Soviet Union's cotton, but only a small amount was processed there. The European Russians got the jobs involved in its manufacture. The same was true of their oil and gas supplies, their rare and precious metals. They gradually got the message that they were simply another colony. Their valuable products were exported to Russia and less than one fifth of all Soviet internal investment found its way back in their direction. Many of these oppressed people emigrated to neighboring Afghanistan and continued their anti-Bolshevik resistance from there. Their descendants contributed to defeating the Soviet army in Afghanistan and they can be found as leaders within the anti-establishment circles in each of the Central Asian Islamic movements.

Remnants of the Soviet days reside in different degrees in the former Soviet Muslim republics. For example, the political leadership of Tajikistan is more Islamic than the others. In Uzbekistan and Kazakhstan there is a healthy mixture of fundamentalists, nationalists and democrats. The overwhelming majority of Central Asian Muslims, including the ethnically Persian peoples of Tajikistan, follow the Sunni Islam observed in Saudi Arabia and most of the Muslim world. Central Asia would probably produce an Islamic state more like Pakistan than Shiite Iran. The Islamic Renaissance Party, founded in 1990 in the Russian city of Astrakhan, sees itself as the leader of Central Asian Islam with branches in Russia, Uzbekistan and Tajikistan. The mosques are full to capacity in this area. Uzbekistan's Ferghana Valley is a major center for Muslim religious and political activities. Cultural revitalization has also been taking place. Stalin, in 1939, mandated that the Central Asian republics use the Cyrillic alphabet, but now Arabic-language schools abound in Tashkent and in other major cities.

The Russians have been intimately tied in with the Gulf enemies of the United States for many years. Saddam Hussein was both a valued ally and the 'Soviets' most profitable military client in the Gulf, indeed in the world. We need to remember that all the members of the Saddam regime were and remain close Russian friends and allies at a personal level. The Baathist party members now carrying out the guerilla campaign against the Americans in Iraq were the creatures of Soviet training and support. Their relationship goes back a long way. In 1972, Moscow and Baghdad signed the Treaty of Friendship and Cooperation and thousands of military advisers and other specialists flowed into Iraq and trained both the military arm of the government and its intelligence agencies. The relationship between the two nations deepened once Saddam came to power in 1979, as Saddam purposely followed the Stalinist model of government by introducing Soviet intelligence and coercive methods. One of the first things he did as leader was to sign an agreement with Soviet Defense Minister Ustinov on military cooperation and strategic consultation.

Soviet friendship and support at all levels of Saddam's regime made it a regional military superpower and positioned the Soviets to have a strategic position in the Middle East, with the construction of eight military facilities, naval and air, for Soviet use. During the 1980's Iraq became the world's largest importer of arms. Between 1980 and 1990 Saddam spent a hefty $100 billion dollars. To a weak Soviet and then Russian economy it was like manna from heaven. But, since Iraq made all those purchases on credit, it was in Moscow's interest to help maintain Saddam's regime so that it could get back its investment and not lose its richest client. As the crises over Kuwait developed and later the problems with the UN and the United States, the Russians became obsessed with the fear of losing its best customer for its outmoded weapons, and of losing face as all that Russian weaponry failed to stop American military might. They lost money; they lost face.

Now they are determined to win it all back by supporting any terrorist group that has as its goal the expulsion of the American military presence in the Gulf. No question about that. News Max.com printed an article by Col. Stanislaw Lunev,[42] dated March 28, 2001. He wrote:" While there is nothing unusual about Russia selling its weapons to foreign nations, it is very strange and suspicious that the weapons she is selling are going almost exclusively to those regimes having a traditional anti-American orientation, and to countries which could not, without great difficulty, be called friendly to the West. This required an enormous Soviet investment in the region, an investment which they saw melt away when Saddam, an uncontrollable client, invaded Kuwait, thereby introducing a dominant American military presence in the region. They watched their great expenditure of money flow down the proverbial drain as their favorite client, driven by a personal megalomania, squandered it all in a short 2 or 3 weeks of military adventure in Kuwait. Russian return to the region and the recovering of their financial losses drives present Russian Middle East policy. Its cozy relationship with terrorist groups provides them with mercenaries as they covertly go about the business of regaining once again a dominant position in Central Asia.

The principal reason Moscow forged a close relationship with Baghdad and made such a deep military commitment is because Iraq has tremendous geopolitical strategic value. Iraq is at the heart of the Persian Gulf and the richest oil-region in the world. Thus, it was a focal point not only of the Arab world, but also of vital Western energy interests. Russia wants to fill-in the space in-between. Their foothold in Iraq enhanced Moscow's influence over other Arab nations and gave the Russians dominance in the one area of the world where the Americans were most vulnerable, i.e., the oil-rich Middle East. The Russians hated their own weakness and helplessness in the face of American power. On the day Saddam moved into Kuwait, American Secretary of State James Baker was visiting his Soviet counterpart, Eduardo Shevardnadze, in Siberia. Within a couple of hours they worked out the draft wording for U.N. Resolution 660 which called for an immediate, unconditional Iraqi withdrawal. This had to be one of the most humiliating and frustrating moments in recent Russian history. They exposed their weakness to the world and, most galling, to the Arab world. The battle against American presence in Iraq is the great Russian opportunity for revenge and we can be certain that they are exploiting this opportunity with tremendous energy. If you have ever attended a Notre Dame/Southern California football game the year after one of those teams had been humiliated on the field, you know the feeling.

Russia, Major arms Supplier

Since the fall of the Soviet Union, Russia has become the major arms supplier for China and India. On a recent trip to New Delhi, Russian representatives signed arms and nuclear deals worth an estimated $3 billion, including cooperation in nuclear and missile defenses. On July 16, 2001, Russia and China signed a Treaty of Friendship and Cooperation for a period of 20 years and automatically renewable unless one of the parties indicates otherwise at that time. In the treaty "Russia recognizes that there is only one China in the world." Analysts suggest that the treaty may have secret appendices outlining the conditions for a common defense, military cooperation in space, cooperation on military technologies, and new weapons sales. Russia is already selling nuclear weapons blueprints, multiple warhead (MIRV) technology, Sukhoi-27 fighter jets, and, most recently, $1 billion worth of A-50 AWACS early warning planes to China that will make it possible for the People's Liberation Army to coordinate its air, surface, and naval operations in areas like the Taiwan

Strait. Russia supports China's claims regarding Taiwan, and China supports Moscow's activities in Chechnya. Finally, both Russia and China have vociferously opposed Washington's plans to deploy an NMD (National Missile Defense) system. Putin, who is restoring ties with Europe by cultivating a friendship with Prime Minister Tony Blair, is also playing out the Primakov doctrine of weakening the United States. Russia also carefully strengthened Moscow's ties with former Chancellor Gerhardt Schroeder of Germany. As France and Germany have sought to strengthen the European Union and offset European military reliance on the United States, Moscow has begun to express an interest in joining the European Security and Defense Preparedness (ESDP) group, which would drive a wedge between Europe and the United States. Russia's offer to construct a common missile defense with the EU may have been made with the same strategic goal in mind. However, Putin, who at first expressed a wish to join NATO, has since disavowed that suggestion. Russia's increasing activities in the Persian Gulf, and the Middle East are obvious. The change in German leadership in 2006, however, presents a major challenge to Moscow's German policy.

Since 1991, Russia has sold Middle Eastern countries more than $8.9 billion worth of modern weapons, including almost $5 billion in sales to Iran alone.

Moscow, in a secret memorandum signed by Vice President Al Gore and Prime Minister Victor Chernomyrdin in June 1995, acknowledged that it had sold Iran such conventional arms as submarines, anti-ship missiles, and tanks. The agreement between the two officials made it clear that the United States would do nothing about the arms sales if Moscow promised to cease these activities by 1999. The weapons sales, however, continue. Moreover, the secret agreement may have been in violation of the 1992 Iran-Iraq Arms Nonproliferation Act cosponsored by then-Senator Gore (D-TN), which stipulates that the United States would impose sanctions on Russia if it persisted in selling weapons of this type to Iran or Iraq. In the summer and fall of 2000 Russia shipped 325 shoulder-launched anti-aircraft SA-16 missiles to Tehran, part of a deal totaling 700 missiles worth $1.75 billion. Because Tehran is known for re-exporting weapons to Islamic radicals in the Middle East, such as the Lebanon-based Hezbollah movement, it is only a matter of time before these latest missiles find their way to Hezbollah terrorists or the Islamic Jihad. U.S. objections to the sale prompted a rebuked from Russian Foreign Minister Igor Ivanov, saying that Russia is not constrained by any "special obligations in spheres which are not restricted by international obligations."

Putin has managed to keep the Russian public on his side in these mini-confrontations with the United States, according to the polls. The shift in public opinion is dramatic. The Russian government's demonstrated determination to maintain friendly relations with Iraq, Iran and North Korea, suggests that Moscow's continued support in the war against terrorism is not assured, and that Russia may ultimately emerge as a very complicating factor for U.S. security planners. Iran is the primary state sponsor of terrorism today, along with Libya, North Korea, Sudan, and Syria. Iran sponsors Hezbollah, Syria and Libya backed Abu Nidal[43] and Libya backs the Japanese Red Army. Osama's al-Qaeda was a bit different. It appears that instead of being supported during the time that the Taliban were in power in Afghanistan, al-Qaeda supported the Taliban, at least militarily.

Chapter Thirteen

PESHAWAR, THE HEARTLAND OF ISLAMIC TERRORISM

Peshawar is the capital city of world Islamic terrorism. As far back as March 20, 1995 a New York Times article is quoted as claiming that the Islamic university in Peshawar is a training site for terrorists. Al Dawat, as the university is known, was founded by Abdul Rab Rasool Sayyaf, a militant Muslim with strong anti-American leanings, in the mid 1980s. There is no end to Peshawar's involvement in just about everything. A story in the New York Times, March 20, in 2002, titled, "Terror Network Traced To Pakistan," reported that "an Islamic university in Peshawar, Pakistan is under investigation as a training site for terrorists who have struck in the Philippines, Central Asia, the Middle East, North Africa and, possibly, in the 1993 explosion at the World Trade Center in New York."

Investigators and diplomats are quoted as saying that the University of Dawat and Jihad and other centers in Peshawar had been training militants for a jihad, or holy war, against governments and other targets they see as enemies of Islam. The Times quoted an unnamed Pakistani military official as saying that as many as 25,000 such volunteers were trained there with the help of a Pakistan military spy agency. Sheikh Rahman, who was, before being convicted of being involved with bomb plots in New York City, the head of the Brooklyn-based Afghan Center, was also connected with the holy war headquarters in Peshawar, Pakistan. It is in Peshawar that the New York terror campaign took shape, and was the headquarters of Sheikh Rahman's international network. Peshawar was also the headquarters of Gulbuddin Hekmatyar's group, which trained four of the key New York suspects. Afghan officials officially warned the U.S. government about Hekmatyar no fewer than four times. The last warning delivered just days before the Trade Center attack. Gulbuddin Hekmatyar's Mujahideen faction, the Hezb-e-Islami, was one of the groups which helped end the Soviet occupation of Afghanistan. The group was blamed for much of the terrible death and destruction of that period, which led many ordinary Afghans to welcome the emergence of the Taliban. Gulbuddin fled to Iran, where he lives a quiet life, waiting for his fortunes to change.

It is a dry, dusty city,[44] just east of the Khyber Pass. If Afghanistan is the birthplace of modern jihad, Peshawar is its staging ground. This city of intrigue is where many of today's Islamic youth from all over the Middle East came to train. At the end of their training they were handed both the Koran and a Kalashnikov machine gun. The area is called the North West Frontier Province and has seen many conquerors and adventurers, like Mahmood of Ghazni, Alexander the Great, Taimur, Emperor Babar, Nadir Shah and Ahmed Shah Abdali. It is known to all the world's security and intelligence services as a haven for guerrillas, spies and religious zealots on the Pakistani frontier with Afghanistan. But, Peshawar is more than that. It is there that al-Qaeda makes money for its war chest by guaranteeing that if you want to be someone else or live somewhere else, they will get you the right documents. A lot more is going on is Peshawar. Its snow-capped peaks and lush green valleys of unusual beauty attract tourists and mountaineers from far and wide while its art and architecture is not less known than the historic Khyber Pass. The biggest tourist attraction is the historic Khyber Pass which is 17.7 km from Peshawar City and extends to Afghan territory and now forms part of the main Asian Highway. This legendary gateway to the South-Asian subcontinent is more than 35 km long.

Another attraction is Gandhara art, largely expressed through sculpture, the valuable heritage of the Peshawar area. In the

Gandhara School of art, creation of the Buddha, after nearly 500 years after his death, they search for an ideal human being who is above the common man, but is not a god, a man who ultimately aims at bringing human beings under the influence of Buddha's moral teachings.

Peshawar derives its name from a Sanskrit word, "Push-papura", meaning the city of flowers. It is so old, 2000 years, that no one can say anything authoritative about its origins. Down through the course of history it has had many names. One of its very early rulers, Sher Sha Shuri, got a bright idea. He turned Peshawar into a boom town by running his Delhi-to Kabul Road through the Khyber Pass. He and his successors then went about turning it into the "City of Flower" by planting a large variety of trees and laying out gardens. It developed rapidly also as a Buddhist center, but as Buddhism declined, so did Peshawar. When Marco Polo visited Peshawar in 1275 he commented: "The people have peculiar language, they worship idols and have an evil disposition". He would be pleased at the many changes that have taken place. The population has now long been Islamic and it is noted for its hospitality. It is a large city with a 1990s population in the neighborhood of 988,000, and prides itself in being the capital of Pakistan's North-West Frontier Province. Its location near the Khyber Pass makes it a natural military and communications center, as well as a major trade outlet with Afghanistan. It is not surprising that in a city of this size, and its unique access to Afghanistan, it houses a large number of industries, from food processing to steel to cigarettes and many other products. Its wonderful location, both scenically and commercially, has made it a target of desire from invaders for everyone from the Afghans and the Mongols, to the British.

Everybody wanted a piece of the action that Peshawar provided. When the British were about building their empire they captured the city in 1848 and turned it into a valuable base for their military operations against Pathan tribes. More recently (1979-89), during the Soviet occupation of Afghanistan, it was the center of relief operations for Afghan refugees and the command center of the coalition of guerrilla groups fighting to expel the Soviet forces from Afghanistan. It was during this period that it started down the road of also being the hotbed and training

camp for Islamic terrorists. The defeat of the Russians embold-
ened the Peshawar-based terrorists to develop a strategy for ex-
pelling infidels from all Islamic lands. The better educated of
them were students at the Al-Azhar University in Cairo, where
they were converted to the concept of "Pan-Islamicism," which
was opposed to the concept of the nation-state. "One Arab Nation" became both their cry and their strategy.

When the Soviets attacked Afghanistan in December 1979,
the initial prognosis in the West was that the native population
lacked the unity to resist. It was felt that the proud ethnic groups
in the country would never unify enough to drive out the communists. The answer, agreed to in Washington, the Middle East,
and Pakistan was to bring about unity on the basis of a shared Islamic culture and religion. The creation of the mujahideen warriors was the result - fighters that would come from around the
Muslim world and take up arms in the name of a holy war. When
the Soviets invaded Afghanistan in 1979, Pakistani President Zia
ul-Haq handpicked the so-called "Peshawar Seven" to infiltrate
into Afghanistan and assist in driving the Soviets out. Later, after
the fall of Afghanistan to the Americans, many of the al-Qaeda
and Taliban fighters who escaped from the U.S. onslaught found
refuge in Peshawar.

U.S. and Pakistani officials have collaborated on many raids
in the area. On one occasion, in August 2002, Pakistani and U.S.
security officials arrested 12 suspected Muslim militants in Peshawar. They had been working with al-Qaeda and Taliban fugi-
tives to carry out attacks inside Pakistan. Police recovered a
cache of assault rifles, explosives, detonators and timing devices
from the building. Pakistan is very loathe to admit the close relationship between Pakistani intelligence and the FBI, but it is very
close, and includes the arrest of senior al-Qaeda figure, Abu
Zubayda, in the city of Faisalabad.

Along with the new fervor to fight the Soviet infidels, a new
set of insights and pan-Islamic ideals developed, capturing the
hearts and minds of young Muslims, along with a powerful new
interpretation of an old Islamic idea - jihad. Later, after the war,
the Afghan Arabs would take their battle-tested skills and sharp-
edged ideology home to Yemen, Algeria, Saudi Arabia, Egypt,
the Philippines, Kenya, and the United States. "Scratch an Is-

lamic militant group today and you find Afghan Arabs behind it," says a Jakarta-based diplomat. Peshawar remains a terrorist stronghold. In January 2006, about 8,000 Islamic hardliners in Peshawar were among those taking part in protests across Pakistan against a U.S. attack on a local village, Bajour, meant to kill al-Qaeda leaders. Some protesters chanted "Death to America" and "Jihad is our way" while burning an effigy of President Bush. Although there was no violence, on standby were hundreds of police armed with tear gas launchers and submachine guns. Supporters of Pakistani religious party Jamat-i-Islami burned an effigy of U.S. President George Bush at a rally in Peshawar. The alliance Mutahida Majlis-e-Amal governs the conservative province and strongly opposes the country's support of the U.S.-led fight against terror. Shahid Shamsi, a spokesman for the alliance, told the Associated Press that demonstrators were also demanding the withdrawal from Pakistan of U.S. troops helping with relief efforts after an earthquake killed 87,000 people and left 3.5 million homeless. He assumed that the real reason the Americans came was to spy on the area and gather as much intelligence as they could for operations like the air strike. They vowed that they would continue to protest until all American armed forces were expelled from the area. Killed in the attack were an explosives and chemical weapons expert, and a relative of the organization's second-in-command to Osama bin Laden, Ayman al-Zawahiri. Pakistan's leader, Gen. Pervez Musharraf, was condemned for not publicly criticizing the U.S. In 2002. Peshawar-based radical Islamic groups made huge gains in Pakistan's parliamentary elections by opposing the United States and supporting the Taliban.

The Jihad Godfather: Abdullah Azzam

Just outside Peshawar, in what was the Jalozai Afghan refugee camp, is the "martyrs graveyard," the Peshawar Pabi Graveyard of the Shuhadaa (legendary defenders of Islam), where some 6,000 mujahideen veterans from the Afghan war are buried. Among them, identified by a small marker that reads "star of the martyrs," is the resting place of one of the most revered "freedom" fighters, Abdullah Azzam. He and his two sons were assassinated in Peshawar by a car bomb blast in November of

1989, while they were driving to Friday Prayers. The physical remains of his sons, Ibrahim and Mohammed, were scattered among the trees and power lines. Azzam's body was found resting against a wall, totally intact except for blood trickling out of his mouth. The assailants were never apprehended.

One cannot speak of Peshawar without at the same time mentioning Azzam, called by Islamic Terrorist organizations across the Middle East the "Godfather,' or the 'Lenin" of jihad. Azzam melded - in a practical ideology - the Arabic forms of Islam with the Deobandi versions.[45] It was an ideology of jihad. Time Magazine wrote of Azzam that "he was the reviver of Jihad in the 20th Century." Those who met Azzam were impressed by his oratorical skills, his talent as a military strategist, and his religious leadership. Today, the military wing of Hamas in the Palestinian West Bank is called the Abdullah Azzam Brigades. Azzam's first impression of Osama bin Laden, when he arrived in Peshawar was that of a playboy and dilettante who had revolutionary potential. Azzam took him under his wing and made a "man" out of him, teaching him everything he knew about military strategy and how to inspire Islamic youth to volunteer for jihad.

In Peshawar, Azzam founded the now-famous Mujahideen Services Bureau. Its purpose was to offer assistance to the Afghani Jihad and the Mujahideen by initiating projects that supported their cause. The Bureau was to become the strategic nerve center of the struggle to rid Afghanistan of Soviet troops. Azzam was the first to call the Arab world's attention to the plight of the Afghanis and his role as bin Laden's spiritual leader says a lot about bin Laden's development. It is estimated that he recruited as many as 18,000 young men from 15 or 20 nations, including the United States. He traveled freely to more than 50 American cities in as many as 25 states recruiting men and raising money for his jihad.

In fact, it was in 1988, at the Al-Farook Mosque in Brooklyn on Atlantic Avenue, that he convened the first Conference of Jihad. Azzam urged his audience to "carry out jihad no matter where you are, even in America." He stressed that whenever Jihad is mentioned in the Holy Book, it means the obligation to fight. It does not mean "to fight with the pen or to write books or articles in the press or to fight by holding lectures." In the end, it was like-minded men who murdered him and his sons. After Sept. 11, it was the name of Osama Bin Laden that was associated with changing world alliances and security, but the real strategist behind all of this was Abdullah Azzam.

Osama bin Laden is the beneficiary of Azzam's tactical genius. It was Azaam's doctrine and call to arms that prompted bin Laden to issue his 1998 fatwa declaring that Muslims must kill Americans. He opposed the Palestine Liberation Organization and Arafat as being too secular. Hamas agreed with him and adopted his program of reclaiming all Muslim territory. For them, as for Azzam, there was no question of implementing a two-states (Israel and Palestine) solution. Israel must be destroyed. The program was laid out by Azzam: "There will be no solution to the Palestinian problem except through jihad ... Jihad and the rifle alone: no negotiations, no conferences, no dialogues." Arafat's real enemy was not Israel; it was the ghost of Abdullah Azzam. After Azzam's assassination, bin Laden took over the organization's leadership. It is clear now, however, that bin Laden has abandoned Azzam's over- ambitious goals, settling for replacing the secular Arab regimes and establishing Islamic states in their place.

Azzam's "Legions"[46]

Azzam dipped into the legions of idealistic unemployed young men looking for meaning in a world in which they were mere observers, a world that was and remains a breeding ground for terrorism. Typically, the novice-terrorist, using a language and concepts he has only artificially absorbed, hides behind identification with the poor.[47] For a young Arab with no realistic hope of finding dignified employment, membership in a terrorist organization offers a not-before-found sense of historical relevance and adventure. And Azzam's reputation brought them in by the thousands. *The London Times* quoted intelligence reports suggesting that militants trained in Al Dawat and other camps in Peshawar have taken part in almost every conflict in which Muslims have been involved: Kashmir, Mindanao (the largest of Philippine islands), Tajikistan, Bosnia, Egypt, Tunisia and Algeria. They have also been very busy in China, in the Xinjiang-

Uighur Autonomous Region, where they are helping the indigenous Wahhabi to form a separate Islamic state.

At the same time, Peshawar is a city whose streets are littered with broken men and women, after 20 years of constant dislocation, caught in the crossfire of opposing Islamic ideologies, heroin addiction becomes a distraction of choice. But, there is little local sympathy for their plight. A survey team of the United Nations International Drug Control Program (UNDCP) interviewed 150 addicts living in Peshawar on the streets, under the bridges and in graveyards. They learned that 46% of the addicts are forced to live outside their homes due to family pressure and public disdain. Half of them use heroin three times a day. The survey said nearly two-thirds of all addicts reported feelings of despair and alienation.

Alongside this distressing image, there are also bright images. An Islamic educational institution designed to instruct youth in strict Islamic principles, Jamia Imam Bokhari, was constructed on the outskirts of Peshawar on a seven acre plot of land. Known as 'the center,' it was built at a cost of nearly eight-hundred thousand dollars, the bulk of which was provided by Saudi prince Salman bin Abdul Aziz and the Saudi Red Crescent society. It caters to 750 students, from home and abroad, having a separate section reserved for young women. The centre is run by an organization, Jamaat-ud-Dawah Al-Koran wa Sunnah, with close ties to the Saudis but based in eastern Afghanistan. The core curriculum consists of Islamic principles, but traditional educational subjects are also offered. Another important Islamic institution, the University of Peshawar, spreads over an expanse of 1000 acres and has an 18,000 student enrollment. It was established in 1950 with 120 students. Groups of terrorists, according to diplomats and the police, still live in and around Peshawar, using as cover some of the 18 Arab educational and relief organizations that registered with the Pakistani authorities during the Afghan war. Some senior Pakistani officials complain about Western pressure to root out these groups from Peshawar saying that "the terrorist groups that became established here got their start under policies that Western countries eagerly supported, as long as the target was the Soviet Union." Chickens do come home to rest.

The Gang of Seven

Most of the Islamic "fundamentalist" parties involved in driving Russia out of Afghanistan were already active years before the Red Army marched across the Oxus River. Many of their leaders were educated at the Al-Azhar University in Cairo, where they studied "Pan-Islamicism," as opposed to the concept of the nation-state. As they developed into full blown Islamic parties President Bhutto of Pakistan allowed them to open up offices in Peshawar, and some were also provided military training by the Pakistani Inter-Service Intelligence (ISI). The Wahhabi of Saudi Arabia also funded their activities. When the Soviets invaded Afghanistan in 1979, then Pakistani president, Zia ul-Haq, hand-picked the so-called "Peshawar Seven" groups—known by most Afghans as the "gang of seven"—who had served Pakistani interests in the past as the primary beneficiaries of funding and arms, to wage the war against the Soviet Union.

Original Peshawar-based "gang of seven," in Brief

1. Hezb-i-Islami (Party of Islam), led by Gulbuddin Hekmatyar, who was affiliated with the Muslim Brotherhood since the 1970s. As a student of engineering in Kabul University, he led most of the demonstrations in Kabul from 1967 to 1972.

2. Jamiat-i-Islami (Islamic Society). Led by Burhanuddin Rabbani, a former professor and theologian at Kabul University, whose party consists primarily of ethnic Tajiks from the north of the country

3. Itehad Islami (Islamic Unity). Islamic Unity is led by former university professor Abdul Rasul Sayaf, who received most of his support from radical elements in Saudi Arabia, Iraq, and other Muslim countries. Sayaf converted to Saudi Wahhabism at the onset of the war. The "University of Dawa and Jihad" was founded by Sayaf in 1985, in Pakistan's North West Frontier Province. Sometimes referred to as the "Islamic Sandhurst," the university provides training for Islamic militants

4. Hezbi-Islami (Party of Islam). Led by Maulvi Younas Khalis, an Islamic scholar, former teacher, and journalist. Originally with Hekmatyar, Khalis, being a traditional Islamist, split from the former in 1979. Khalis's group, primarily led by Haji

Din Mohammad, led the military actions against the Soviet Army. Its major military commanders were: Abdul Haq, Jalaludin Haqani, Abdul Qadir, Qazi Amin Wardak, and Mullah Malang. With his group now barely in existence, Khalis is entirely removed from the political arena.

5. Mahaz-i-Milli Islam (National Islamic Front of Afghanistan). The National Islamic Front is led by Pir Sayed Ahmad Gilani, leader of the powerful Qadiri Sufi sect. Gilani, prior to the war in Afghanistan, was the representative in Kabul of the French auto company Peugeot. He also worked with Lord Bethell of the London-based Radio Free Kabul. Gilani is no longer an important leader.

6. Jabha-i-Nijat-Milli (Afghan National Liberation Front). The Liberation Front is led by Sibgratullah Mojadidi, a religious leader from Kabul and royalist. Although his party had no significant military command, Mojadidi was frequently chosen as a compromise leader, and was the first interim President of Afghanistan following the collapse of the communist regime in 1992.

7. Harakat-i-Inqilab-i-Islami (Islamic Revolutionary Forces). Led by clergyman Mohammad Nabi Mohammadi, whose party's membership was derived from intellectuals. He is presently based in Peshawar.

New York is the financial capital of the world, Rome the Catholic religious capital of the world, and Peshawar the terrorist capital of the world.

PART FOUR

CENTRAL ASIA
ITS POTENTIAL ROLE
IN DEFEATING
ISLAMIC TERRORISM

Chapter Fourteen

CENTRAL ASIA'S CRITIQUE OF WAHHABISM

One major challenge facing U.S. policy makers in the war of ideas is finding the most effective way to communicate with and influence Muslim audiences. It is important to remember that Muslims and Arabs will only acknowledge criticism of Wahhabism as legitimate if Muslim scholars and experts make it. Muslims and Arabs will portray any criticism of militant Islamist ideology by Western experts on Islam as an "infidel's" attack on Islam's sacred spiritual heritage. In its strategy to defeat Wahhabi militancy, the United States must turn for help to Muslim scholars who advocate tolerant Islam. They need to make use of the arguments such scholars and clerics have developed, and nowhere does this take place more effectively than in the Central Asian republics. Central Asians Muslims have developed ways to counter Wahhabi ideology by relying on the traditions and concepts of local, tolerant Islam. Most Central Asian Muslims are "Bukhara,[48] and they have much older traditions and have much more authority within the Islamic world than advocates of Wahhabism. Their arguments with the Wahhabi are based on a very precise knowledge of the Koran and Hadith, the sayings of the Prophet—a kind of knowledge that is very rare among Western experts. So, the key to resolving the United States political and cultural divide between it and the Arab world lies in dialogue with the moderate Islam of Central Asia on what they have done for decades to successfully stave off extreme Wahhabi religious fundamentalism.

Important Shift

In Central Asia the shift from Sharia Islamics, the supranational Muslim community, into Islamic nationalism continues to take place. Wahhabism is engaged in a life-and-death struggle in Central Asia; its success or lack of it will be of great significance for the future of Central Asia and the ability of the world to contain Islamic terrorism. It will determine whether or not Wahhabi terrorism can achieve their goal, their dream of the world-wide Caliphate dream. The growing Islamo-nationalist movements in the region are challenging them. For international terrorism the CA developments are a matter of life and death because if 59 million Muslims in Central Asia reject the Wahhabi religious fundamentalism, Islamic terrorism will be dealt a severe blow, likely a death blow, to their ambitions.

Islamo-Nationalism

Moderate Islamists take the Shariat (Islamic law) seriously but they want its implementation to take place within and circumscribed by state institutions that honor parliaments and elections. They insist that foreign policy objectives be determined by the state, not by some amorphous Muslim agenda that subsumes all states under its sovereign domination. The Islamic Renaissance Party in Tajikistan is such an Islamo-Nationalist party, the only officially registered Islamic political party in the country. Their task is two-fold: first, to develop within an Islamic framework a government that respects both Islam and parliamentary institutions; secondly, to unseat the present neo-Bolshevik regime that is itself struggling to come to terms with the new realities of the region, the post-Soviet realities. It will take some time however for the IRP and similar groups in Central Asia to put their programs into action because Islamic terrorists have created such a fear in the region that any group retaining an 'Islam' orientation knows that government authorities can exploit the fear as a pretext to crack down on legitimate political dissent. IRP members claim that they are harassed and intimidated by local authorities in Soghd Province. Police have been known to turn up at meetings of the IRP's female membership—not to check passports—but to discourage political activism. At the other end of the spectrum, the avowedly Wahhabi-type group, Hizb ut-Tahrir, fearful that the moderate IRP may garner enough support to not only bring down the present government but also marginalize Hizb ut-Tahrir, continually wages a campaign to undermine the IRP. In medio stat virtus is not a popular slogan in Central Asia at this juncture of its political development. A party activist, a Mr. Yakubov, was quoted, in May 2006, by Radio Free Europe: "Firstly, Hizb ut-Tahrir is a foreign party -- so they have no right to work in our society. Secondly, their platform runs counter to the Tajik Constitution." Top IRP leader Husainzoda argues that the IRP presents Tajiks with a useful alternative to the Islamist agenda of Hizb ut-Tahrir. He says that fact should please Tajik officials. "In some areas—in those regions where groups like Hizb ut-Tahrir and others are active—we cannot create a strong presence," Husainzoda says. "But in those areas where the Islamic Renaissance Party has a strong presence, there is no sign of Hizb ut-Tahrir or any other illegal groups." That is a sensible statement but the government, fearful of both the radical and moderate politicians who include Islamic ideas, attacks both groups equally. But the political trends are in the opposite direction. Muslims in Central Asia and the Caucasus are no longer isolated from the Muslim world. Among their activities, they study abroad, especially in Pakistan, the Gulf, and Turkey.

Moving in the Right Direction

When militants of all stripes in Central Asia are repressed or expelled or obliged to flee they often joined other refugees living in Afghanistan and Pakistan. Thousands of Tajiks were hosted in northern Afghanistani camps. In the short term, Tajik authorities can remain in power by suppressing moderate Islam, but this will come back to haunt them. In the long term, because of a basic desire for living in peace and tranquility the supranational, radical, internationalist Islamic movements have no future because they do not represent any historical Central Asian reality, and are unable to assimilate because their world-wide caliphate goal deprives them of a given nationalism and culture. The positive influences that secularism offers to a culture will, in the end, dominate. Just as there no longer is the presence of the Inquisition in the Roman Catholic world, so both radical Wahhabism and neo-Bolshevik Central Asian governments will fade. The present is a delicate time, a time when all parties, including the government are attempting to find a path that will ultimately represent the people of Central Asia. We need to be patient, and to exercise delicate diplomacy. We in the West need Central Asia to succeed in its battle with Wahhabi-type terrorism, both for the good of the Central Asian people and for our own survival. Wahhabism finds in its Puritanism, its tirades against degenerative influences of the media, mass culture, individualism and liberalism, a powerful political tool, but they are fighting against historical trends in Central Asia. Wahhabi offer an alternative to moral degradation, social irresponsibility and the corruption of the religious and political establishment. This is very appealing to conservative and isolated villagers throughout Central Asia but television, access to the internet, reports from abroad all help to educate, to break down isolation. It is true that the Wahhabi play on the deep disillusionment with the prospects for economic development, and feeds on widespread despair over the many forms of moral and political decay. Wahhabism offers immediate answers for the critical social problems resulting from the current period of transition, but it disqualifies itself for the future both because it identifies race, nationality and creed with Wahhabism a very grave mistake on their part. They should have learned from the Russians.

Local Central Asian authorities have learned how to manipulate Islamic theology for their advantage and how to keep Islam within private limitations, all under the banner of Muslim theology and Islamic language to shape their new ideology of "the independent Muslim state" Their staying power has had to do with this rather than the nebulous concept of a world-wide Caliphate. United States foreign policy, therefore, should adapt itself to seeing to it that the long-term historical trend is not disrupted in Central Asia by our bureaucratic sluggishness and our seeming inability to transcend momentary realities. We need to open our hearts and treasure to Central Asia; what happens there will determine the configuration of our long-term security.

The Wahhabi Arrive

To burnish their credentials as the champions of Islam, Central Asia's local leaders opened their doors to Saudi Wahhabi who, in the beginning of the 1990's came to the newly independent Central Asian states under the pretext of building mosques and supplying Korans. But, very soon, the local leaders discovered that the Wahhabi promote their own ideology, which encouraged local opposition forces to support an Islamic Caliphate rather than the local, post-Soviet governments. They encouraged the local Muslim clergy to launch campaigns that could lead them to gradually become directly involved in state power. So, long before September 11, Central Asian governments recognized the danger that radical Islamists posed to their very existence. They undertook tough administrative measures against Wahhabi supporters and similar Islamic fundamentalists. The leaders of these nations, for that reason, were criticized by human rights organizations and this criticism has had an impact on U.S. politicians who, not knowing who or what they were dealing with, and having the best of intentions, became sympathetic to Wahhabi complaints that their civil rights were being abused. The Wahhabi took advantage of legitimate complaints to inspire others to think in terms of removing the governments of the day. This scenario is still playing out, with the Wahhabi hoping that, riding on the wave of anti Bolshevism, their day may soon come. However, at the same time, Central Asian governments did not remain idle. They took steps to de-legitimize the ideology of Wahhabism, to limit its ideological influence on local Muslims, and to inculcate immunity to Wahhabism in the hearts and minds of local youth, in order to discourage them from joining radical Islamist organizations and terrorist groups.

Education Helps

The Central Asian governments have created and developed an educational system – from kindergarten to university level – that teaches and promotes the social principles of tolerant Islam, by publishing a wide variety of textbooks, monographs and studies for all levels of education, from primary schools (even using cartoons) to university. Providing education to the most uneducated imams is also a priority, for the government knows that at the local level, the 'teacher,' both inside and outside the mosque, is the local imam. Not neglected are the wide range of counselors, local and central administrators, plus a variety of TV and radio shows that challenge the Wahhabi interpretation of the Koran and Hadith, providing listeners with a vision of tolerant Islam. Students of madrasas and universities in Tashkent and Bishkek study Arabic intensively, and upon graduation can not only read and interpret the Koran and Hadith, but also teach in Arabic. Graduates of these educational establishments become knowledgeable imams for mosques and theology teachers for public schools. Most American analysts who have been influenced by the negative stereotype of Central Asian governments as dictatorial are not even aware of these important initiatives. In spite of the fact that these stereotypes are true to a certain extent, this does not alter the fact that the United States and Central Asian governments share a common enemy – Wahhabism, and that Americans can learn valuable lessons for the war of ideas from Central Asian religious leaders, academic researchers and governmental officials. They can pass on to us their enormous practical experience in winning the hearts and minds of Muslims.

Cooperating

In July 2006 Kyrgyz President Kurmanbek Bakiev and Uzbek President Islam Karimov agreed to form even closer cooperation in combating what he called "international terrorism" and "religious extremism." "I had the full backing of Uzbek President Islam Karimov on the fight against destabilizing factors in Central Asia," Bakiev said after meeting Karimov Moscow on July 22. Kyrgyz state media gave extensive coverage of the meeting of "the leaders of the two fraternal countries." This meeting was followed on July 25, 2006 with a meeting of the security chief of each nation to discuss ways to strengthen bilateral cooperation. Kyrgyzstan's Busurmankul Tabaldiev and his Uzbek counterpart Rustam Inoyatov agreed to exchange information and conduct joint operations against "religious extremists and terrorists" in order to prevent terrorist attacks in their countries. On August 29, 2006 Kyrgyz Foreign Minister Alikbek Jekshenkulov today defended the government against the attacks of human rights campaigners who criticize it for collaborating closely with neighboring Uzbekistan on security issues. In an interview with Radio Free Europe's Kyrgyz Service, Jekshenkulov said Kyrgyzstan is in no position to "fight terrorism" alone and has to enlist the support of its neighbors. "If there is cooperation between the security services of Kyrgyzstan and Uzbekistan on security issues, is it something bad? Not only Kyrgyzstan, but even the world's leading states are unable to fight terrorism alone," he said. "That's why he have to cooperate with the whole international community [in general], and with our neighbors in particular on those issues."

Both meetings augur well for further rapprochement between the two Central Asian neighbors, whose relations soured last year following Bishkek's decision not to send Andijon refugees back to Uzbekistan. Vitaly Ponomaryov, the director of the Moscow-based Memorial's program for monitoring human rights in Central Asia, pointed out that this was a step in the right direction since the "common enemy" of Tashkent and Bishkek is Hizb ut-Tahrir (HT). And, it is true that the number of cases of detention of Hizb ut-Tahrir members has been on the rise in both southern and northern Kyrgyzstan. On July 19, 2006 Interior Minister Murat Sutalinov said that police are arming themselves with the best available weapons and technology to fight HT. In another sign of Kyrgyz-Uzbek cooperation, a police spokesperson in Osh confirmed to akipress.org on July 20 that Gulmira Maqsudova, the daughter of Akram Yuldoshev, was arrested in Osh on July 18 on forgery charges. Akram Yuldoshev, who has been imprisoned in Uzbekistan since 1999, is the purported leader of Akramiya, the group behind the unrest in Andijon in May 2005. In all of this, the Kyrghiz government has moved quickly to deal with the threat of Wahhabism.

On April 5, 2004 the Government adopted order KP № 226 "Concerning approval of the State program of counteraction to religious extremism in the Kyrghiz Republic in 2004 – 2005". This order states that the government has instructed the various Ministries, State Committees, administrative departments, and the local self-government institutions to develop and carry out concrete plans to implement the State program. In the new plan officials will be held personally responsible for implementing government plans at all levels to deal harshly with extremism in all its forms. Every 3 months, a special commission will review the effectiveness of the actions taken. The Plan envisions a qualitative change in Kyrghiz by focusing on the stabilization of religious activity and the encouragement of inter-confessional dialogue. The government, the Order states, will deal harshly with any persons or groups to act in such a way as to "impact negatively on all the processes of democratic and economic transformations in society". The implementation of the Program is based on a wide use of law-enforcement measures that are preventive in character. Obviously, the same discussion about where to draw the line in law enforcement is taking place in Central Asia as is taking place now in Europe and America.

Devil in the Details

The devil, of course, is in the details. Improving the general legal structures in the region is seen as important so that government actions will be consistent with the law and the protection of human rights. Striking a good balance is a desired if difficult goal to achieve in an atmosphere of fear and violence. Finally, the government must put in place legislation that gives it authorization to, in effect, censor printed, audio, and video materials that encourage any form of illegal religious-extremist activities. The realization of these government goals in the KR will require the coordinated activity of the ministries involved: the State Committees, administrative departments, and the institutions of local self-governments. In judging such actions on the part of the Central Asian governments we need to recall the relief many have experienced in Britain and other nations when their respective governments decided to "get tough" when faced with suicide bombers and other activities on the part of Islamic extremists. Keeping law and order in volatile areas often demands hard choices.

A second government document, the Plan of Measures on Realization of the State Program in the Kyrghiz Republic, consists of a list of 20 specific tasks to be carried out and the names of the officials responsible for their implementation. The tasks are contained in seven different areas. The time frame for implementation was set as the year 2004-2005. Targeted are a host

of religious extremist groups, including extremist Shiite missionaries, and the Akhmadia, Falungun, and Moon Churches.

About Resources
However, the State program is not provided with sufficient
financial resources[49] to accomplish its goal. For example, in the
Plan there are no instructions to the Ministry of Finance to finance the various activities outlined in the Program. An international appeal to States, international organizations and NGOs for
financial help in implementing the Program is in order, since
what happens in Central Asia will have domino effects in other
parts of the world. The CA nations especially need funding to
create the sort of databanks used in the more developed world
for sharing intelligence.[50]

The Mosque
Given the competition taking place in Central Asia between
the government and the followers of Wahhabi, especially as
found in the HT movement, the imam in the remote regions is an
important asset to social stability. They do not receive a salary
and are often given about one guitar of land to live on. Many of
them support their families by becoming farmers and receiving
payment for religious ceremonies like weddings and funerals.
The imams are aware of the HT but are grateful that neo-
Wahhabi HT teachers and propagandists are not very plentiful in
the rural and mountainous areas. Very little of their leaflet propaganda finds its way there. Nevertheless, the Imams are fully
aware that HT presence has been growing in Central Asia, and
they consider it their duty to work closely with the local authorities, especially with the local militia and the local security service agencies. They regularly advise local authorities to register
any Muslim preacher who comes to their areas with the local militia. They have agreed, and issue permits for preaching only if
the local imam gives his seal of approval.

The average congregation numbers 450-500 parishioners.
They admit that the atheistic heritage of Communist rule continues to impact on the general population. Working to bring religion to the youth, they say, is a very difficult task, but they are
pleased and surprised that local youth are actually more active in

the mosque than the elders. Their mosques cannot afford to build madrasas but do manage to have evening classes for as many as 100 youngsters of all ages. They study the Koran and Khadises rather successfully. The more ambitious have already learned 5 chapters of the Koran by heart, and the brightest of them are recommended for advanced studies at Bishkek Islamic University. Any Kyrgyz students having an imam's recommendation can receive scholarships to Islamic universities in Egypt, Jordan and Pakistan. All she/he needs is some money for a ticket and lodging, the ability to pass tests in Arabic, and familiarity with the Koran. This would be a wonderful area of U.S. assistance. Investments of this kind would reduce the temptations offered to unemployed youth by HT radicals.

Unfortunately an uneducated clergy are sometimes discouraged over their inability to match the HT teachers, who are seen as disciplined, intelligent students of history and economics. The clergy, on the other hand, are perceived as backward, and this is very distressful to the young, for many of them see the imam as the bearer of the Islamic message that they so desperately need at this juncture in their history. Unfortunately for the community, imams need not be scholarly nor be known as persons of integrity. Some of them are heavy drinkers, and some take bribes. There were no seminary facilities to properly prepare and educate imams during the Soviet period. They are trying to offer imams at least a modicum of education, and they have asked the local Islamic universities, institutes and madrasas to help in this project. It is also the government's conviction that education will lessen the influence of radicalism. Foreign universities help, but some of those students are being recruited by Wahhabi and terrorist organizations while studying abroad. The Muftijatthe official Islamic spiritual leadership), keeps close tabs on hundreds of students studying abroad in Islamic colleges in Egypt, Iran, and elsewhere. It also requires that all mosques be government registered.

The struggle to be relevant goes on. According to Uzbek law enforcement bodies, there are as many as 20,000 to 30,000 HT members in Uzbekistan alone. Experts estimate that the growth rate may have doubled since 2003 and is growing apace. One government official put it this way. "At the present time the number of new members entering into HT exceeds the number of those whom authorities have the time to arrest." If moderate religion ever had to step forward and lead the CA people, the moment is now.

Chapter Fifteen

WAHHABISM AND ISLAMIC REVIVALISM/ FUNDAMENTALISM

The increasing popularity of the Wahhabi among today's Muslim youth can be explained by a worldwide rising tide of revivalism among Islamic people. Therefore, making the distinction and explaining the difference between Islamic fundamentalism and Islamic revivalism is essential if we are to understand the complexities and even seeming contradictions that plague Islam today. Perhaps a brief comparison with American revivalism will be helpful. Just as we can compare Christian and Islamic fundamentalism, so it is appropriate here to compare American and Islamic revivalism, for the site might be different but the mentality is similar. We Americans went through our own revival when America was still young, so let's try to understand the revivalist mentality. High morality did not characterize many Americans at the end of the eighteenth century. Immoral activities, according to the clergy of the day, were rampant. Ministers complained the profaning of the Sabbath, the prevalence of vulgarity, vigilante justice, drunkenness, gambling, and lewdness. The interest in religion was at a minimum. Something had to be done to bring America back to God. The ministers and prophets developed their own style and brand of revivalism. The 'wild West' spirit, a life raw and full of passion, formed it. Itinerant preachers were the usual fare for most rural folks, and among them one could find a sprinkling of conmen, making a good piece of money in their spiritual journeys and visitations.[51] "Those who attended such camp meetings...generally expected their religious experiences to be as vivid as the frontier life around them. Accustomed to 'braining bears and battling Indians,' they received their religion with great color and excitement."

Holy Eruptions

Sometimes the religious fervor 'erupted into "godly hysteria," falling, jerking,... and "such wild dances as David performed before the Ark of the Lord." The emphasis was to 'wallow in God', creating an experience of the heart. The person of Christ was sung about, shouted about, wept and cried about, but the concrete imitation of Christ was not all that prevalent. American revivalism was far more subjectively emotional than objectively rational. A preoccupation with religious experience and perfectionism supplanted a rational moral assessment of societal and corporate justice and charity. But, it was not only the frontier that became religiously engaged. In New England, Timothy Dwight, the grandson of Jonathan Edwards, stood out as a promoter of America's Spiritual Awakening. Dwight, a former chaplain in the Revolutionary Army and educator, was appointed President of Yale. He brought the revivalist movement to the campus and in 1802 a third of the student body converted and got 'saved.' Once a year, at revival time, under a big tent, people lustily praised God and had their sins forgiven until the next tent meeting the following year. It was fun.

The nineteenth-century historian Joseph Tracy dubbed the Protestant revival in the mid-eighteenth-century American colonies the Great Awakening. The revivals were many-sided. They played themselves out in New England and the middle colonies in the 1740s; later they occurred in the southern colonies in the 1760s. They ranged from Calvinism with its belief in predestination, to Arminianism which insisted on the individual's ability to affect salvation, to various forms of mysticism. Some called for laymen to preach in the place of the regular clergy, accusing them of ignorance and worse. Book burnings were not uncommon, to preserve their faithful from temptations. The itinerant preachers are even credited with creating a revolutionary mood as the Founding Fathers plotted their revolutionary agenda.

Paul Tillich remarked: "For the kind of Protestantism which has developed in America is not so much an expression of the Reformation, but has more to do with the so-called Evangelical Radicals."[52] So, when we see images of crowds shouting and screaming in the name of Allah, making irrational statements, moved only by the kinetic energy of slogan-shouting crowds, we need to recall that America has its own bit of similar history. Those who shared this spiritual emotionalism in different denominations felt more in common with each other than with non-charismatics of the same church. Many truly believed that they were at the dawn of the greatest revival the world had ever known. Both Catholic and Protestant Pentecostalism have within them the seeds of irrational belief, the same kind of irrational belief that moves Islamic terrorism. American Christianity has its share of religious emotionalism that is, as is happening with the literature of Wahhabism, flooding every nook, and cranny of America. This will help us to understand the intensity of revivalism among Islamic peoples.

Islamic Revivalist Roots

Revivalism did not confine itself to America. It is a worldwide phenomenon that among Islamic peoples has its roots in the collapse of the Ottoman Empire at the hands of Ataturk. The collapse of the Empire devastated the Arab world, as they watched the Empire lose its historic cultural characteristics and mold itself into 'another European nation'. Ataturk's achievements in Turkey are an enduring monument to his name. The world honors his memory as a peacemaker who upheld the principles of humanism. Accolades have been strewn on him by such figures as Lloyd George, Winston Churchill, Roosevelt, Nehru, de Gaulle, Adenauer, Bourguiba, Nasser, and Jack Kennedy. A White House statement, issued on the occasion of "The Atatürk Centennial" in 1981, pays homage to him as "a great leader in times of war and peace". He remarked in 1933: "I look to the world with an open heart full of pure feelings and friendship".

But the Wahhabi now curse his memory. We need to understand why.

Ataturk was born in the Ottoman city of Selânik (Salonika), now Thessalonica, in modern Greece, where his birthplace is commemorated by a museum at the present day Turkish Consulate. He was given the name Mustafa. He studied at the military secondary school in Selânik, where he acquired the name Kemal. (meaning 'perfection'), in recognition of his academic brilliance. He later entered the military academy at Monastir (now Bitola) in 1895, and graduated as a lieutenant in 1905. He joined a secret group of reform-minded officers called Vatan (Fatherland), and became an active opponent of the Ottoman regime. In 1907 he joined the Committee of Union and Progress, a.k.a. the Young Turks. They seized power from Sultan Abdul Hamid II in 1908, and Mustafa Kemal became a senior military officer, traveling to wherever his assignments took him. In July 1913 he returned to Istanbul and was appointed commander of the Ottoman defenses of the Gallipoli area on the coast of Thrace, and then military attaché in Sofia. He made his name as a brilliant military commander, and took the surname 'Ataturk'). In October 1918 the Ottomans capitulated to the Allies, and Kemal became one of the leaders of the party that favored a policy of defending the Turkish-speaking heartlands of the Empire, while agreeing to withdraw from all the non-Turkish territories. Ataturk consolidated his power by pushing through the Maintenance of Order Law, which allowed the government to shut down organizations it deemed to be subversive. This law was immediately applied to the Progressive Republican Party, the main opposition party opposing Ataturk's desire to reform the nation and bring it up to the standard of a developed Western nation.

With no significant opposition left to oppose him, he easily won the next election. He did away with the colorful fez (the Ottoman hat) as a symbol of feudalism and encouraged the male population to wear European attire. While the hijab (veil) for women was never formally banned, women were encouraged to wear western apparel and to enter the country's workforce. From 1926, the Gregorian calendar replaced the Islamic calendar. In 1928 the government decreed that a modified Latin alphabet, which facilitated publishing and made Turkish easier to learn replace the Arabic script. Citizens between the ages of six and forty were required to attend school and learn the new alphabet. The conservative clergy fiercely opposed these reforms, trying in vain to maintain its traditionally strong influence. As a result of these reforms, literacy increased dramatically. Ataturk also lifted the Islamic ban on alcoholic beverages, much to his own personal delight because he enjoyed consuming large amounts of the national liquor, raki.[53] He is reputed to have consumed vast quantities. In 1934 he promulgated a law requiring all Turks to adopt surnames. The parliament gave him the deferential name Atatürk, meaning "father of Turks," and assumption of that name by other persons is still forbidden by law. And in a very bold gesture Ataturk abolished the 1300-year-old Islamic Caliphate on 3 March 1924 and established a western-style separation of church and state ("mosque" and state) in Turkey. While promoting a secular Turkish state, he maintained the traditional Ottoman tolerance of religious diversity and freedoms, but viewed these freedoms in the western Enlightenment sense of freedom of conscience.

Science and Democracy

Ataturk considered science and rationalism as the basis of morality and philosophy. An authoritarian by nature, nevertheless, he was clever enough to create a political system that could adapt to the introduction of democracy fairly easily, by introducing sweeping secularist and modernizing reforms, resulting in domestic and international peace. But he also left Turkey with a divided identity, not quite European, and alienated from the Islamic world, though remaining a Muslim country. The Wahhabi have never forgiven him, especially for his success in the international arena, a success Turkey continues to enjoy today. Success in modernity is far from the minds of fundamentalist Islam. The Arab world, as a whole, is in a revivalist mood and has been for a long time. Islamism came back into prominence a century ago in response to the conquest and transformation of Asia and North Africa by capitalist Europe. The Islamic revivalists argued that in the process of conquering European soil during the Ottoman expansion, Islam became Europeanized, thereby losing its soul to worldly objects. The way back to a dignified and purified

Islam, therefore, was by reviving the original spirit of Islam. Imagine how the Muslims saw the world at the end of the 18th Century. Previously they boasted that in the Ottoman, Afavid and Moghul Empires they had created the most powerful and prosperous super-state of that era. And now, it all lay in ruins, and they were subject to European whims and fancies. Their world had been turned upside down.

What to Do?

The dialogic struggle that must first ensue before there are answers to a myriad of questions that Muslims are asking themselves is to decide whether to recreate the past glories or become part of and compete in a wider world economic and scientific order. The Islamist movement is complex and multi-layered, with competing Sunni and Shiite backers. For example, Saudi Arabia, where the ruling class is Sunni, has done everything in its power to counter Iranian Shiite influence, an influence that has grown since the 1979 overthrow of the shah. The strong current in modern political Islam in the Middle East is based on the Ikhwan-ul-Muslimeen, or Muslim Brotherhood, founded in 1928 in Egypt by Hassan al Banna and exported to other countries. The Brotherhood grew into a mass movement across the region in the 1960s. It condemns the separation of the state and religion and aims to establish a theocratic state. Some took up arms, including Egypt's Islamic Jihad, Algeria's Armed Islamic Groups (GIA), Hezbollah in Lebanon, Hamas in Palestine and numerous groups in Pakistan. Others advocate the development of democratic Islamic states, as in Turkey, where the main Sunni Islamist parties have been coalition partners in successive secular governments, and some "Islamic democrats", as they call themselves, are part of the movements for human rights, democracy and, albeit less consistently, for the national rights of Kurds.

Islam Tried Moderation

Several times in recent history Islam was written off. Lenin wrote: "Flourishing Afghanistan is the only independent Muslim state in the world, and fate sends the Afghan people the great historic task of uniting about itself all enslaved Mohammedan peoples and leading them on the road to freedom and independence".[54] In the 1950s, 1960s and 1970s, in Syria, South Yemen, Iraq, Somalia, Libya and Ethiopia, there were left-wing coups and the creation of state capitalism. These left wing political movements appeared to further the destruction of Islam. Modernization, it seemed, as happened under Ataturk, was about to annul Islam as a political force. The Islamic peoples were unable to fight against the communist-inspired governments, but suddenly, with almost no warning, the Soviet Union collapsed. Like a sleeping giant, Islam awoke and saw an opportunity to go back to its fundamental beliefs. The process reached its peak during the 1980s, when thousands of Islamists were trained and sent to Afghanistan to fight against the Soviet-backed People's Democratic Party of Afghanistan, which took power in 1978. Afghanistan is estimated to have been the largest covert CIA operation ever conducted (assisted by the Saudis), involving Islamic fundamentalists.[55] Politics makes strange bedfellows indeed.

While we did not Notice

For years Islamic terrorist groups have been attempting to find a place in the sun, but we hardly noticed. Very quietly, as far back as 1978, the U.S. National Security Council set up, in collaboration with the CIA and the Saudi and Turkish intelligence services, Islamist propaganda networks intended to infiltrate the nationalist Muslim organizations in the Soviet republics of Central Asia. Large quantities of weapons and Korans printed in the Gulf States were introduced into Uzbekistan, Tajikistan and Turkmenistan. Likewise, the Israeli intelligence agency, Mossad, under successive Israeli governments, discreetly supported the Muslim Brotherhood in the Occupied Territories in the 1960s and 1970s, while the Brotherhood was exclusively attacking Yasser Arafat's left nationalist Palestine Liberation Organization (PLO). However, this support ended during the first Intifada begun in 1987, when the Brotherhood gave birth to Hamas, which melded the jihad with the struggle for the liberation of Palestine from Israel. Hamas[56] formed in late 1987 out of the Islamic Center in Gaza. The Center opened in 1973 and began making its mark among the populations by preaching against pornography, alcohol, homosexuality, and drug abuse. The mosque became the point of reference for questions of Islamic identity and Islamic morality. Shiite Islam used a bevy of rationales to point out why Muslims should not be attracted to modernism, nationalism and communism, showing how they had failed everywhere to provide a better life for their people. As time went on they were able to point to the economic failures of South Yemen, Egypt, Libya and others that had flirted with communism and nationalism. The Ayatollah Khomeini leadership "eliminated" thousands who thought otherwise. The clergy assisted by radical followers harassed and persecuted leftists and the Kurdish national movement. Iranian revolutionary success was followed by the Taliban success in Afghanistan. The predominantly Pushtun Taliban emerged in late 1994 as a movement made up of taliban (literally "students") from madrasas who were living as refugees in Pakistan.

However, since Arafat's PlO had political ambitions of its own, nationalistic ambitions, Hamas had to move very delicately as it began to consolidate itself within the Palestinian authority. Hamas, ever since, has operated on a twin-track policy of jihad and nationalist struggle. Hamas, as well as other revivalist movements in other places, as in Turkey, were able to cut out a niche for themselves in every Arab nation. They launched programs such as public education, social welfare, medical supplies, improved sewage and water supplies, garnering public support and admiration. With every dose of medicine went a cup of fundamentalist education. Hamas alone has received as much as $150 million a year, channeled from Saudi Arabia and its Wahhabi religious establishment. Upwards of 30,000-40,000 people receive food baskets every month. Even more importantly for the future, the same Saudi/Wahhabi sources provide for the establishment of schools (madrasas) throughout the Islamic world, in which the students get a thorough education in fundamentalism.

Many of these students, as they progress, are inculcated with the ideology of Islamic terrorism and are eventually trained in the use of firearms. Hundreds of thousands of fighters have been recruited and trained in the madrasas, Pakistan alone having established about 4000 madrasas. However, in spite of all this progress, without the 1979 revolution in Iran, political Islam might have remained relatively marginal, for in Iran Islamic fundamentalism organized itself as a state, allowing Shiite Islamists everywhere access to government coffers and to asylum if they need it. Islamists from all over the Middle East opened offices in Teheran, received cash and arms, and were trained in military camps by the Iranian Revolutionary Guards.

Before the Taliban arrived, none of Islam's extreme orthodox sects had built a base in Afghanistan. The Taliban version of Islam was borrowed from the Deobandi in Pakistan, whose political wing. Saudi funds and scholarships brought these Deobandi closer ideologically to the ultra-conservative Wahhabism. Between 1994 and 1999, an estimated 80-100,000 Pakistanis trained and fought in Afghanistan. Ironically, it was these same Taliban who were supported by and felt obliged to the United States government, for they saw themselves as foot soldiers for U.S. interests in the region! They were encouraged by the U.S. to join with other Islamic fundamentalist groups in a jihad against the Russian occupation of Afghanistan. They assumed that as a reward for such battlefield sacrifices against Soviet occupation their prize would be the freedom to establish their fundamentalist umma.[57] Backed by U.S. and Saudi financial support, the Taliban preached their extreme fundamentalism in the former Soviet Central Asian republics. This now comes back to haunt the U.S.

The Political Shape of Revivalism

Americans familiar with the role played by urban churches in their own country during the late-nineteenth century, are aware of the power of religious groups. Researchers who have examined the wave of Protestant conversion in urban Latin America, the Catholic Church's main stronghold, during the 1970s and 1980s will also recognize parallels. For the urban poor and lower-middle class, religious schools offered islands of civility and moral clarity. In the face of growing class- and status-differentiation, these institutions provided avenues of participation for believers otherwise consigned to society's margins. As in the late-nineteenth-century United States, the pervasiveness of religious associations gave a deeply religious hue to interactions in civil society. That society was not made up of modern liberalism's individuals freed from ethno religious bonds, but individuals and groups bound by ties of kinship, ethnicity, and religion.

One telling indicator of the Islamic public's heightened interest in religion is the rapid development of a market for inexpensive Islamic books and magazines. The literature provides a means for people who had never had an opportunity to study in religious schools to familiarize themselves with the fundaments of their faith. It also stimulated the emergence of a new class of teachers and preachers, with target audiences different from those of the classically trained ulama, a community of learned men. More important yet, the new preachers make their message relevant by adapting their topics to political and economic concerns. Revivalism dressed in current political terminology is the background to the great religious resurgence seen across the Muslim world in the 1970s and 1980s. Described in the language of modern political theory, the resurgence was primarily an affair of civil society, not the state. This political form of revivalism created a great reservoir of social capital comprised of networks and solidarities dedicated above all else to public piety and expressions of Islamic identity.

The Jadids
    The early supporters of Islamic reforms and restructuring of Muslim society were called the Jadids, from the Arabic word for "new" or "modern." Initially, they acted primarily as educators. They deplored the religious and cultural plight of Muslims in the Russian Empire and advocated changes in Muslim education in order to culturally unite all Turkic peoples. The leader of the Jadids, Crimean Tatar Ismail Gaspirali, even proposed a single language for all Russian Turkic peoples based on that of the Ottomans. The influence the Jadids exerted on the intelligentsia in Central Asia steadily strengthened in the early years of the twentieth century. The "golden youth" of the local intelligentsia embraced the ideas of the Jadids and were friendly toward the new generation of businessmen, merchants, and industrialists who were accumulating modern-style wealth and shared their desire for change. Aspiration for further development in Islamic thought, politics, economics, and culture became firmly rooted in this circle of reformers and started to grow beyond them to the larger society. Despite the energy of the Jadids, it would be mistaken to assume that they operated in a favorable environment.

The spirit of conservative Islam was very strong in the emirate. The conservatives did not favor reforms; they cherished stability and order among the Muslims. Therefore, the Jadids proceeded with caution, working to spread their ideas among the general population.

In 1910, the Jadids established a secret organization that they called Tarbiya-Atfal (Children's Upbringing). In 1912, they began publishing the newspaper Bukhara-al Sharif in the Tajik language and Turon in Uzbek. Two years later, they established a cooperative that they named the Society of Sacred Bukhara to publish textbooks. They opened a public library, the Marifat, as part of this cooperative, and the Barakat Bookstore, which became a discussion club for the young intelligentsia of Bukhara. Looking back to these years, Russian historian Vladimir Medvedev remarked in 1991: "These activities [of the Jadids] would not be considered so modest by our contemporaries who remember how similar activities resulted in the end of the Soviet republic only a couple of years ago. It is unlikely that in Bukhara at the beginning of the century these activities were treated with more tolerance."

With their parents' financial backing, many of the young Jadids went to Turkey to study, because they were attracted by the opportunity to study in a land that mirrored them in many ways and yet was well into democratization. The transformations taking place in Turkish Muslim society were in accord with the Jadids ideals. They witnessed their older brothers, the "Young Turks," taking power and starting to implement decisive reforms. They returned to Central Asia excited about the possibility of creating an Islamic society at home that could absorb the transformations taking place in the outside world without losing their own Islamic essence. They began to introduce their own program of political and economic reforms. Between 1914 and 1916 they advocated lower taxes, limited powers for the local bureaucracy, and participation by the Jadids in local government. In short, they shifted the emphasis of the Jadids' program from educational activism to political struggle.

This process came to a gradual halt by the appearance of Soviet Russia. The Soviets, in spite of their flattering condescension, treated Islam as a backward, superstitious religion that, with all religion, needed to be neutralized by the infusion of revolutionary, messianic Communism. The flowering of the jahid ethos first experienced setbacks in the face of Soviet overwhelming power. It then was forced underground. Political struggle was a dangerous undertaking. It could result in a prison term or even a death sentence. To fight openly in the political arena against traditional Muslim power without Soviet support meant risking everything. Although the vast majority of the Jadids were freethinking intellectuals, they were not ready to sacrifice their lives.

Collapse of the Ruble

Then, an economic setback further complicated both economic and intellectual progress. The collapse of the ruble zone in 1993 was a hard blow for the Central Asian nations to absorb. It forced them, just as Gorbachev's decision to cut off billions of dollars yearly to Cuba, to scurry for ways to survive. They did not have the luxury of planning a long-term, careful, studied approach. Suddenly, the focus shifted from modernizing Islam to economic survival. Independence from Soviet power gave them the opportunity to chart their own course. At the same time, the new Central Asian leadership, basically appointed to power by Gorbachev, had little interest in the reshaping of Islam. They set about trying to develop state economic and political models that would allow them to compete in a growing global economy. The physical and ideological buffers that kept Central Asia isolated and focused on internal matters were beginning to crumble. The time had come for a new direction, the time for action. The CA leadership responded, initiating emergency measures.

They closed unprofitable state enterprises, spoke of nationalism, and cleverly retained a public devotion to Islam, but indicating by their attitudes and actions, that modernity was the answer to ages of backwardness. The departure of the Soviets was accompanied by new attitudes, new challenges, but also new possibilities. Soviet style bureaucratic enterprises, designed more to give every person a job than to make a profit were either downgraded or closed. The CA leadership quickly identified itself with the experience of economic reforms in the Newly Industrialized Countries (NICs) and called on the intellectual and entrepreneurial elite of their nations to pitch in and provide ideas, leadership and hard work.

Uzbek's President Karimov took a very practical approach and announced that ideology has its function in society but its function is not to engage in endless debate without action. The nation was on the ropes and everyone had to come together regardless of intellectual or emotional differences. To a great extent his approach was successful. Nor did he hesitate to declare that the state would play a leading role in guiding, nudging, and even requiring certain approaches and methods to use in the common struggle. Karimov stated very bluntly that a unified and determined citizenship, undistracted by either ideology or terrorist activity, was necessary for development. He made it very clear that the government intended to come down hard on anyone interfering with a peaceful work atmosphere, the necessary ingredient for progress.

Karimov was also quick to publicly identify an economic model for his people to follow. He said that mixed models would only confuse the population and make steady and organized progress impossible. The model he chose was that of East Asia, as exemplified in South Korea, urging his people to imitate Japan's high personal savings rate, pointing out its beneficial effects. National wealth also had to be poured into an improved transport and communication infrastructure.

President Adayev declared that Malaysian economic policy "is a good example to follow." In economic terms, the "model of development" discussions had two important implications. First, reference to the "model of development" was used to preserve the role of state regulation and the power of state institutions in the Central Asian economies. The government, the people were told, had a plan, a model of development and everything was going top be fine. Second, it was used to justify some unpopular economic decisions in order to "sell" the package of reforms to the public. Finally, there was among the people a genuine belief in the existence of a concrete program or "model" that may have "magically" changed the economies of the republics. Particularly in the beginning, it was believed that because CA was quite rich in natural resources they would not have to pay a high social price for implementing such reforms. In terms of the CA foreign policy formulation and establishing deeper relations with the international community, the discourse on the "model of development" performed two important functions. First was the establishment of a positive image of the CA nations in the eyes of the world community. Second was promotion of the republics' and ruling elites' self-identity in the international arena.

The Image Offensive

Establishing a positive image of CA before the world community as a good place for foreign investment and tourism was a complicated issue. On the one hand, their geographical location was intimidating, lying as it did aside two of the most radical Islamic regimes, Iran and Afghanistan. On the eve of independence and during the first few years after the disintegration of the USSR, many experts, especially among Russia's academics, warned that the CA nations might come under the influence of Iranian or other radical Islamic groups. On the other hand, the nations faced political turmoil and other problems. The ruling elites were challenged by a radical opposition, in which the Islamic groups played an important role (especially in Tajikistan). Therefore, for the CA elites, creating an image of their republics as secular states was one of the most important tasks. But they were fully aware that foreign investment was also very cautious about investing in areas that had the possibility or even likelihood of political instability.

The CA leadership needed to project the image that Central Asia was, unlike its neighbors, secular, interested in technological development and trade. It also had to project the image of political staying power. It is at this juncture that we need to be most understanding. In an atmosphere where religious institutions were, at times, at odds with one another, when radical Islam was both infiltrating society and at the same time creating fear and uneasiness in the general population, a strong hand appeared to be the only answer. In this sense, reference to the "model of development" was one of the most effective and quick tools in demonstrating their particular features in the post-Soviet period. The articulation of the "Turkish secular model" or "South Korean model of development" had assisted the CA elites in displaying to the international community that they were not devoted to former communist ideas, and that they were not going to establish Islamic "fundamentalist" states either.

Looking for Self-Identity

Another important issue was the search for self-identity in the international arena. The problem was that throughout the Soviet era the CA elites were persistently taught that they belonged to a special world (which was neither part of the West nor the Third World). They strongly believed that they were a part of the Eastern European - or at least Eurasian – superpower which belonged to Asia geographically, but culturally, politically and economically was a part of Eastern Europe. In this sense, the CA elites found that they needed to rethink their identity when they discovered that they no longer belonged to the huge and powerful Soviet state.

The painful lesson of the Belovezhskii Agreement in 1991 (when Byelorussia, Russia and the Ukraine dissolved the Soviet Union) was aggravated by harsh political and economic realities when they were pushed out of the ruble zone. But it was all so new and there was so much optimism that no one panicked.

These two events made the issue of self-identity of CA especially significant. Was CA a part of the Third World? Could CA nations continue to be considered Eurasian states? These questions, which have been discussed frequently by the public in all of CA, clearly demonstrated that the CA elites and public were not ready to "return to Asia" and accept their "Asianess."

Apparently, the CA elites would have liked to preserve their special status of being neither the East nor West. In the post-Soviet era, the CA national elites continued to identify themselves more with Europe than Asia. Indeed, President Adayev perfectly reflected this paradox by saying,

"Historically, Central Asia played a special role in establishing relationships with the East and West, being a sort of link between them." In this respect, the "model of development" discourse was a transitional concept or a bridge for the CA elites and foreign policy-makers in their search for a place in the international arena and in establishing their identities.

"Model of Development": the Experts' Assessment

During the 1990s, discussions on the issue of the "model of development" were quite intensive both within and without the region. However, there was a sharp difference in emphasis on various aspects of the "model of development." Outside CA the most important message was that the Central Asian elites were technocratic and oriented to secularism. Within the region, the discussion focused mainly on the "model of development" as regards the economic transformation of the Central Asian republics. Occasionally, there were references to the political aspects, such as the limitation of democracy, activities of political parties and press, etc. -- and the local policy-makers frequently referred to the South Korean, South East Asian and Turkish models of economic development.

Olivier Roy's Opinion

As time goes by, radical Islam is becoming an increasingly potent force in Central Asia. Olivier Roy, in Paris, put it this way: "The main threat in Central Asia is the growth of Salafi (Wahhabi) Islam, which preaches total rejection of modernity, of culture and the arts." U.S. officials admit that they have yet to develop tactics to win hearts and minds of discontented Muslims in Central Asia. That critical area of the world, one of great interest to the United States, remains a significant challenge to American policymakers. While the State Department sorts out what sort of positions to take vis-à-vis Central Asia, they need to keep their eye on our own interests, which is to defeat Islamic terrorism. In the order of priorities, it is clear that at this juncture in Central Asia's move toward democratic institutions, defeating Wahhabism is a priority.

We cannot do everything at once, and certainly we must not bite the hand that is helping us by their offensives against local Islamic radicals to defeat Islamic terrorism. In England today, the British people's famed reputation for providing sanctuary for every world dissident has had to be modified. In the cold light of the reality of suicide bombers who blow up British men, women and children in cowardly acts that kills civilians who are simply going about their daily lives making a living for their families, policies have changed. As Prime Minister Blair has said, "the rules of the game have changed." While we are legitimately concerned about the long-term evolution of democracy in Central Asia, we need to cut a little slack with Central Asian governments when it comes to their defending themselves against very dangerous and unfeeling Wahhabi allies.

Chapter Sixteen

A CLOSER LOOK AT CENTRAL ASIA TODAY

When Uzbekistan ordered the eviction of U.S. military personnel from the Karshi-Khanabad airbase, the dimensions of the future struggle among the major powers for influence in Central Asia became evident. Russia is back in the competition, a competition that marks the beginning of a Russian-led counter-revolution. The stakes are very high. Central Asia (CA) has become the new battleground where major powers will compete for hegemony. Central Asia is where the major battle against the Wahhabi will take place. Russia needs Central Asian support in its struggles against the Wahhabi in Dagestan and Chechnya. China needs Central Asian support for its struggle against the Wahhabi in the Xinjiang-Uighur Autonomous Region, where Muslim activism becomes increasingly strident. CA is also a future major supplier of oil. The lines are being drawn, as China, Russia and the United States woo the leaders and peoples of CA. The Russian advantage is that they've been there already. The American advantage is that they are more appealing to the grass roots of at least 4 of the CA nations. The China advantage is not having been involved previously.

The collapse of the ruble zone in 1993 was a hard blow for the Central Asian nations to absorb. It forced them, just as Gorbachev's decision to cut off billions of dollars yearly to Cuba, scurry for ways to survive. They did not have the luxury of a planning a long-term, careful, studied approach; however, neither did they follow the crash Russian approach, which, they observed, had dire effects on the Russian people. The CA leadership, however, did take emergency measures. They closed unprofitable state enterprises, enterprises designed more to give every person a job than to make a profit. They quickly identified themselves with the experience of economic reforms in the Newly Industrialized Countries (NICs) and called on the intellectual and entrepreneurial elite of their nations to pitch in and provide ideas, leadership and hard work. President Karimov took a very practical approach and announced that ideology has its function in society but that function is not to engage in endless debates without action. The nation was on the ropes and everyone had to come together regardless of intellectual or emotional differences. To a great extent his approach was successful. Nor did he hesitate to declare that the state would play a leading role in guiding, nudging, and even requiring certain approaches and methods to use in the common struggle. Karimov was also bold enough to say that since a unified and determined citizenship, undistracted by either ideology or terrorist activity was absolutely necessary for progress, the government intended to come down on anyone interfering with a peaceful atmosphere for work and progress.

Therefore, for the CA elites establishing an image of their republics as secular states was one of the most important tasks, as was showing the world community that the technocratic-oriented elites would firmly stay in power in the CA nations. In this sense, reference to the "model of development" was one of the most effective and quick tools in demonstrating their particular stance in the post-Soviet period. The articulation of the "Turkish secular model" or "South Korean model of development" had assisted the CA elites in displaying to the international community that they were not devoted to former communist ideas, and that they were not going to establish Islamic "fundamentalist" states either.

Tajikistan
The discussion of all these matters in Tajikistan represents what is going on in the other CA nations. The Tajiks feel that the

Sharia would guarantee the stability of legislation, preclude the ability of the powers-that-be to interpret the laws, and make the legal code of the state understandable to everyone. Besides, even under Soviet power ordinary Tajiks, whenever they needed to be in contact with state bureaucrats, acted in accord with the norms of the Sharia, which were acceptable to the corrupt Central Asian bureaucracy. Therefore, the desire of most Tajiks to reestablish the Sharia that originated in the Middle Ages, with norms that seem strange to Westerners, is quite natural for an ordinary Tajik who has suffered all his life from the Soviet system's colonialism. The question of degree naturally arises: Does the Tajik opposition intend to create a pure, classic Islamic state that would emulate the Iranian model and literally copy into its constitution all the postulates of the Sharia? The jury is still out on that subject because political events continue to unfold.

The desire of the Tajik opposition to root out the neo-Bolshevik system of governance in their country and establish a system based on the principles of Muslim justice is beyond doubt. It is also understandable that the opposition wishes to use the principles of the Sharia to develop a new constitution. But the following factors should be kept in mind. The educational level of Tajikistan's population, thanks to the Soviet system of compulsory free education through high school for every youth, is immeasurably higher than that in Iran. Furthermore, the republic's young people, who make up a substantial number of the political activists among the population, are not inclined to accept without reservation outdated precepts of the Sharia, like the requirement that women wear a yashmak and the practices of stoning adulterers, the cutting off of thieves' hands, and so on. Tajiks are not likely to sacrifice to the integrating demands of the Islamic umma the national traditions of Tajikistan that harken back to pre-Islamic times and are steeped in clan and tribal relations.

Remembering Iran

The opposition leaders understand the harm caused by the Iranian experience and its unpopular image in the eyes of the world. Politicians competing for political supremacy in Tajikistan are aware that the republic will not be able to strengthen its economy without outside help and that fundamentalist Iran cannot be the sole source of such help. Therefore, even the opposition leaders are inclined not to overemphasize the fundamentalist features of a future Islamic state in Tajikistan. Finally, the creation of a classic, purely Islamic state in Tajikistan would be resisted in every possible way by the neo-Bolshevik elites and the bureaucracy that sustains them. Although they have lost their former total control over the state apparatus and have had to share power with some nationalist forces, the neo-Bolsheviks' leadership remains a potent force in the political arena and will continue to exert a significant influence on Tajikistan's economic life. So it appears that even if the fundamentalists in the Islamist opposition were to become the predominant political power in Tajikistan, it would not be a totally negative development. Islamic forces would be replacing the republic's neo-Bolshevik regime.

Basically, Islamic terrorism ideology is a hybrid and simplistic blend of Islamic fundamentalism fuelled by longstanding resentments and hatred, mixed with political and religious ambitions that feed off of these feelings and resentments. Of course, nothing is quite that simple. There are also smoldering resentments within the Islamic community itself, based on the various interpretations of the Prophet's message, and they are breaking out all over the Muslim world. Islam is in ferment everywhere on a massive scale. Militant Islam ideology seeks to eradicate all forms of Islam other than its own strict literal interpretation of the Koran. It comes packaged with a set of now well-known political grievances, often directed at U.S. foreign policy, and justifies violence as a means of purging nations of corruption, moral degradation, and spiritual torpor.

This modern strain of madrasa Islamic ideology has been around for several decades. It is taught to small children in fundamentalist classes throughout the Islamic world, fueled by petrodollars from Saudi Arabia. It continues to inspire militant groups such as al-Qaeda, the Taliban, Islamic Jihad, Abu Sayyaf, and many others. It is a movement that is on the move, fired up by the intensity of feelings its ideology has created among younger Muslims. Even in the traditionally more "moderate" Muslim nations of Southeast Asia, a culture of militant jihad is now spreading rapidly. One's credentials as a "true Muslim" are increasingly based on a willingness to use violence. In just the past year, the walls of buildings throughout northern Pakistan have become hand-scrawled billboards advertising "jihadi training," complete with phone numbers. People are calling.

There was a time, just a few yeas ago, when the number of suicide bombers in a group like Lashkar [e-Tayyiba] may have been 10 or 20. Now it is close to 400. Vali Nasr, a specialist on Muslim extremists at the University of San Diego, Calif., (and a Shia Muslim) agrees. "I've been to Pakistan over the past 20 years, and the Pakistan I see today is unrecognizable to me, even though I've been working on fundamentalism from the beginning," he says. There was also a time when a seminary was a place where a student spent years at the foot of educated scholars and became well versed in all aspects of Islamic jurisprudence, law, philosophy, theology." He laments that those running such schools today are petty mullahs with a distorted understanding of Islam. They interpret Islam in terms of the violent jihad rather than interpreting jihad in terms of Islam. They have it backward and, consequently, so do countless thousands of their madrasa students. These students are instilled with a false consciousness that if they do not offer themselves for battle, even as suicide bombers, they are not true Muslims. Their mullahs are reaping a devastated youth, dead, maimed or alienated from the wider society, a culture of death and despair. That the ancient traditional definition of jihad as an internal struggle for a just cause could have been so massively co-opted by extremists needs explanation.

Democracy is Evil

The ideology of militant Islam is very hostile toward democracy and liberal ideas because democracy separates the state from religion. Democracy not only has no political role for the clergy but actively opposes such a role. It advocates the separation of Church and State. Such ideas, if they were to spread in the Middle East would spell the end of clerical control, so today's militant Islam has primarily to-do with clerics retaining power which they have exercised for centuries. Many of these clerics will go down with the militant Islamic ship. Ironically, it was in Iraq that, under Saddam Hussein, that mullah power was successfully challenged. Saddam secularized Iraq and the ensuing benefits were seen in the fact that Iraq became the most progressive Arab nation. We have to give the devil his due. What is going on in the Middle East today, to a great extent, is the desperate attempt to retain theocracy. The enemy is democracy. The propaganda of anti-democracy comprises a large part of the commentaries broadcast on Al-Jazeera, Al-Arabi, and other Arab television networks. The ideological message has gone out: Muslims must not only accept the militant Islamic interpretation of the Koran, but must fight to the death to preserve it. At the moment, the religious leaders continue to have a large following, but at an increasingly slower rate.

Mullahs not In Accord with Mohammed

The Mullahs are making what will very likely turn out to be their last historical stand. The tide of history is turning against them. In the meantime they will continue to call the people to engage in a violent campaign for Islamic ideas and will flood the airways of Islamic television with discussion panels hosted by ulema (Islamic theology experts) calling on the Arab population to take up arms in the struggle to preserve Mullah rule. They will continue to present jihad as qital (armed struggle). The Koran very explicitly forbids armed conflict (jihad as qital) if its objective is the acquisition of wealth or power, and never in an offensive manner, but only after extreme and repeated provocation. (7:199). Mohammed himself was the ideal exemplification of this approach. "Fight for the sake of God those that fight against you, but do not be aggressive." (2:190). Islamic war propagandists manipulate various verses of the Koran, for example, "Fight against them until fitna is no more," (2:193). Fitna, in fact, refers to the response Muslims may use when the political system is carrying on a wide-ranging and brutal attack on the religious system. This is not the case in the Middle East today. The reality is that democracy is spreading, thereby threatening the Mullah political establishment. This is the real struggle: the Mullah attempt to rule an increasingly restive population desiring democratic institutions. In the end, the enemy of militant Islam will be the people of Islam.

A Flawed Interpretation

In 1993, a Harvard University professor, Samuel Huntington, published a book, "The Clash of Civilizations." He interprets clashes such as the attempt of Islamic terrorists to drive the West out of the Middle East as a clash of civilization. He speaks of the inevitable contradictions between the Christian and the Islamic worlds as being the objective basis for the majority of modern and future conflict. His own cultural experience as an American living and working in Boston should have given him a totally different assessment. To go from saying that different cultures need to adjust to each other, to maintaining that cultural difference inevitably lead to battle is a very long stretch indeed, a dangerous one to state as based on academic research. He observes the contrary happening every day in Boston, not perfectly, but reasonably well and without major conflict. He grants to ambitious and greedy leaders and movements a false importance and ability to determine the future based on cultural differences.

The work of the United Nations and its agencies, while flawed, gives proof that his theory is flawed. The theory is also contradicted by the fact that most conflicts are, in fact, a clash among movements, if not of the same culture, then belonging to the same national heritage. The professor has mistakenly characterized the public awareness of peoples of various cultures and backgrounds on a scale never before known in history as something ominous. It is true that it will take time for all of this to be absorbed. But it is moving ahead rapidly. Mobility among peoples is creating a universalized culture. All one need to do on any given day is stroll the streets of almost any city anywhere in the world and one might well hear the songs of Whitney Houston and Celine Dionne, together with photographs of Elvis Presley, Michael Jordan or Madonna. To stem the flow of intercultural absorption, ruthless and ambitious men, using the cover of a legitimate and respected religion, as Islam, call for a jihad that has as its purpose the personal consolidation of power and self-aggrandizement before history passes them by. Professor Huntington has bought into their rationale. He wrote: "Civilization identity will be increasingly important in the future, and the world will be shaped in large measure by the interactions among seven or eight major civilizations. These include Western, Confucian, Japanese, Islamic, Hindu, Slavic-Orthodox, Latin American and possibly African civilization. The most important conflicts of the future will occur along the cultural fault lines separating these civilizations from one another."

Instead of writing: "The most important conflicts of the future will occur along the cultural fault lines separating these civilizations from one another", he could have written, "The most interesting and challenging interactions of the future will occur along the cultural fault lines distinguishing one civilization from another."

Exposure of one culture to another is a recent phenomenon and as peoples adjust to this they will enjoy tasting and experiencing the plentitude of music, art, food preparations and intellectual exchange that has never before been possible in history. We are not on the verge of a cataclysmic age at all; we are on the verge of a more beautiful and tolerant society. Cultural differences, as we become more aware of them in a world of instant communication, are a source of joy and anticipation rather than a source of future conflict. The author's analysis is written from the perspective of terrorist propaganda. This is unfortunate.

When people get to know each other better with the help of the mass media, the terrorist will find it ever more difficult to convince a large portion of his native population to engage in mass killings or blow themselves up in the name of religion or anything else. Right now they are playing on unfounded fears and manipulating the minds of religious people, all to fulfill a private agenda of greed and personal power, but they will be exposed. Today's youth want to live a life. In contrast to Huntington, political scientist Francis Fukuyama believes that income levels and the degree of modernization, i.e., access to the latest technologies, constitutes the differences in political and social outlook (Karl Marx will be pleased to hear this), and that everyone and every society is converging toward a set of universal values.

An Unfolding Process

The Islamic world is passing through a stage in which the growing secularization of its society is frightening to a population that clings to its religious heritage for fear of the unknown.

Leaping into that darkness can take a lot of courage. This same process took place in the Christian, especially Catholic, world over the last century in Europe and America. Christianity has, in general, become secularized and it took a lot of adjusting and a lot of faith that secularization would not lessen religious piety. As it turns out it has deepened it, for it is no longer enforced, therefore chosen freely and with a healthy mind. Modern Islamic terrorism, although employing the one common language, that of religion, is to some extent unconsciously rooted in the same national liberation ideologies that brought independence to a host of nations during the 19th and 20th centuries than they are in Islamic tradition.

Al-Jazeera, Al-Arabi, and other Arab stations spend a considerable part of their broadcasting time teaching the Koran and hosting discussions with the ulema, ways to participate in the holy jihad against the West. Arab historical legacy is colonialism and they want to liberate themselves and their people. This they have a perfect right to do, and all the major powers are going to suffer while this process takes place, while the sins of our fathers are expiated.

When liberation goals have been achieved and when the great powers come to terms with their inability to any longer "rule the world," then the descendants of the present-day terrorists will want to live in peace and harmony with their former enemies. This phenomenon is part of the history of peoples.

The West and Islam are not destined to a struggle of civilization, not at all. The opposite direction, nuanced by cultural heritage, is where the Middle East is going. The use of religion as a vehicle for power still exists, but it is a dying strategy in a world that increasingly finds it disgusting. Interestingly enough, of all the Muslim leaders it was Saddam Hussein who understood this most deeply.

It is a pity that he felt it necessary to wrap it all up in greed and a desire to be the central leader in the central government in the Middle East. Of all the nations in the Middle East it is Iraq, because of its advanced state of secularization, that is most likely to lead the way socially and economically, in spite of its present difficulties.

Presidential System in Central Asia

All the Central Asian countries now have presidents but, initially, their leaders were appointed by the Soviet Union before it collapsed. They have established what they refer to as "presidential systems," that gives the executive branch the power to rule by decree with the force of "constitutional law." The executive branch dominates the other branches, undercutting the separation of powers, making it more difficult to provide sufficient checks and balances. All of them have held elections, yet none has fully conformed to international standards for free and fair elections. Three of these governments have former communist leaders who have extended their mandate in extra-constitutional ways. Even in the most open and liberal of these countries, Kazakhstan and Kyrgyzstan, the parliaments have been routed by presidential decree.

In short, none of the countries can be said to have truly succeeded in making the transition from democratic structure to democratic function. As a consequence, many of the formal institutions of government have acquired a showcase quality. The formal institutions exist but it is the informal institutions that actually guide the processes of policy decision-making. The legal and regulatory framework exists and purports to protect the rights of individuals and legal entities, but in reality many critical public decisions are made on an ad hoc basis and with the interposition of favored individuals whose interests are directly affected by the outcome. The existence of the formal institutions of democratic governance creates expectations that the government cannot realize, leading to disillusionment and cynicism. In such a situation, it is, ironically, the least democratic of the leaders of the region who cynically take the greatest credit for progress and reform. Turkmenistan's president, Saparmurad Niyazov, has boasted that in Turkmenistan there are no civil rights violations of government's opponents because the government has no opponents. That's very convenient.

Questions to be Answered

The experience of these countries in the past decade raises important theoretical and urgent practical questions. What accounts for the resilience of authoritarian practices in societies that have adopted democratic, market oriented institutions? What accounts for the tremendous divergence between structure and function? What role can the good offices of outside institutions play in promoting democratic change and reform?

In addressing these questions, it is important to begin by noting that, at least in the first decade of Central Asian independence, values have played a more important role than institutions. It would have been helpful if the West had paid more attention, up close, and if the Russians, prior to the dissolution of the Soviet Union, had not looked the other way when CA leaders crossed the line.

Missed Opportunity

The West lost a wonderful opportunity in 1991 to join hands with the Central Asian people. In each of the five countries of Central Asia, Kazakhstan, Kyrgyzstan, Tajikistan, Turkmenistan, and Uzbekistan, the initial cry in 1991, both from the leadership and the man in the street, was for the democratization of the political structure and the transition from state capitalism to market-oriented economies. In fact, all five states quickly adopted some form of representative government using internationally accepted standards for the separation of legal and regulatory powers. The future looked bright. Possible models of development dominated discussions from coffee shops to the inner sanctums of government, especially in Kazakhstan. Various developmental models were analyzed, including two of opposite poles: Turkey's secular political structure, Iran's theocracy and China's gradualist reform versus the Russian crash program. Kazakhstan's then President Nazarbaev declared a goal: "Kazakhstan in 2003: Prosperity, Security and Welfare Improvements for all Kazaks." The West, delighted at all this progress, foresaw great democratic changes on the near horizon. However, the euphoria that gripped the West was misplaced. Western assumptions should have been accompanied by Western investment in time, understanding, political support and money. That did not happen. Therefore, having been left to fend for themselves, the CA power structures began slowly but surely to gravitate back toward the known Soviet ways of doing things. Shame on us for not having foresight.

Their parliaments did very little in the way of parliamentarianism and their legislatures did little legislating. The power was in the hands of the President. The judiciary failed to honor due process, freedom of speech, and free assembly. The Soviet habits, developed over seventy years, quickly overwhelmed the delayed introduction to democracy. Widespread discouragement among the people at the slow pace of reform resulted in growing apathy. Also, at this point, the Central Asian nations were oriented towards integration with Russia and seemed to lack, psychologically and intellectually, the dynamics for real independence.

They wanted to escape being titled 'Asian states' because they were, in spite of Russian occupation, proud to be considered 'Russians.' After all, they reasoned, who wants to be called an Asian or be identified as part of the inferior Third World. For various reasons they had strong feelings about belonging to what they called "Eurasia" and they did not perceive their countries as a part of Asia or the Third World. They wanted to be a bridge between Europe and Asia and a member of the European community. This, they believed would give them status.

In spite of the fact that political progress was slow, and they had to deal with inter-ethnic volatile relations, the power elites of Kazakhstan, Kyrgyzstan and Uzbekistan had little difficulty in keeping their peoples under control. President Karimov of Uzbekistan in declaring that his reign would be characterized by "enlightened authoritarianism" as the nation moved toward democracy. He gave himself a wide berth when it came to loosening the reins of power. Having started out with a background of gradual but effective transformation of the economy from agriculture to an industrial-agricultural leader, the President was self-assured that all would be well. Although the nation has an Uzbek population of 57%, it also has a large proportion of Russians, Germans and other minorities. While still a member of the Soviet Bloc, Kazakhstan's leader at that time, Dinmuhamed Kunaev, was admitted as a full member of the Soviet Politburo, and the people were very happy about that. They wanted to belong to the wider world.

A survey study found that the "Turkish model of development" was considered the most attractive among the Kazaks until 9/11. Since that time things have changed. The leadership of these nations began to worry that what happened in the United States was a bad omen for them. They feared that such enormous destruction imposed on them by the Wahhabi could forestall economic and social development. They could become targets of Islamic terrorism unless they put more public emphasis on their Islamic roots. However, it can also be said that there has been a healthy development in political coalitions since that time, more solidarity, especially in Kazakhstan and Kyrgyzstan. Also, President Bush, signed into law the Belarus Democracy Act in the autumn of 2004. This legislation authorizes the president to support the development of democratic political parties and establish non-governmental groups in Central Asia that promote democracy. Another bright spot was the announcement, in February 2005, that the five Central Asian states would sign a treaty before the end of 2005 creating a nuclear-free zone in the area. Actually this did take place on September 8, 2006, a great achievement. It would be the first security-related treaty concluded among the five since their independence from the Soviet Union.

The Central Asian states are in the throes of a healthy "traditionalism," albeit with political overtones. One can observe it in public ceremonies and in frequent references to their history. Late in 1998, Uzbekistan's president, Islam Karimov, was awarded the country's highest honor, the "Order of Emir Timur" in an attempt to maneuver the people to heed the government's call for loyalty to national goals. In Turkmenistan, president Niyazov recently introduced genealogical descent in choosing people for public sector employment. This was in emulation of "the experience of our ancestors, who chose their leaders, military commanders, and judges from among the worthiest compatriots, men with high moral standards."

Kazakhstan

Kazakhstan is the largest of the CA nations. It has oil. Its mixed population of Kazakhs and Russians are relatively experienced in developing a viable economy. The Kazakhstan communist party leader, Nursultan Nazarbaev, once the Soviet departure was a fait accompli, quickly shed his pro-soviet allegiance, transforming himself into a leading defender of Kazakhstan independence. He fostered development of economic and cultural ties among the Central Asia people. Since then, the newly discovered oil and gas resources attracted the attention of the Western powers, together with China and Russia. The year 2005, however, saw a gradual shifting of allegiance back toward Russia, and Kazakhstan now is the CA nation most favored by the Russians for closer economic and strategic cooperation. Russia's Vladimir Putin has not hesitated to increase Russian military presence in the Caspian Sea region, placing a flotilla based in Astrakhan that contains two frigates, twelve patrol ships and a handful of support ships. This flotilla includes the Tatarstan, a new naval ship launched in 2003. The rationale for the flotilla's presence is to have a force available to Russia and the CA nations to combat terrorism and interdict the movements of narcotics in the area.

Access to CA oil is a prime target of Russian foreign policy decisions relative to Central Asia. There is a strategic Russian plan to compete fiercely with America's plans for capitalizing on CA oil resources and export routes. When it comes to oil, the best of friends can part. Iran and Russia each has different ideas about who should dominate this vital region. The interplay of strategic plans and counter-plans continues apace. In July of 2005, President Nazarbayev, who is proud of the fact that that Kazakhstan's oil reserves are estimated at 1 billion tons, announced the signing of a 55-year production-sharing agreement involving the Kurmangazy oilfield in the Caspian Sea. A subsidiary of Kazakhstan's state oil company will hold a 50 percent stake in the project, while two Russian oil companies, Rosneft and Zarubezneft, will likely control the other fifty percent "Profits from this project are estimated at $50 billion," Putin said. Nazarbayev added that the joint investment would reach approximately $22 billion.

In the background, however, is the ever-present specter of opposition to increasing Russian presence in the area. A powerful opposition movement, Democratic Choice of Kazakhstan, arose as early as 2002 and has every intention of curbing President Nursultan Nazarbayev's Russian-Kazakhstan plans. Since economic cooperation necessarily impacts on ideological relations, the United States needs to be far more active in the region.

Kyrgyzstan

That good things can come in small packages was exemplified by the rapid democratic reforms that ensued upon independence in the tiny, remote, and mountainous country of Kyrgyzstan. Its post-Soviet leader, President Askar Akayev, took Central Asian leadership in pressing for reform. Kyrgyzstan, in 1993, was the first of the CA nations to move out of the ruble zone in 1993. Kyrgyzstan, which moved to reforms immediately, consistently carried out the recommendations of the World Bank and IMF to develop a western style civil code, to privatize industry, and to adopt, in form at least, an open political system. It also was the first country of the Commonwealth of Independent States (CIS) to join the World Trade Organization. However, its geographic location as a remote mountainous state puts limitations on its economic potential.

During the Soviet era Kyrgyzstan acquired a modern industrial base (light manufacturing, agricultural machinery, electric power, metallurgy and others) and transformed its agricultural sector from pastoral to export-oriented large farms. The native Kyrgyz account for only 58.6% of the population with roughly one third of the republic's population of European origin. President Adayev, considered a liberal, had been the vice-president, then president of the Kyrgyz Academy of Science from 1987 until 1990, when he became President of the republic in 1990. He was one of the first Central Asian leaders to leave the Communist party, fostering a liberal political environment, and was admired by such International organizations such as the World Bank, and IMF. He opted for what he called the "Korean Model of economic development" and decided to explore the opportunities for joint co-operation with foreign companies. Because of its natural beauty, the "Switzerland of Asia," it did succeed in attracting multinational corporations and banks.

Darker Side

However, there was a darker side emerging politically. The Kyrgyz government undertook both to restrict the freedom of opposition parties and launched a massive propaganda campaign to present its own vision of Kyrgyzstan's future. Using the general concern about terrorism, the government, in September of 2005, introduced a constitutional reform process that strengthened its control of the media and opposition parties. However, like a deus ex machina appearing on stage to rescue the heroine, a significant shift of power took place on 10 July 2005. For the first time in the history of this nation the voters chose as President a southerner, Kurmanbek Bakiev, as its new president. Long time president, Akayev, damaged by widespread fraudulent elections a few months before, lost all credibility and was ousted. The political fault lines in Kyrgyz politics had always been between the more populous and affluent (relatively) north and the poor and less populous south. Akayev had already begun to falter when, in March 2002, he allowed the transfer of Kyrgyz territory to China. China increasingly figures in Kyrgyz politics, as does Russia. Both nations are pressuring Bakiev to close the U.S. military base in Kyrgyzstan.

Russian leaders have not hidden their desire to drive the United States out of Central Asia. Moscow spearheaded the drive to get the Shanghai Cooperation Organization to adopt an early July resolution that called on the United States to set a deadline for withdrawal from air bases in both Uzbekistan and Kyrgyzstan. So, Bakiev has the tricky task of balancing Kyrgyzstan's foreign policy between China, Russia and the United States. He will not be able to give full attention to that until he begins to accomplish the task for which he was elected by the people, namely, reforming the state structures to reflect more democracy. Serious discussions are taking place to reshape the constitutional amendment process. The results of these discussions could well produce an island of democracy in Central Asia, although analysts do not expect that to happen quickly.

Uzbekistan

President Karimov of Uzbekistan, shortly after having taken the reins of power, made his intentions clearly known. He said, "we have our own notion of democracy" in explaining his early persecution of his political opposition. The most heavily populated of these Central Asian republics, Uzbekistan, quickly established itself as defiantly nationalist. Uzbekistan's strong-willed president, Islam Karimov, who, only a few years before had been a dutiful communist, rapidly became an enthusiastic champion of an independent political path and engineered the "Uzbek cultural renewal." Like the legendary Kemal Ataturk, he was determined to develop a national identity based on playing a Saddam-like role in Central Asian politics. This was his primary goal. Economics and culture took second place in his prioritizing order. Of the five CA nations, it has remained the most identified with neo-Bolshevism. Uzbeks are proud of the fact that because 71.1% of the population is Uzbek it is the most homogenized of the five states, and, they say, the intellectual and cultural leader of the region.

Karimov began his presidency in 1990. He has certainly not been a liberal and even opposed the very political reforms initiated by his mentor, Gorbachev, that gave the Uzbeks more authority to decide their own fate. His motto has been, "stability at any cost." He has shrugged off accusations of being a dictator. There is general disappointment in the area among opposition leaders that the United States has not used its influence to act more decisively in putting the brake on repression. No doubt the decision of the Uzbek government in 2005 to close the United States Air Force base under hostile conditions and rhetoric will open new avenues of opposition among the U.S. senators and congressmen. Uzbek officials delivered a diplomatic note July 29, 2005 to the U.S. Embassy in Tashkent, renouncing an agreement that 1,000 American military personnel have the use of the Karshi-Khanabad base, known as K-2. The cooling of relations between the two nations has been developing for some time. This became very evident when U.S. Secretary of Defense Donald Rumsfeld did not visit Uzbekistan during a 2005 tour of Central Asia. The cooling of relations became evident in 2004 after the velvet revolutions[58] in the former Soviet Union occurred in Georgia, the Ukraine and Kyrgyzstan. The Uzbek government believes that the United States played a role. As U.S.-Uzbek relations grew increasingly tense, President Karimov turned to Russia, which was delighted to make points with the Uzbeks by backing them in the dispute. Russia has a lot to gain if CA-Washington relations continue to sour. During visits to Kyrgyzstan and Tajikistan, Rumsfeld sought to downplay the strategic significance of the K-2 base. At the same time, the Secretary of Defense convinced Kyrgyz and Tajik leaders that tenuous political conditions in Afghanistan warranted the continued presence of American military personnel in Central Asia.

Turkmenistan

Turkmenistan has a population of 4,863,169, 89% of whom are Muslims. The capital is Ashgabat and its president, who has been quite ill, is Saparmurat Niyazov. Its size, however, did not prevent it from experiencing a wave of stealing. Yolli Gurbanmuradov, the former chairman of Turkmenistan's foreign bank and more recently the deputy prime minister in charge of Turkmenistan's multibillion-dollar oil and gas industries, was imprisoned for stealing $100 million dollars from the State treasury. But, when the prosecutor was asked how much stolen money had been retrieved, he said "180 million." Turkmenistan's nationalism exceeds even that of Uzbekistan. It is a small nation skirting the southern borders of Central Asia. It is so poor that in Soviet times economic survival, except for the coal and oil industry, depended on Soviet largesse. Even the maintenance of its cotton industry depended on irrigation subsidies. When those subsidies were discontinued, production in many areas came to a sudden halt.

Niyazov boosted his nation's confidence by announcing that, based on its gas and oil wealth, Turkmenistan would adopt a position of "positive neutrality." This resonated among his hard-pressed peoples, although no one is quite sure of its meaning. The nation does not have a good human rights record, a fact conveniently kept out of the public eye by Western governments in the interest of fostering good relations. Good relations can lead to a sharing in the wealth that will be created by Turkmenistan's immense gas reserve. However, Turkmenistan did not fare so well with the European Bank for Reconstruction and Development (EBRD), which forthrightly suspended its lending programs to the Turkmenistan government in April 2000 because it had made so little progress in government reforms.

Tajikistan

The smallest and poorest of the Central Asian countries is Tajikistan. Tajikistan would also likely have moved in the direction of reform if the country had not fallen prey to an internal contest for power in the first year of independence. The contest plunged the country into civil war. Tajikistan is a landlocked, mountainous country lacking good transportation routes. The war resulted in a blockade by its neighbors, further compressing the already collapsing Tajikistan economy. The modest level of civil normality maintained in Tajikistan was largely a result of the presence of foreign (mainly Russian) peacekeeping forces. After a decade of independence, Tajikistan has become one of the world's poorest countries. The tiny economy is based largely on subsistence barter relations and foreign assistance from donor organizations.

CA Governments/Mosque Relationships

The Turkish Model Again

In looking for common ground between state and mosque, it has been suggested in many quarters that the Central Asian nations move to adopt the Turkish model of Islamic government, one that seems to have satisfied its people without resort to Islamic extremism. Even U.S. President Bush made that suggestion. The Turkish model, he said, according to the majority of prominent religious figures, is the most suitable for Kyrgyzstan for many reasons. First, Muslims of the CA countries belong to the same moderate Islamic Hanafi Sunni sect as do the Turkish Muslims. Second, both in Turkey, and in the surrounding countries of the region they share the same negative attitudes to Wahhabi ideology. Thirdly, Turkey and Central Asia share the historical experience of interaction between Islam and state institutions. That is why, from the first days of independence, the Spiritual Department of Muslims of Kyrgyzstan has kept in touch with Turkish Islamic organizations. The religious figures of Kyrgyzstan, sharing the government's fear of outsiders, have not allowed Turkish spiritual authorities to assume the role of "the senior brother". Turkish religious leaders made numerous offers to send "volunteers" to Kyrgyz to take positions as imams in local mosques. However, the religious management refused to accept those offers. The Kyrgyz Mufti, Kimsanbai hajji, has managed to find a middle ground by allowing Turkish imams to read the Koran during the month of Ramadan, to teach in religious educational institutions, and to build mosques. Turkey aspired to fill the ideological vacuum that developed in Central Asia after the breakup of the USSR and offered a helping hand to adjust the local governmental system to the "Turkish model."

In itself the Turkish initiatives were appealing because the Turkish model had already proved its viability on the world scene. However, the CA political elite were preoccupied with the problems of strengthening their political role in society and had little interest in the Turkish model. The CA leadership was, and for the most part, remains far more attracted to Russia, and through it, Europe. However, initially, the Turkish Fund did receive permission from Uzbek authorities to open an Islamic university in Tashkent, but before this could be realized, the rise of terrorist activities in the Ferghana valley and in Tashkent led President Karimov to reverse that decision.

The Kyrgyz government, very wary of terrorists in clerical clothing, in 2003, unveiled an impressive program to minimize Wahhabi influence in the country, named, "The State Program" project for the counteraction of religious extremism in the Kyrgyz Republic for the years 2004-2005. The government has determined that, in general, fundamentalist religions of every denomination are suspect. While that may be an oversimplification on their part and even objectively unjust, nevertheless, given the tensions caused by fundamentalist Muslims, it is understandable. Too many bibles and Korans have been part and parcel of many religious services, so all are suspect. Obviously, the government equates any form of fundamentalist religion a danger to the state and a safe haven for HT Wahhabism. As terrible as this may sound, it must be put in the context of dealing with serious problems that arise out of fundamentalist mosques. Put in that light, it is understandable. Church authorities feel it is unjust for them to have to register and some insist that they will continue to worship regardless of the government's decision. This stance does not take into account the nervousness of government officials in the face of the tension and increased violence that is gripping the nation. True, such a report made to a Human Rights organization would be taken very seriously and a negative response would likely be forthcoming.

Uzbekistan

Uzbekistan, which is pursuing the harshest policies against religious extremism, receives the most criticism from Human Rights groups. Several Jehovah's Witnesses have been prosecuted under the Criminal Code for unlawful missionary activity. The last criminal prosecution against a Jehovah's Witness was in late 2004. Once again, in their determination to limit the spread of religious fundamentalism and to break the link between it and any form of Wahhabism, the state immediately investigates any case in which the church did not strictly follow the state's regulations. The requirement of Uzbek law is that the church, to be allowed to operate, should be of a certain size in membership. This does sound very restrictive to Western ears, but if groups, as with Hizb ut-Tahrir (HT), use small churches or mosques as a venue to discuss the overthrow of the government, then the state has a right to step in. The state regulation requires that if a place of worship has only a handful of members, the members should travel to the nearest larger church center. Is this a violation of the peoples' right to worship? Per se, yes, but since it is also a well known fact that the radical Islamic Movement of Uzbekistan(IMU) and the HT use mosques to recruit suicide bombers, it is not unreasonable for the government to treat such meetings with suspicion. It is, after all, duty-bound to protect the state. The only thing worse than criticism for actions taken, is criticism for action not taken, especially if it results in a loss of life. It is a well-known fact that the Wahhabi use the mosque to establish conspiratorial cells consisting of three to five people. Ergo, the straight-line logic is that any religious meeting of just a handful of men and women could be seen as a potential threat to the area. In Tajikistan a radical group opening and brazenly calling for the overthrow of the government are so closely tied to the Wahhabi that they call themselves and are called by the general public, the Wahhabits. The tight restrictions are also reflected in the region's view that madrasas are centers of extremism that threaten the political status quo. In Uzbekistan, some directors have been removed from their posts, and the schools themselves are barred from receiving funding from Saudi Arabia because of the Wahhabi connection.

China

China is mentioned here because the CA rules on religion and those of China are consistent with the agreements made at the Shanghai Conference, as we saw in Chapter One. China is stepping up its attack on religious fundamentalism. New religious affairs regulations went into effect on March 1, 2005. The new rules, while pretty much a reflection of old rules, do give a keener insight into the targets of the Chinese crackdown. The Chinese make a distinction between the official open-to-scrutiny churches that can easily be monitored, and the "underground" churches operating far from the eyes of the Chinese security services. The world press has covered the story of the Chinese government's quarrel with the followers of the Falun Gong, and the Wahhabi inspired Uighur Muslims. Citizens do complain about government intervention but, at this time, the government pretty much has its way. Certainly one very legitimate concern on the part of those who study religious persecution is that a totalitarian government may, purposefully, and under the cover of state security, abuse the religious rights of its citizens. China has certainly been given a lot of press of doing exactly that. However, Government actions anywhere need to be judged not by the rules of any particular NGO, but by the social context of the nation involved. Also, in international relations, it is not so much a question of having a blind eye to the violation of human rights anywhere. It is a question of taking action at a time and place that one can reasonably assume will produce some positive results.

Turkmenistan

In July 2005, President Niyazov directly interfered with Turkmenistan's only official institution for training Muslim imams. All Turkish staff members were required to return to Turkey and 20 students were expelled. It could well be that the President over-reacted, but the act itself, in the context of the religious extremism threatening public order, is a matter for local authorities to determine. No one was arrested; no one was subject to any physical harm. No doubt the move was part of the government's determination to nip terrorist plans in the bud. Certainly the rest of the training center's staff was very upset, but responsibility for national security, exercised within a poorly developed legal system, is bound, at times, to cause false alarms and overzealous enforcement. Other such government actions have been reported. A variety of Protestant fundamentalist groups and Hare Krishna members have had run-ins with government officials. In one case, a Protestant church's rental contact was cancelled, and a Baptist pastor is on trial for refusing to register his church. Not until the CA nations feel comfortable in their new role as independent nations and sort out the ways and means of establishing democracy, there will continue the ebb and flow of growing pains in every sphere of CA life.

Chapter Seventeen

HIZB UT-TAHRIR

Most Central Asian experts, including American intelligence units, agree that today the Hizb-ut-Tahrir (HT) (Party of Islamic Liberation), a Wahhabi look-alike, is the most popular Islamic movement in the region. Imran Waheed, spokesman for Hizb ut-Tahrir in London, was not shy. "Hizb ut-Tahrir has a very clear objective, which is the re-establishment of the Islamic Caliphate and it is working toward that." That statement did not go over very well in Britain, where British Prime Minister Tony Blair banned Hizb ut-Tahrir in August 2005. Nabi Rahimov, a deputy prosecutor in Tajikistan, said of HT, "they are trying to topple the constitutional government by force and violent means." It represents the pan-Islamic movement in that it is working for the goal of creating a Sharia-based "Caliphate" and is convinced that it can get a start in that direction in Kyrgyzstan, even though most of its members are ethnic Uzbeks living in and around the Ferghana Valley (Uzbekistan, southern Kyrgyzstan and northern Tajikistan), a bastion of Wahhabi faith throughout the last century. In true terrorist fashion no one knows where its leadership is based. HT is believed to be getting its financing from "Arab charities." You can translate that into Wahhabi funding and, like the Wahhabi, they have outreach in many Western countries. They are able to maintain their secrecy by continuing their custom of having each module consist of only five members, one of whom is the leader. No two cells interact directly. Every four cells are grouped under a

`Naquib' who, in turn, belongs to a regional council headed by a `Muta'amad' (head of a region). The Muta'amads work independently under the Amir's (Supreme Leader) supervision. The structure configuration is on a "need-to-know" basis. HT followers probably number between 20,000 and 60,000, some of whom belong to military units. Although the Central Asian nations and the Russians have listed HT as a terrorist organization, and Uzbekistan blamed HT for several incidents of violence; yet, the United States continues to refuse to so list them. There is a belief in Washington that HT is a force of moderation in Central Asia, a surprising summation given their history and the description and assessment of them by Central Asian, European, Russian and Chinese intelligence services. Central Asian governments have spent years trying to repress Hizb ut-Tahrir. That effort has not produced results since, by all estimates, the group's core of younger members is growing as unemployed and desperate youth, frustrated with the political arena turn to Hizb ut-Tahrir for help and hope.

Twenty-nine Hizb ut-Tahrir members are currently on trial on charges related to the group's activities in Uzbekistan. The youngest is 19, and most of the others are under the age of 30. In Kyrgyzstan, former President Askar Adayev allowed Hizb ut-Tahrir to organize informational and even charitable events despite the ban, but the new President, Kurmanbek Bakiev, has cracked down on the group and has declared that they should be eliminated. In the summer of 2006, Kyrgyz National Security Service official Talant Razzakov spoke to Radio Free Europe/RL's Kyrgyz Service, and spoke of Hizb ut Tahrir's ties with the Islamic Movement of Uzbekistan: "Only those who 'graduated' from the [Hizb ut-Tahrir] school can subsequently join the IMU," he said. Aalybek Akunov is a professor of political studies at Kyrgyz National University. He has a more benign view. He told Radio Free Europe, also in August 2006, that poverty and high unemployment encourage young people who live along the Uzbek-Kyrgyz border to join Hizb ut Tahrir. "The main reason is, of course, an economic one—poverty among people living in that area," Akunov said. "There are many unemployed people. The economic future is precarious. There is despair and exhaustion. They are tired of waiting for changes in government policy on both sides [of the border." Akunov warns that Hizb ut-Tahrir ideas will continue to resonate unless economic problems are solved. Again, the leader of the Islamist movement in Tajikistan, Deputy Prime Minister Hoji Akbar Turajonzoda, is quoted in a Radio Free Europe broadcast August 28, 2006 as warning warns of a plot to "remake Central Asia." He says: "A more detailed analysis of HT's programmatic and ideological views and concrete examples of its activities suggests that it was created by anti-Islamic forces. One proof of this is the comfortable existence that HT enjoys in a number of Western countries where it has large centers and offices that develop its concept of an "Islamic Caliphate."

Utopian Government

For the HT, the term "Islamic Caliphate" refers to a utopian form of government that the HT is convinced existed from the very beginning of Islam, a government in which both religious and temporal authority were in the hands of the Prophet Mohammed or his immediate successors. This is their dream and also their ambition. Hizb ut-Tahrir first emerged in the Uzbek-controlled part of the Ferghana Valley after the collapse of the Soviet Union. It then spread to other parts of the valley claimed by Tajikistan and Kyrgyzstan. It can also be found in Russia and Kazakhstan. So fearful are the Central Asian governments of the Wahhabi-inspired HT that any person found to be in possession of Hizb-ut-Tahrir literature could be sentenced to at least 10 years in prison. Therefore, to be identified as an HT member makes one either famous or infamous among the Muslim population of Central Asia. The manner in which the average CA Muslim describes a member of the HT reflects his political stance. The American equivalent would be the description of a politician. If one person calls him a "redneck" and the other calls him a "far lefty", we might not have learned anything new about the world, but we know a great deal about the two people. We have their political profile.

The local mass-media regularly publish information on how the police have uncovered "a printing house" that was set up in an apartment somewhere in the city that is being used by HT." The report will no doubt relate in great detail that the apartment was equipped with machines for manufacturing leaflets and books. Certainly, HT actively uses modern information technologies for reception, duplication and distribution of agitation-and-propaganda materials. That is why they place the printing houses and office equipment in city districts. Statistical data of law-enforcement and judicial bodies of the CA countries and numerous publications concerning HT activity creates an impression that the HT party confines its greatest activity to urban areas. However, it would be more accurate to say that HT has a two-pronged attack, simultaneously recruiting both in the countryside and in the city.

Active in Mosques

Usually HT[59] agents attend mosques, whether in the city or the countryside, to get to know and mingle with the youth. They offer them brochures written in the local language that explain an edited version of what HT is all about. They mention that in the following month they will be back to see how well they understand the brochure and to answer any questions. They also imply that they will bring some games or other appealing donations with them to contribute to the mosque's youth. That approach always works. At the follow-up meeting the youth are invited to join. Any young person who agrees is signed up immediately, and takes an oath of fidelity and secrecy. It is not unusual that many unemployed youth are eager to join. Perhaps for the first time in their lives someone is making them feel important and useful. According to the Osh Public Prosecutor's office and the Osh city court, almost all HT prisoners were formerly unemployed and undereducated. In one area not one educated or gainfully employed youth had been arrested for HT activity.

But recruiting work in urban areas has a greater risk than the same work in a rural environment. Probably therefore, according to our data, HT pays increasing attention to the creation of its support base in rural areas among common people. It has obvious advantages: in villages it is easier to communicate, people basically know each other. They are connected by family-related ties and will not report what they see or hear to authorities, even if there are ideological disagreements among them. In the rural area there is no need to distribute leaflets. In the casual atmosphere of the countryside membership is most often accomplished with a handshake or over a beer. A private home or local "gjapy," teahouse, is usually the locale for even private meetings after the new member becomes active. Recruitment is basically carried out by one relative contacting another. Rural poverty, unemployment and absence of an opportunity to receive proper education are not only the most acute village problems; they are also what get the HT recruiter's foot in the door. HT representatives are most active in rural villages during the autumn-winter time, when peasants pretty much sit out the long winter at home.

Some observers, in order to bring the point of Hizb ut Tahrir danger to Central Asia, compare the reconstruction of a Caliphate to the Bolshevik's slogan: "Proletarians of all countries be united!" Ironically, the struggle, especially in Uzbekistan, comes down to one between the neo- Bolshevik former Soviet republics in Central Asia against the newly structured hard-line Islamic HT. However, there is one important difference. The neo-Bolsheviks are working their way away from totalitarianism, and HT is working its way toward it. Both parties have a utopian ultimate goal: The Bolsheviks dreamt of establishing world-wide Communism; Islamists dream of establishing a world-wide Caliphate. Also, both parties dislike real democracy and seek the establishment of a mythical democratic society in which an entire peoples' consciousness is changed by means of propaganda. Both parties use identical tactics –the distribution of leaflets, the special literature of propaganda, and the organization of their activities by means of primary party cells. The structure of HT in Central Asia resembles a secret hierarchical pyramid consisting of sets of Cells ("Khalaka") - a party nucleus that is composed of three members. The cells meet and organize political meetings and prepare propaganda leaflets for distribution to the population.

Exploit Tension

Like all revolutionary groups, HT extremists are ready to exploit any tensions they detect in Central Asian society. The well-organized and controlled structure of the party has managed to increase its membership and sympathizers in geometrical progression. The HT works secretly, so we have only sketchy information about its specific locations and its membership. The words HT and "Wahhabi" are interchangeable operationally, since "Wahhabi" has become a generic word for those who wish to create the Caliphate. Any terrorist who wants to attain fame and fortune as a terrorist can hope to be identified as a Wahhabi. It takes a long period of time, great trust, and the willingness of the individual to sacrifice his or her own personal future on behalf of creating a better Islamic world. HT members were previously routinely identified as Wahhabi, but CA leaders now prefer to call them HTs because, for one thing, since they are locals, the HT label separates them from the foreign Wahhabi. That makes it easier to accuse them of subversion and insurrection, very serious charges. Nevertheless, the five thousand local HT prisoners in Uzbek jails are contemptuously referred to by the general population as "those Wahhabi." The knee-jerk reaction to a terrorist attack or plot in Central Asia is, "The Wahhabi did it." In one sense that is correct, i.e., the Wahhabi philosophy and Wahhabi money is so pervasive that any Islamic terrorist action taking place in Central Asia, Russia or China gets, and to some extent deserves, the Wahhabi label.

HT came to the attention of the international community in Tashkent, Uzbekistan in 1995. They were accused of being responsible for a series of terrorist explosions. In April 1999, in response to this charge, HT published its first leaflet containing its views on the current political and economic conditions in Uzbekistan. Following that first public initiative, and attracting the attention of CA citizens, they began a barrage of publishing, more than a hundred thousand leaflets once or twice a month. Once again only foreign funding, i.e., the enabler states makes this outlay of money possible. Since that time HT has increased many times over, especially in Uzbekistan. Now that they have made their mark, it has not been difficult to attract influential people from state institutions to the HT party. There are indications that confirm this assumption. In 2002, the NSS (National Security Services) chairman publicly declared that the deputy of parliament, Zhogorku Kenesh, and KR's ombudsman, Mr. Tursunbaj Bakir uuly, were connected to radical Islamists. The new Islamic state envisioned by HT would encompass the Ferghana,

Andijon, Namangan (Uzbekistan), and Osh (Kyrgyzstan) regions. HT definitely plans to be the wave of the future.

There seems to be very little intelligence on the sources of HT funding. Despite numerous investigations of HT activities, the information on financial sources remains limited. The HT organizational structure explains, at least partially, why it is so difficult to penetrate. HT is organized in such a way that it guarantees strict secrecy about its activities both inside and outside the party. A new member of the party swears on the Koran that she/he will never disclose any information. Their response to questions is always the same: Allah Akbar! Many believe that HT has already infiltrated the government to such an extent that is might be very prudent indeed to join.

Financing

Local HT branches financially depend on the central committee, which, in turn, appoints staff treasurers who are in charge of gathering donations. HT staff treasurers collect money from private donations by means of informal payments and the direct taxation of party members. Each member of the party is obliged to a monthly donation that is from 5% to 20% of his/her income. In addition, local HT organizations set up small private enterprises for self-financing, everything from bake sales to selling used clothing. The HT leadership takes special care to fund events designed to attract the youth in the 17-25 age range. The money raised also funds the everyday expenses of party functionaries: editing, duplicating, distribution of party literature, renting of premises, office equipment, payment for phone calls, Internet services, the translation of foreign documents, the support of families of arrested members, and salaries for HT functionaries. The financial status of HT is solid enough to support a wide network of HT branches worldwide and a comfortable life for party leaders in a number of Western countries where they operate large centers and work diligently both to raise funds and to lobby for the creation of the "World Islamic Caliphate". Their finance slogan is: "Our party has the right to demand financial help from infidels during jihad," through kidnappings and robberies.

The Jewish Question

Local residents maintain that the general population, while sympathetic toward HT, has been annoyed at their anti-Semitic message, and the almost obsessive focus on Middle East issues. Muslims in the region do not approve of the current policy of Israel, but that has never been translated into anti-Semitic demonstrations as, say, frequently occur in Russia. In the town of Bukhara Jews freely visit synagogues, and the property and lives of the Jewish population is secure. Of course, as in any country, one finds individuals who are prejudiced and intolerant, but they have no decisive influence, and are social pariahs. The former deputy Mufti of Kyrgyzstan and the director of a large madrasa in a town near Bishkek, Mr. Khabibulla hajji, had very friendly relations with local Jews. At the same time, many do not approve of the Israeli policy toward Palestinians. The daughter of the former state minister of culture and a famous public figure, Mrs. K. Konduchalova, is married to a Jew, and she lives in Israel. The Jewish philosopher, Mr. Aaron Brudnyj, is married to the daughter of Muslim writer T. Sydykbekova. There are many such examples. People in Central Asia understand that war in the Middle and Near East is connected more to policy, than to religion. The majority of the people are of the opinion that anti-Semitic HT leaflets and messages are a by-product of the imagination of HT ideologists. The HT is learning that it needs to justify its policies with the local population before they will be totally embraced.

Government is stepping up the Pressure

In spite of the many advances the HT has made among the general population, the regional governments are stepping up their efforts to crush the movement, with a significant number of their members already imprisoned, especially in Uzbekistan. Authorities have detained, according to press reports and legal experts, more than 10,000 HT members, although official Tashkent sources give the total at about 6 000. However, in recent years a former HT group, Hizb an_Nusra, disenchanted with extremism, has broken away from HT. Government officials are hopeful that as the general population experiences increased acts of gratuitous violence, more such defections will take place.

That may be wishful thinking. HT members have received a degree of sophisticated military training in Pakistan that previously had not been seen in the republic. In private homes, the SSK (security force) found many weapons, explosives, components for the preparation of bombs and identity cards stolen from the American military base. Local officials admit that the social and economic situation in Central Asia lends itself to the formation of extremism, and no group exploits poverty more cleverly than HT. However, these same officials point out that as economic conditions improve in an area, so do defections from HT. That is not always true. In the more affluent agricultural Uzbek Lake Aral region of the Ferghana valley the opposite occurred. Officials are resigned to experiencing contradictions and surprises in the ebb and flow of Central Asian politics. Due to historical developments in the region, especially in Uzbekistan and Tajikistan, there was always a public need to put Islam in some institutional framework. This pressure sharply increased after the Central Asian nations became independent. Islam caught fire. The mosques are crowded with the region's youth. The mosque provides companionship and at least momentary relief from the drudgery of everyday life in the region. The HT party, quick to observe and analyze social patterns, began to associate itself with the religious needs and policies of the mosque. This filled a vacuum left by the State's lack of interest in affairs religious. HT affiliates introduced a host of programs attractive to the young. Money seemed to appear out of thin air. Most officials in the region expressed their frustration at not being able, financially, to compete with the money flows from the Saudi Wahhabi that made all of this possible.

HT Becomes Political

In due course, the HT, having established a strong base in the mosque, began to move onto the political stage, carrying with them the call for a return to Islamic fundamentalism. This, they proclaimed from every rooftop, is the solution to society's problems. Secure in the all-important religious arena, and moving quickly along political lines, they have become the unchallenged Islamic alternative to the post-Soviet governments of the region. Casting their political message in an Islamic religious framework has bought them friends throughout the region. They are on a roll.

Only They can Do It

HT advertises itself as the only political entity that can restore the people to its rightful place as a leading Islamic state. The leadership has taken shrewd advantage of the fact that under communism the knowledge of Islam has faded. Islamic revivalism is the key to HT's success. They are convincing the youth, with great sophistication, that if they go back to their Islamic religious roots they will be able to totally transform their society, giving Central Asia a place in the international sun. HT indoctrination has produced dramatic change. For the impressionable, and for those who are ashamed of the low visibility of Central Asia on the world scene, the idea of a "great jihad," or "jihad of the heart" is enormously appealing. The youth are offered an opportunity to place Central Asia on the world stage. The message is heady, dynamic and energizing, a drawing card for signing up as an HT member. Recruits are especially fascinated with HT slogans of justice and equality, public order and assistance to the poor. They have become convinced that only radical solutions can change their lives.

On the other hand, there are many thoughtful people in Central Asia who understand the problem of radical Islam, and are frustrated that the Wahhabi groups are making such rapid inroads in spite of Government's best efforts to contain them. And, when Uzbek officials do make some progress they are, internationally, accused of violating human rights. They are also frustrated by the fact that the HT, coming as it does in the sheep's clothing of religion, is making progress on the coattails of religion. They point out that the majority of the Central Asian population, because of the religious restrictions in place during the Soviet hegemony, has no scholarly or theological knowledge of Islam. So they are relatively easy to impress. Under Soviet rule, Uzbeks were banned from studying either Islamic literature or becoming acquainted with the relatively moderate Hanafi tradition that predated Soviet hegemony. That tradition, unfortunately, has been supplanted by the HT religion-for-convenience interpretation of the Koran.

Uzbek authorities took part in 2003 in the questioning of 3418 prisoners accused of being in collaboration with HT and made a judgment that radicals brainwashed approximately 1303 of them. 736 of these prisoners were released. Authorities are convinced that if the essence of Islam is properly explained to the youth of Central Asia they will quickly abandon the radical, self-serving version promoted by those seeking fame and fortune in Islamic radicalism. However, they also acknowledge that it is a race against time, so they have immersed themselves in developing a wide array of programs that educate the young not only about true Islam, but also about the world around them. Education, they are convinced, is the key to the moderate Islam that characterized the pre-Soviet Central Asian Islamic community. Many men of good will are engaged in the ideological struggle being waged in Central Asia against any further infiltration of radical Islam. They comprehend all the difficulties inherent in such a challenge and purposefully direct the activities of state institutions, as Islamic University, making the best use of the mass media, especially radio and TV broadcasting.

Major Confrontation on the Horizon

It is clear both from government announcements and HT responses that a major confrontation between them is looming in Uzbekistan, a confrontation that will have no borders. The proliferation of HT propaganda increases as the political temperature of the nation rises. Mass arrests of HT members have taken place in Tashkent and throughout the nation. There is a growing fear now that any opponent of the government will be smeared with the same HT brush. Observers there see this as a deliberate strategy on the part of the government. Once the general population becomes convinced, so the government reasoning goes, that their safety and that of their children depends on making certain that no one can tie them to the HT, membership will drop. Of course, Uzbek leaders can look at history to see if that strategy, in the long run, works. But then, politicians are not fans of looking beyond their term of office. The dark clouds of terrorist activity and government response are gathering. The battle between HT and the government of Uzbekistan is now in full swing, and no one can safely predict the outcome.

A large percentage of the HT membership consists of 25 - 35 year olds who come from the more traditional areas of the nation. Although not all are confined to Uzbekistan, the majority of HT members are ethnic Uzbeks living throughout the entire region, especially in southern Kyrgyzstan and northern Tajikistan. They have not been quite as successful in Kyrgyz and Turkmen primarily because the populations there are not as religiously oriented as their neighbors, but they feel it will happen. In time, their increasing contacts with other youth in the region will result in a greater political consciousness. In Kazakhstan HT activity is concentrated in the southern Kazakhstan region that borders Uzbekistan. Russia and China are keeping a close watch on events in Central Asia with a practiced understanding borne of their own personal struggles with Wahhabism. Hopefully, the West will come to realize, before it is too late, that what is taking place in Central Asia today will have a direct impact on their future security and way of life.

Chapter Eighteen

SWITCH FOCUS TO CENTRAL ASIA

Change will come to Central Asia rather slowly since the political/economic base is neither strong nor developed. Once again, however, we must remind ourselves that they never were sufficiently strong or developed, so that false expectations on the part of the West do not, of themselves, hasten the process of change. Patience and observation that there is general movement in the direction of democracy are essential in the formation of our foreign policies that impact on them. All five states, with the possible exception of developments in Kyrgyzstan since March 2005, generally resist any change that could threaten the present leaderships' power. It is not easy for any government to loosen its hold on power, but this becomes even more difficult when engaged in eliminating terrorist attacks that threaten the very fabric of the nation. This condition also has another side effect, namely, a hesitation to join international forums and alliance that might make immediate demands for change. When one does not own a pair of skis, one might avoid the embarrassment of others discovering this by refusing to accept an invitation to go skiing. This is one of the main reasons why efforts to foster regional cooperation have largely been ineffective.

The decision on the part of four of the CA nations to join the Shanghai Cooperation Organization was for them a courageous step, one they knew they had to make at some point in time. The fact that the big powers in the group, Russia and China, were far from fully democratic in nature made it easier for them to become members. They reasoned, correctly, that Russia and China would not make a strict adherence to the Western concept of civil rights a condition for mutual friendship and solidarity. And they knew full well that Russia and China shared a dual purpose in inviting them: a) to remove as much as possible American presence and influence in the area, and b) their need for oil and gas supplies. They are also fully aware that Russia has every intention of regaining its big power status by recouping, in some manner, its loss of the CA states when the Soviet Union imploded. They also make note of the kind of assistance, or, from their perspective, lack of it, offered by the United States. They look at the three billion dollars the United States gives in military aid to Israel and also to Egypt every year, and contrast that with the roughly $250 million total given to the five of them, understanding a nuanced version of the expression "money talks". They are not inclined to enhance American power and prestige in their region at such a cheap price.

They are also aware that although joining the SCO provides them with a measure of coordinated regional strategy, they must begin a process of trusting each other and developing bilateral engagement. For example there is a need to reduce tensions that have developed because of economic considerations and cross-border incursions involving Wahhabi terrorists. An example of an economic consideration is the need to develop a mechanism to handle water distribution, especially in the Kyrgyz Batken Valley and Tajik Soghod Province. Tension over water rights does not good neighbors make.

Central Asia has not lived in a vacuum for the last hundred years plus. It has lived with total political domination by the Russians, pre-Czar and post-Czar. More than one hundred years of occupation. That is a record hard to beat. Now, that is simply an historical event, not a judgment on the Russians. They have enough problems. What is important for our purposes is that one hundred years of occupation and total political domination has certainly had a psychic effect on those good people. The beginning of the growth of nationalism and nationalist movements in Central Asia began when the populations in that region learned, unbelievably, that the Russians were leaving. And, no one had even attempted to remove them. They just left. This movement out of occupied territories took place under the leadership of Mikhail Gorbachev under the banner he waved high, glasnost and perestroika. Nationalism, something new for them, since they were all "Soviet citizens," continued to increase in popularity, but with one eye on Islamic internationalism. Groups began to talk about something greater than nationalism, the internationalism of one huge Central Asian Caliphate, a mega state based on Islamic law. They gloried in the real and mythical history of the region, remembering many heroes and incredible accomplishments. The initial flush of being Uzbeks, Kyrgyz, Tajiks, Kazakhs, or Turkmen began to take on the hues of the Islamic flag. However, this tendency did not prevent them from highlighting their national values and ethnic cultural originality. This took unconditional precedence over universal Muslim values and ideas of Islamic umma unity.

Theory and Reality

The theory was nice; the reality was quite another thing. To lose the newfound freedom to be Uzbeks, Tajiks, Kyrgyz and Kazakhs was not going to happen. They had waited over one hundred years for this. At the same time the goal of joining with the other CA states to form one mega state, of whatever political hue, is not their goal. In fact, these heightened nationalistic feelings have, for the most part, produced a people who want to be a nation that is guided by Islamic principles. They have been nobody for so long that now they yearn to be Uzbek, or Tajik, or Kazak. There is no doubt about this. The dominance of nationalism over religious sectarianism is seen in the many clashes between Muslims--Uzbeks and Kyrgyz, Tajiks and Uzbeks, Meskhet Turks and Uzbeks. Nationhood is now a fait accompli. Nationalists will clash with Islamic fundamentalists who prefer Islamic unity to national exclusivity. The influence of the fundamentalists will continue to increase, and the challenge both of the Central Asian political leadership and the wider world community is to work with the leadership to contain Islamic devotion so that it does not become Islamic extremist explosion.

The choices now being made in Central Asia are going to affect the rest of the world. If outsiders take sides too quickly and then, later, begin to arm opposing sides, Central Asia could be in for a long night of terror that could spread to the rest of the world communities. The sprouting of oil, pipelines and mineral resources makes the world aware that Central Asia is a region where the West can access non-OPEC-controlled energy, and they are keen on that. Vice President Cheney looks to the Kashagan oil field and natural gas in Kazakhstan, Turkmenistan, and Uzbekistan. He is keen on exploiting those resources so that we can become less dependent on Middle East oil. He certainly has a point but perhaps is a bit too optimistic, at least at this time, because Kazakhstan oil reserves are in the order of 9-7 billion barrels. Natural gas reserves in Kazakhstan, Turkmenistan, and Uzbekistan equal only 3.4 per cent of the world's reserves.[60] This pales in comparison to OPEC countries' production levels. Production levels in Central Asia may reach 4 million barrels per day (bbl/d) in 2015, compared to 45 million bbl/d for the OPEC countries in that year, making it cost more and, unless more oil reserves are found, be exhausted sooner. Central Asia will not free us from reliance on OPEC oil, but it can help us free ourselves from Islamic terrorism. Our government should put the oil question in a low priority and focus instead on, as they volubly profess, ridding the world of the scourge of Islamic terrorism. We need Muslim allies and it is not yet too late to acquire them. Regrettably, the conflict in an Iraq brimming with sectarian violence and the murderous settling of old scores from the days of Saddam, is distracting us from the real issue. Pitting the Sunni minority against the Shiite majority in an orgy of self-glorification, Saddam, in effect, threw out the baby of Islamic unity with the bath water of religious extremism. He understood the problem perhaps better than any other leader in the region, but transfixed by an uncontrolled ego, he failed to make the real contribution that he might otherwise have made.

Helping the CA Peoples

The true test of leadership is to take a people where they are at and bring them to where they should be. The people of Turkmenistan live under the idiosyncratic regime of President Sapamurat Niyazov, who wants to build a palace of ice in a land of insufferable heat, who says he has had private visions that convince him he must rule for life, etc. etc. A People's Council was created under the president. This council does not have any real power, but its existence enables neo-Bolshevik propaganda to claim that the Turkmen leadership has returned to the traditions of the Turkmen people, who are long accustomed to solving most vital current problems together. An antidote to all of this is to have a long range plan to gradually help the people of Turkmenistan so that their nation will change for the better, enabling enlightened leadership to emerge. If the United States feels that it is good for us to interact in that part of the world then it must have a plan to assist them in ways that they articulate to us, not as part of some grand plan to have power in Central Asia. There are similar problem throughout Central Asia. Some of them reflect a conviction on the part of the CA leadership that Islam is too potent a social and political, as well as religious, force to leave it beyond the state's control.

The governments feel compelled to establish Councils for Religious Affairs that control the selection, promotion, and dismissal of Muslim clergy .This is not paranoia but it does need to be noted and understood. We do need to share their anxiety that there have been as many as three successive mini-revolutions already in Central Asia since they gained their independence from the Soviet Union 15 years ago. And there is a thread that runs through the three events, a thread of relationship with extra-territorial, even extra-regional entities that support, defend and agitate for political Islam. Tajikistan in 1992 is a good example. There, efforts were made by rebels in the southern provinces of Kulyab and Kurgan Tyube, with Afghan and Pakistani connections, to establish an Islamic state. With an ongoing developmental model still taking shape among Islamic separatists, there is no pure and unadulterated line of attack. There are, rather, many shades of ideological positions. Democratic, nationalist, radical, purely religious elements make up the pattern of political meanderings that are important to the Organization of Islamic Conference and the Organization for Security and Cooperation in Europe. The U.S. minimized the Tajik accord and continued encouraging Central Asian states to ally themselves with the Taliban Government in Kabul. We could not have been diplomatically more off base. Conspiracies were spotted around every diplomatic corner while the obvious rise of Islamic sentiments with grass roots support was not even noticed. However, there is a growing understanding, at least among former high level intelligence and diplomatic circles in the United States that Islam is becoming, increasingly, a seamless garment and not some isolated pockets of praying mullahs. While Washington slept or issued unfriendly threats of sanctions to Central Asian governments, the very forces the CA nations were combating were and remain our real enemies.

9/11 happened and, suddenly, the U.S. sought and received permission to put military bases in Central Asia and spoke of creating a common front with that part of the world in order to fight the growing threat of Islamic terrorism. Then, as we saw in earlier chapters, the U.S. turned on these same governments for not respecting human rights while conducting their war against Islamic terrorism. As a result of those outbursts we now need to beg in order to continue our presence in that part of the world, but a qualified diplomat acceptable to the Islamic world sent as a special envoy could yet save the diplomatic day. However, there is no sign from Washington that that will happen. It is the only real viable option left to us to defeat terrorism. We could attain our own self-serving goals in Central Asia and at the same time befriend the wonderful, and sometimes naïve people who live there. It just takes some study, effort, commitment and enlightenment of our own.

Islam and the Central Asian Economy
    While the chances of creating a classic Islamic state seem remote, building a new Central Asian economy on the basis of the Islamic model of organizing entrepreneurial activities appears to be quite feasible. As it has been tested in Saudi Arabia, Kuwait, and the United Arab Emirates, the Islamic model of modern economic activities is oriented around the individual and is regarded by those involved as occurring with the participation and patronage of Allah. It has an economic ethos of its own. A business decision is made by choosing from among alternatives the one that accords with Allah's will, as interpreted by the owners or bosses. The entrepreneur then focuses on the "personality" of his employees, which means that he concentrates on apprais-

ing their subjective qualities rather than the results of their work. The basis for a manager's moving up the career ladder is the personal trust and respect that he has for his subordinates. A subordinate's main function is to serve as a buffer for his boss so that if something bad happens it can be blamed on the circumstances or on the subordinate rather than on his superior's decisions. However, initiative on the part of subordinates is frowned upon.

This model differs dramatically from the Western system of organizing business activities, which is typically distinguished by labor mobility and short-term employment contracts, rapid promotion of employees up the career ladder, narrow specialization among employees in their professional orientation, spontaneous and open management over subordinates' activities, individual responsibility for making decisions, individually defined subordinate duties and responsibilities, and a low level of employee integration into the firm. Unlike the Islamic model that is oriented around personality, the Western business model is more concerned with role, power, and function.

U.S. needs to catch Up

As the Central Asian populations become more distracted by the insurgency, the West needs to study it. It is the West that now needs to come to grips with the hidden contours of the fundamentalist Islamic presence in the republics of Central Asia. We are, to a certain extent, captive to widely accepted stereotypical ideas about Muslim political passiveness, conservatism, and adherence to tradition. The United States in particular must better understand these powerful politico-religious forces if it is to craft an intelligent policy toward the region and avoid blunders like those that befell Soviet policymakers in Egypt and Afghanistan in ignoring Islamic realities. Soviet and Russian inattention to Islam had deep roots. Marx and his Bolshevik followers were blinded by the Hegelian dismissal of Islam's ability to play a role in modern society. But, in the end, the Bolshevik repressions were unable to disrupt the fabric of Islam in the Soviet Union. But the new generation of Russians has lived to see the day when, not only has Islam survived, but the term "Wahhabi" is used by post-Soviet governments to denote militant Islamic groups ready to use force to achieve political-religious goals.

The United States and its allies suffer from a severe shortage of Islamicists who can remedy our lack of knowledge of the history, content, importance of Islam to hundreds of millions. American scholars, with rare exceptions, are unable to fruitfully speak with Muslim mullahs and officials. As a result, "Islamophobia" is widespread at a time when there are serious questions to be answered, questions the answers to which are of far-reaching importance to strategic policy-making in the West. How might the situation in this region change if these Central Asian republics unite with their neighbors to the south or became active participants in the pan-Islamic movement? How would these prospective events affect the geopolitical interests of the United States and its allies? American foreign policy makers cannot remain indifferent to the fate of the Central Asian Islamic republics or unaware of the forces driving developments there. The struggle for the hearts and minds of Muslims is taking place all over the world. Since we have been welcomed and can be welcomed again by slight changes of attitude and policy, we can join with them, helping them to create what they want, a moderate, enlightened Islamic state.

Islam Not Monolithic
The Muslim world embraces a billion people, extending across Africa and Asia from Morocco and Senegal to China and Indonesia, as well as several million adherents in Europe and North America. Profound and explosive differences of ideology and policy can be found among Muslim states and movements that have led to little tangible integration beyond the rhetorical level. The catchall term 'Islam' fails to convey the substantial differences among the many Islamic sects, races, nations and culture. The Islamic world is no more monolithic and homogeneous than the world of Christianity. After the United States mobilized an international coalition against Iraq, Saddam Hussein attempted to define the war as a war between Islam and the West. But few believed him. Under the leadership of George Bush senior, although certain radical Islamic elements considered the war a jihad, most of the Muslim Middle East states joined a US led coalition in a war against their fellow Muslim state. There are 44 Islamic countries and the differences among them are clearly

discernible in their approaches to economics, foreign policy and societal structure. Iran, Turkey and Egypt are all Muslim Islamic countries, but they have little else in common. Iran is Shiite, not appealing to Sunnis. Shiites are not appealing to Sunnis. Seventy sects and offshoots of Islam characterize the Muslim Diaspora. Islamic terrorists exploit these differences for their own personal benefit and one day, after more education and more contact with the outside world, these fomenters of useless revolutions and carnage will be seen exactly for what they are. That will be the beginning of the real Islamic revival. Let us all try to contribute to bringing this day about, instead of taking sides and posturing.

There is no natural tendency for all of these sects to coalesce into a single force. Fear and bundles of money are the two weapons the Saudi Wahhabi use to bring about a worldwide anti-democratic, anti-Western Islamic Caliphate. The recent Islamic revivalism in some parts of the Islamic world is a response primarily to political and economic crises rather than a spontaneous spiritual rebirth of a messianic nature. Islam has no powerful, organized central body or hierarchy that can coordinate, mobilize and regulate a universal Islamic Caliphate. Every Islamic movement must be judged within the political context of its own country, its own agenda, and its own ideological orientation. Moderate Islam advocates the adoption of democracy as the vehicle for bringing the non-violent transfer of power within the nation. Reform of both the state and the society is at the heart of their political agenda.

Moderates see no contradiction between Islam and Western philosophies and institutions. But the lure of undreamed of access to Saudi money, together with the glorification of martyrdom on the part of wealthy Saudi power brokers who stay far away from the battlefield can increase the number of young Islamic terrorists a thousand fold. The vast majority of people in the Muslim countries are among the most impoverished in the world. Growing economic difficulties, rising expectations, increased unemployment, and lack of educational and occupational opportunities have embittered large numbers of people, particularly the young. The politically motivated and fundamentalist-based Wahhabi come dressed in the appealing garments of affluence and 'pure' doctrine. Muslim youth, distressed, impoverished and alienated, flock to Saudi financed lectures and schools, and emotionally dedicate themselves to the reincarnation of another Ottoman Empire. It gives them a "life." As the editors of the Middle East Report wrote in a recent special issue on democracy in the Middle East, "The high profile of Islamist groups owes more to the character of state repression in the past than to the exceptional religiosity of Muslim societies."

Secularism Failed
The current Islamic revival is also the result of failed secular ideologies. A generation of Muslims has been bitterly disappointed by a series of successive ideologies of Marxism and Nationalism. Experiments in Arab socialism failed. Arab socialism produced state classes whose relatively privileged positions set them apart from the masses. The turning point for many was the Arabs' crushing defeat in 1967 at the hands of Israel -- a nation that was perceived by many Muslims to have been victorious because it had not lost touch with its religious roots.

As a result, Islamic reformists began to embark upon a new direction moving closer to the religious norms and values of their societies to renovate the socio-political structure. As John Esposito observes, "at the heart of the revivalist movements lies the quest for authenticity, identity and tradition." Despite the frequent comment that Islamic revivalism is a reaction to the negative pressures of modernity, it is a mistake to call these movements reactionary; they do not fit the profile of "reactionary." The prime sources of support for the Islamist movements are students, college graduates, teachers, intellectuals, and young men and women from rural areas. Olivier Roy contends: "Rather than being a reaction against the modernization of Muslim societies, Islamism is a product of it." In nearly all Middle Eastern countries, a process of modernization has occurred that brings with it both secularization and religious revivalism.

American foreign policy should not ally itself, at this point in history, with progressive forces if by 'progressive' we mean forces that glorify secularism to the detriment of moderate Islam. We must understand that Islamic revivalism is not, per se, anti-western. It is, rather, a process of soul searching among Muslims who tried modernity, who tried socialism, and discovered that it failed them in spite of the promises held out in the West. After all, Saddam Hussein 'modernized' Iraq. The Shah 'modernized' Iran. There is a time and place for all historical trends and options, but now is not the time to pontificate on modernizing Islam. Let us give Islam the opportunity to rediscover and restore its soul. Our foreign policy is in tatters because we do not understand this simple need that Islam has to resurrect itself from having moved in the wrong direction. In attempting to do so they skipped by that which was essential to their integrity and wholeness. They now realize this and we should be in the forefront of understanding what they need and assist them, not just for their good but also for ours.

Wahhabi not a Household Word

Central Asians are a ready-made lifeline in our struggle to survive in a morass of misguided, even though well-intentioned, policies, and most Americans do not even know who they are or in which part of the world they are located. A major shift in the State Department focus on defeating Islamic terrorism is needed if the West is to defeat it without a major, perhaps cataclysmic struggle.

The "revival" of Islam in today's Central Asia is, therefore, neither an absolutely new phenomenon nor the rebuilding from its foundation of a religion that had been forgotten or rejected. In its fullness it went underground during the Soviet occupation, but it has now dramatically reappeared. The revival has sprung from the increased national consciousness of the Central Asian intelligentsia, the development of the idea of cultural uniqueness, a growing interest in national cultures and national languages cleansed of Russian neologisms, and an interest in a national history free of Bolshevik ideological interpretations. It is a very healthy development and the rest of the Arab world can benefit.

Poets and Writers Weigh In

The status of popular Islam has begun to change substantially not only because it is coming out into the open but also because it is no longer just "popular" Islam, limited to the spheres of informal, personal, marital, and family relations among Central Asian Muslims. Various opposition forces are drawing it into a political struggle against the remnants of the Bolshevik system that clings to power, but is considerably weakened. National writers and poets laid the groundwork for revivalism in the 1960s and 1970s. The 1970s witnessed a boom in historical novels. Ferghana *Before the Dawn* described the rich past of the Uzbeks. Mamadali Makhmudov's novel *Immortal Cliffs* dealt with events of the nineteenth century in Central Asia, accenting the unity of the Turkic peoples in their struggle against the encroachment of Russian conquerors. Aitmatov showed the world that modern Central Asia was a region of rich ethnic culture, ancient Muslim traditions, and people of high—and not Soviet—morals. Central Asian writers articulated the revival of Muslim culture that was maturing in the minds of the young national intelligentsia.

As early as the 1970s, the youth of Central Asia had begun to reject the official communist ideology. The Islamic revolution in Iran contributed considerably to the growth of Muslim consciousness within the population of Central Asia. Portraits of Iran's Ayatollah Khomeini often appeared on city streets and in local newspapers, while the innovations of the Iranian fundamentalists with respect to returning society to the laws of the Sharia were widely discussed in intellectual circles.

The Enlighteners

Across the board, exciting things are happening. The Afghan jihad, its success in defeating the Russian occupation has become one of the most important stimulants for the Islamic revival in the Muslim regions of Central Asia. Islam thus provided another important boost to the movements for cultural and political renewal. No one ethos will apply evenly across all five Central Asian republics, but the language of Islamic doctrine is well suited to the ideological needs of movements that have appeared on the political scene in the past two or three years.

Central Asian writers and poets, journalists, university professors, students, and even young Muslim ecclesiastics who want to become independent spiritual advisors to their brethren, are now called the new Muslim enlighteners. These enlighteners want to establish a close relationship with popular Islam. They study the Koran, the Sunna, and Islamic history and civilization.

In conducting these educational activities among the population, the new enlighteners stress the need to restore social justice to a society whose intellectual edge had been dulled by years of Czarist and communist rule. The new Muslim enlighteners are proving to their fellow citizens that one can be a cultured Muslim, observe all that Islam prescribes, and still be open to dialogue with the outside world.

Enlighteners portray the ideal modern Muslim as a man who "stands on two legs". He is intimately familiar with Islamic dogma, Muslim traditions, and the history of his nation while he also possesses the most modern knowledge of world civilization. This ideal is well known in developed Muslim countries; former Soviet Muslims, however, still in the process of catching up with their history, have yet to adopt it. Mahmoud Ahmadinejad, elected as Iran's new president in June of 2005 claims to desire such a society. "My mission is creating a role model of a modern, advanced, powerful and Islamic society."

The Jadid Model

Jadid is the Arabic word for "new," but, in fact, Jadidism was a quest for cultural and social renewal among Muslims in the Russian Empire in the first decade of the 20th. So, it would be more accurate to use the word in the context of seeking to present an old message in a new way. Regrettably, Jadidism did not survive the Bolshevik revolution in 1917. Its desire for knowledge and rational thinking in religion and politics was too much of a threat to Stalin's megalomaniac authoritarianism. The Jadids perished in Stalin's purges. But their ideas have been given new life in today's Central Asia. The head of the history department of Carleton College, Adeeb Khalid, published a book on the subject in 1998 entitled *The Politics Of Muslim Cultural Reform: Jadidism In Central Asia.* In the book he describes the difficult task ahead of Central Asian scholars, politicians in their struggle for self-discovery and cultural authenticity. "The three and a half centuries between the collapse of the Timurid order and the Russian conquest constitutes the least understood period of Central Asian history...The literary production of the period still remains largely in manuscript form."

At the heart of the Jadid philosophy was the desire to teach morality while at the same time imparting knowledge and the art of critical analysis. This, they hoped, would replace the memorization of passages of the Koran in Arabic by the ability to read Arabic. The Jadids were ashamed of the lack of intellectual content deriving from the lack of interest in literacy. Illiterates, they said, cannot help a nation develop itself. They were determined to rid their people of an educational system that they described as a curator of ignorance. Any change of intellectual comprehension on the part of the peasant, however, was a problem for the elites in society. Functional literacy has always been a challenge to any government. For some leaders, it is welcomed; for others it is a threat. Julius Nyerere, prior to becoming President of Tanzania, often said that the first thing he would do if he became President was to put an electric light bulb in as many huts as he could. His position was that independence without literacy would simply be a continuation of dependency with new rulers.

Jadid writings and influence barely surface in today's Central Asia, but it is likely that in the varied mixture of Islamic interpretation of life in the mosques and learning centers of Central Asia they may make a comeback. Self-Identity remains a desire in the heart of every Central Asian man and woman. The revival of the Jadid tradition would be a wonderful counter culture to the culture of violence now being perpetrated by the Wahhabi. In continuing the cause the Jadids started out with at the end of the nineteenth century, the new Muslim enlighteners are similarly facing a monumental task: they have to offer a blueprint for building a new society based on the principles and norms of Islam. But they are juxtaposing this model not against the medieval system that existed a century ago in Central Asia but against the Soviet Bolshevik scheme of social relations, which makes their job somewhat easier than their predecessors' because the Soviet model was never really accepted by a majority of the region's people as legitimate and "native." A typical former Soviet Muslim readily rejects the Soviet model. The enlighteners' task today, therefore, is not so much to criticize Bolshevism as to play a constructive role as theoreticians in designing and bringing into being a new social order. Although individual enlighteners have joined politically oriented associations such as the Uzbek Birlik and other organizations that advocate national renewal, the new Muslim enlighteners do not participate actively as an organized political entity. They have nonetheless prepared the ground for Islam's return to the political arena in Central Asia by providing a new language for the ideologies of modern political movements and parties in Central Asia.

The Moderates

So who are the moderate Muslims in Central Asia? No simple identification is possible, but one can certainly use a generic definition: The political forces that advocate the revival of Central Asian society through the repudiation of the Soviet Bolshevik model and the restoration of Islamic civilization. They want to recover the most important trait Islam lost during the Soviet period, i.e. the active participation of religious figures in political life. The creation in June 1990 of the all-union Islamic Revival Party (IPV) may be considered the beginning of the conscious political organization of Islam in the region. The skeleton of renewal exists. It needs now the flesh to bring it alive. This will be very difficult to accomplish in the near future because the Islamic terrorists have both confused the issue of reviving Islam and for the time being have derailed its progress by associating the revival of Islam with murder and mayhem. Magda Makhloof, professor of Turkish and Persian Studies at Ain Shams University in Cairo, comments: "These days, many are afraid to speak of Islam because of what's going on with Wahhabism. There are those who use Islam as a mask to cover terrorism. Therefore it's scary to speak of Islam."

The hope that soared upon independence, that promise of a bright future, has been dissolved in the acid environment of hate and destruction. We all must wait, Muslim, Christian and Jew, until the present terrorist forward motion slows down and the Central Asian peoples discover exactly who they are. In the meantime let us give them a lot of slack.

Chapter Nineteen

EUVGENY PRIMAKOV

Euvgeny Primakov deserves a chapter by himself for the simple reason that he has had, in the area of Islamic terrorism, a greater negative impact on the lives of Americans than any other person alive, excepting perhaps Osama bin Laden, even though his name is hardly a household word in America. He is, without a doubt, the leading Russian politician from this cohort of former KGB officers in power today. He is the real Master Spy, the Prime Mover behind Islamic terrorism, a man whose life is dedicated, day and night, to the fall of America as a great power, a man for Americans to watch and get to know. The destruction of America is his daily bread, his obsession and his religion. His stature in the Russian government is unassailable. BBC correspondent Alan Little says Mr. Primakov was the only member of the current cabinet "who could point to any real achievements". When former Russian President Boris N Yeltsin was, by law, obliged to name a Prime Minister, the last person he wanted to choose for that job was Primakov, a man who would outshine him, be applauded for his fame and personality at every event, either public or private. Yeltsin knew that Primakov was also the favorite choice for the average Russian citizen who missed the stability of Soviet times. He knew that Primakov would bring prestige and soberness to the Yeltsin administration. Yeltsin, an inveterate drinker, knew that without a façade of "soberness" he would not be taken seriously, so he chose Primakov, this wily diplomat and steely opponent of American dominance and respected international negotiator, as Prime Minister. The day his appointment was announced in Moscow, the Russian ruble resumed its rally and then registered gains as it went from 20 rubles to the dollar to 11 rubles. Primakov, the clever fox that he is, knew that the Russian people, while happy to see the end of authoritarian rule, missed the stability and security of the Soviet days, so he made a clever and assuring move. He chose as his top aides two prominent and popular economists from the Soviet era, Viktor Gerascshenko and Yuri Maslyukov. Gerashchenko headed the Soviet central bank, later the Russian central bank. Since the German government had only recently announced and complained that only part of a Dm800m ($475m) Russian debt payment due at the end of August had been paid, Gerascshenko's reputation as a man who could get things done was further appreciated. Primakov is known as a careful pragmatist, but he can display an independent mind. As Prime Minister he and a small handful of colleagues were the only members of Mr. Yeltsin's team to oppose the decision to begin a war against the rebel republic of Chechnya in 1994. That adventure, like the Soviet invasion of Afghanistan, brought nothing but heartache, shedding of blood, and waste of treasure to the Russian government.

Background

Born in Kiev in October 1929, Primakov began his lengthy career in 1956 as deputy head of the state committee for radio and television, a propaganda unit. He was a member of the Soviet Communist Party for more than 30 years and in 1989 -1990 was an alternate member of the politburo. Gorbachev picked him as his closest aide and special advisor for foreign policy issues during the reform period of the 1980s. His consistent pro-Arab stance has won him great support and honor in the Middle East. The nations there consider him a great friend and a man who truly respects their culture and ancient traditions. An incident that took place in March of 2002 in Moscow symbolizes Primakov's unique power and prestige in Russian society. A struggle as to who would win the battle to control ownership of Moscow's TV6. Entrepreneur Euvgeny Kiselev expressed his appreciation that Euvgeny Primakov had sided with him on the issue. The Russian Press commented: " Kiselev said he is particularly satisfied with his union with Primakov, noting that the communist former prime minister has direct access to the President: 'It's always useful to have the kind of partner who, in a crisis, can appeal to the head of state.' " Of course, what Kiselev did not say is that he knew very well that with Primakov on his side even the President of Russia would not dare to demure. Primakov is indeed a heavyweight. He has played many roles in Soviet and now Russian politics. One role was that of head of the Soviet SVR, Foreign Intelligence Service. At that time the SVR was a unit within the KGB, but Primakov, when appointed its head, insisted that it be a separate agency. He wanted a free hand in using the SVR as a powerful tool in his continuing determination of secretly undermining U.S. hegemony.

On the other hand, his presence and wisdom in the government is of great value when a top Russian leader gets his hands caught in the cookie jar. In late March, 2003, President George W. Bush discussed the sales of night vision goggles, anti-tank Kornet missiles, and Global Positioning System (GPS) jamming equipment with Russian President Vladimir Putin. U.S. intelligence caught the Russians with their hands in the cookie jar. Washington accused Moscow of selling sensitive military equipment to Saddam Hussein in violation of U.N. Security Council sanctions. During a March 24th, 2003 telephone conversation Putin not only denied sales to Iraq, but went on the offensive, accusing the United States of selling military equipment to countries that supports international terrorism. The Associated Press described the exchange as "tense." While the Russians were asking for more time for the UN inspectors to do their work, the Russian company, Aviakonversia, as far back as 2000, was busily supplying the Iraqis with military equipment they might need in case of hostilities with the U.N. sponsored military action.

Aviakonversia president Oleg Antonov did not deny the sales, but explained that, technically, he had not done anything wrong because his company sent the component parts, not the assembled product! His righteousness was comical, not doubt no more so than to him. Surely, Mr. Antonov is also busy sending component parts to Iran, North Korea and terrorist organizations. The U.S. provided the Russian authorities with names, addresses, telephone numbers and even shipping details, and went to great lengths to declassify its intelligence information in a good-faith effort to gain Russian cooperation to stop the sales, but was rebuffed.

We do need to call the Russians to task for many of these anti-American actions. For one thing, the U.S government can remind the Kremlin that the profit made by selling six GPS jammers (about $500,000) could be more than compensated for if the U.S. signals the U.S. Overseas Private Investment Corporation (OPIC) and Export-Import (ExIm) bank to deny Russia billions in credits. A little hard ball is needed here. Putin can always call on Primakov, Russia's top magician of diplomacy, for advice.

Primakov's Book[61]

In 2002 Primakov published a book entitled: *The World After 9/11*. It is significant not for what it says but for what it does not say. Primakov comments that there has been a decline in state-supported terrorism and that it was breaking up into smaller groups run by isolated organizations. The statement simply blew smoke in our eyes. He writes that at the end of the XX century: "State support of some terrorist groups continued, but it obviously had being decreasing".[62]He continues: "If an organization that committed a terrorist attack on the U.S.A. was connected with any state of the Middle East, Africa or South- East Asia, at least one of intelligent services of leading world states - External Intelligent service of Russia, American CIA, British MI-6, German BND, or French, Chinese, Indian or any other service would know about it"[63] He says this with a straight face while he sees to it that in one way or another anti-American terrorists get what they need. He is a master at deflecting blame. He does not do it with blustering anger or indignations; he does it with the smoothness of political and intellectual silk. At the same time he acknowledges that the planning and execution of the 9/11 operation required "a big number of assistants' for 'infiltration into a number of US airports, avoiding checking points while boarding aircrafts, simultaneous hijacking of four airplanes with passengers, escaping surveillances of airport's radars and simultaneous strike on pre-elected goals. Such an organization must be mighty, rather numbered, well financed and acting autonomously."[64] It is clear, using his words, that only state-supported terrorists could have accomplished all of this. He is the Master of diplomatically intermingling.

Speaking of bin Laden, he stresses that the head of Al-Qaeda "inherited $250 millions after his father death. For twenty years Osama at least doubled or even tripled this heritage...Thus, the financial capacities of Osama bin Laden were sufficient for the creation and activation of his organization"[65] By picking the exception, he attempts to prove a false rule, i.e. that the terrorists pay their own way. He then goes on to repeat banal facts, like the hostility of the royal family to bin Laden, about his intention to fight against Iraq in 1991, about religious differences with Iran, Sunni vis-a-vie Shia, in order to prove al-Qaeda's independence. What he proves to the attentive reader is that he is covering up Russian involvement. Primakov is losing some of his previous subtlety and cunning. He is slipping a bit, but still going strong.

He takes a jab at the U.S.A. and, in so doing, undermines his own argument about the independence of Al-Qaeda: "Ironically, American special services took part in the creation of bin Laden and his organization".[66] He shifts the goalposts. He now wants to say that if it is proven that bin Laden and his al-Qaeda do receive external financial and technological assistance, America must take the blame. Making such statements Primakov does not bother to support them by facts, believing that Russian readers will trust him as a former Soviet and Russian top-spy. He then stretches our credulity further by making a connection between al-Qaeda and the Chechen militants, making the case that Russia has a perfect right to carry on a war against the Chechens. One can easily get lost in the interlacing corridors of this incredible mind.

Suggests Sharing Intelligence

Primakov then goes on to try to convince the outside world that there should be a greater sharing of intelligence information. "Under the new circumstances it is necessary to increase cooperation between intelligence of different countries, especially exchange of information". What he really wants to know is to what extent other intelligence gathering might know about his agency's relationship with his terrorist clients. He does not stop there. He even calls for the opportunity to influence this information: "such cooperation must include collective analytical perception of the information intelligence" However, he is careful to establish a caveat, saying that such joint operations and cooperation "does not negate the independent existence of the national intelligence services, that should continue their job in the national interests of their states". In other words Russian agencies can continue their clandestine activities against the U.S.A. even in this new atmosphere of 'cooperation'. Obviously, the collective analysis of information enhances the effectiveness of Russian clandestine actions by having access to the secrets made inside the enemy's camp.

Russian cooperation with terrorist organizations and rogue states accomplish two important objectives: 1.It convinces these organizations and states that Russia has returned as a world power to be reckoned with and relied upon in their encounters with America. 2. It is able, with its other face, by offering to assist America in its fight against terrorism, to request from America loans, technology transfers, and assistance in rebuilding its decrepit industrial base. Oilfields in Russia that were brought on stream prior to the break-up of the USSR are gradually deteriorating and require increasingly hefty investments to maintain the current production levels. Exploration and development of new deposits is extremely capital-intensive. There is wariness about moving billions of dollars from accounts in Western banks so both Putin and Primakov desperately need to cajole the West into providing G-8 money and expertise.

Have they deceived us or are we just plain gullible? Lenin said that the best way to overcome the West was to: 'tell them what they want to hear'. Putin, guided by Primakov, is a master at this subtle art. Hitler duped Chamberlin, and the result was a world war of enormous proportions with uncounted dead. It is not inconceivable that by its own logic rather than the will of men like Putin (surely he does not want it) World War III might occur through miscalculation. Terrorism has had and will continue to have as a byproduct of its activity, many incidents, and incidents of the right timing and character can escalate to major conflict. In ratcheting up support for the "axis of evil" Putin is playing with fire, a fire that could engulf him and the rest of the world. Prior to the American invasion of Iraq, the Russians signed an agreement that included deals on oil, agriculture, irrigation, electricity, and transportation, a deal worth $40 billion. Until the American invasion, beginning in the 1990s, Russia, with concessions valued at some $7 billion, had become the single largest shareholder in Iraq's vast oil wealth, all this while pretending that it was listening to and agreeing with the Americans. What they now have on their hands is a massive multi-billion dollar debt. But, they never learn. They are now bitter and looking for revenge. And, with a government full of ex KGB agents, they know exactly how to do it. It's a crazy world.

Primakov the Innocent

Primakov plays the innocent. We should, he says, stop our unfair accusations against Iran and North Korea as they plunge ahead in the development of nuclear weapons. He fails to highlight the fact that the wherewithal to construct the machinery that will produce these weapons is being supplied by Russia. He also does not mention that once Iran and North Korea have a credible nuclear arsenal, which Russia will help create, American lives would be in danger, thus blocking America's ability to control even further proliferation. At that point the balance of power shifts to the Russians.

They will be on friendly terms with the now nuclear supplied enemies of America. This is the dream. They cannot wait. To that extent Iran and North Korea have become Russian proxies and mercenaries in their long-term goal of surpassing the United States in power and influence. Primakov wants to see it all happen before he passes away. He certainly is sparing no effort.

He then almost comically, to those who know his past, calls for a "Terrorism-fighting charter" that should be signed by all states. The charter would call on all nations to establish a firm control on all financial (not intelligence, arms or technical!) sources of terrorist organizations and to monitor the movements of known terrorists within their respective territories (Russia does not need to be involved in these activities on its territory.)" He writes as if these activities today take place in the open. The transfer of arms and technology to terrorist organizations would scarcely be affected by such legislation and Primakov knows this. He is just posturing. He has always been a good showman.

His Dissertation

Euvgeny Primakov's doctoral dissertation contained such sensitive information that it was never published. Copies are located only in special (available only to top officials) library departments both of the top secret International Department,[67] and the Institute of Social Sciences. Primakov, in the 1960s, while acting as Pravda's official correspondent to Egypt, was actually (secretly) the ID's personal envoy to the President of Egypt, Gamel Abdul Nasser, who at that time was also General Secretary of the Arab Socialist Union. Primokov spent most of his in close proximity to Nasser studying attentively his ideology, culture and goals. His dissertation is a reflection on this study, and he gave copies of it to key older party apparatchik, in the hope of conscienticising them to an appreciation of the importance of supporting Arab nationalism. He shocked his colleagues by reporting:

\# Nasser is not a communist

\# Nasser is, in fact, anti-communist

\# Nasser was strongly influenced by the theory of Fascism (the dreaded enemy of communism).

Much to the ID's surprise, it was not Nasser who adopted the Bolshevik model of government, but Hafiz Assad and Saddam Hussein. He shocked the ID regulars by asserting that Nasser was not an ideological ally, that his understanding of "socialism" is not the Soviet understanding; both sides had used the same word, with different meanings. He made the case that since Nasser considered himself a political friend, it was time the ID stopped looking gift horses in the mouth. Nasser's ideology, he told them, doesn't mean a damn. We can note here that it was in Primakov's dissertation that Gorbachev's "new thinking" was crystallized.

Primakov is the leading Russian expert on the Middle East. The West should know more about him. He was born in the Georgian city of Kislavorsk, in the Stavlovol region (Gorbachev's home territory). He was on the Security Council of the

Soviet Union, whose members were Gorbachev's closest advisors. His Jewish mother was a gynecologist. His father evidently abandoned the family when Euvgeny was quite young. Primakov's supporters and detractors all agree that he is highly intelligent, pragmatic, and endowed with a natural political shrewdness. At an early age, he expressed a desire to study at the School of Eastern Languages, a renowned academic department of Moscow University, entry to which requires, not only a keen intelligence, but luck, or influence, or both. His mother made the right connections, because the town of Kislavorsk was a popular vacation spot for high-ranking party officials. These men were provided with women, some of whom become pregnant after a transient affair. An unwanted pregnancy means a trip to the gynecologist by the official in question, who arranged and paid for an abortion. It is likely that Mrs. Primakov's familiarity with many of these men enabled her to arrange her son's entry into the University.

Foreign Minister Igor Ivanov, ex-Prime Minister Euvgeny Primakov's appointee, reflects Primakov's moderately anti-American, pro-Arab feelings of Soviet-era diplomats. Ivanov is not trusted by Putin's inner circle, but he has not been replaced.

In early 1997, then-Foreign Minister Primakov and his Iranian counterpart, Ali Akbar Velayati, issued a joint statement calling the U.S. presence in the Persian Gulf "totally unacceptable." Primakov sought to build a Eurasian counterbalance to the Euro–Atlantic alliance, to be based on a coalition including Russia, China, India, and Iran. These efforts made it likely that the United States and its allies would eventually become the target of Russian-Iranian military cooperation. More worrisome for U.S. policy planners is the geopolitical dimension of Russian-Iranian rapprochement. The Russian Federation and the Islamic Republic cooperate over a broad range of policy issues, with military ties being an important aspect of relations between the two countries. Since the collapse of the Soviet Union, Iran has refrained from actively promoting its brand of Islamic radicalism in the former Soviet republics. Despite fashioning itself as defender of all Muslims, Tehran did little when the Russian military slaughtered tens of thousands of Muslim civilians in the first Chechen war (1994-1996), and it put forth only weak protestations against

Moscow's excessive use of force in the second Chechen war (1999-2001). Moscow and Tehran also have cooperated against Afghanistan's radical Taliban regime by supporting the anti-Taliban Northern Alliance opposition coalition. They supported Armenia rather than the pro-Turkish, pro-Western Azerbaijan; and oppose a "western" route for exporting oil from the Caspian Sea basin through Georgia to Turkey.

KGB general Oleg Kalugin told former CIA agent James Donaldson that Primakov had a very close connection with the KGB. This connection probably started at Moscow University (which he attended with Gorbachev). It's improbable that an out-sider (someone not directly connected with the elite) could enter the University—especially the prestigious Middle-East depart-ment—and complete the curriculum, without being tapped by the KGB. He also worked later worked for Pravda, and a KGB con-nection is a sine qua non for employment on this Central.

Committee Newspaper

Primakov's first overseas assignment was as Cairo corre-spondent for Pravda. Simultaneously he became an employee of the International Department. His covert assignment (all Interna-tional Department assignments have a covert aspect) was to act as liaison between the International Department and the Egyptian leadership. In consequence, he developed a very close personal relationship with Gamal Abdel Nasser. He was described by friends as a man who knows how to party, how to entertain a wide array of friends and officials. His parties often lasted late into the night, and sobriety was not de rigueur. But the highly disciplined Primakov rarely gets maudlin or tipsy; he retains the affability that has made him among the most popular of Soviet officials. His unique attribute was, however, his ability to make deep and lasting friendships with Arabs. During this Cairo inter-lude, a camaraderie developed between Primakov and Saddam Hussein. He met with Saddam many times during the seventies and eighties, both in Moscow and in Baghdad. "I believe that we developed a very close relationship when I could talk with him without any diplomatic precautions, and when I took into con-sideration all his psychological characteristics."

The depth of this relationship emerges in his Pravda article of February 27, 1991. He writes: "My good relationship with Saddam Hussein is not a big secret." Primakov's true skill lies in his ability to form, and retain friendships with opposing Arab factions. For example, he writes, "When I was a Pravda correspondent in the Middle East, in the 1960s, I wrote about my trips to Iraq, about my meetings and conversations with Mustafah Barzani, leader of the Kurdish rebels."

Barzani

Barzani immigrated to the Soviet Union, and lived there for twelve years, during which time he and Primakov grew ever closer. The KGB and the International Department arranged for Barzani's political asylum. The article continues: "Then Barzani returned to Iraq after the Revolution of 1958 which overthrew the Monarchy of Muli Saif. For some time he was the Vice-President of Iraq (the President was Abdel Karim Kassaim.) He escaped to the North and began the war against Baghdad. And then, at a certain moment, it was possible to sign a peace agreement with the Kurds. But suddenly Saddam Hussein said to me, 'No, I cannot sign this agreement, because there is no guarantee that the Kurds would not resume conflict.' I answered: 'Yes, there is no such guarantee, but if the Kurds break the agreement and Baghdad adheres to the agreement, then the Kurds will not get any support from the Soviet Union. Do you understand what this means.' After thinking about this, Saddam agreed."

This conversation demonstrated Primakov's ability to introduce open-minded tolerance and impartiality into ID thinking relative to the Kurds. For example Primakov, as Deputy Director of the Institute of International Economy and International Relations, of the Academy of Sciences, spoke of the Kurdhish-Iraqi problem: "In this capacity, I met with Mustafah Barzani in Moscow, in the middle seventies, while the war between the Baghdad regime and the Kurdish rebels was going on. Mr. Barzani told me how the attempt to assassinate him was organized. He was in a reception for sheiks. One of the sheiks brought a radio-controlled bomb with him to the function, and the driver, who was outside the house, triggered the device". Barzani told Primakov that the assassination attempt was organized by Saddam Hussein.

"My first meeting with Saddam Hussein took place in 1969, prior to his becoming President, but he was, already, the most influential member of the Iraqi leadership. I noted with great interest that Saddam, as the minister responsible for the Kurdish problem, took very seriously his mandate to entice the Kurds to the negotiating table. After I became better acquainted I noticed, at an early stage, the many features of his character that became more overt and articulate later, when he became President of Iraq. His cruelty and stubbornness played handmaids to his unbounded ambitions."

"Some of my most interesting discussions I had in Baghdad were with Tariq Aziz (Iraqi Foreign Minister during the Gulf War) who was, at that time, Editor-in-Chief of the Baathist Party newspaper, Ak Sora." In his article Primakov continued: "The time was unstable…Every office of Saddam and Tariq Aziz had machine guns on the desks, at the ready." Primakov, almost alone among the leading opinion makers, maintains that in reality the United States and the Soviet Union (their respective rhetoric notwithstanding) are consensual allies vis-à-vis the Arab world. He believes it to be in the USSR's interest to maintain close ties with both Israel and the United States. In the Soviet euphoria that followed the dramatic rise in oil prices in the West, Primakov cautioned that, rather than bring the West to its knees, oil shortages would generate such attention to energy saving and alternative fuels, that the long-term loser would be the Arab oil cartel. Strategic bonding with Israel and the United States is high on his list of priorities. He "loves" everybody.

Deemphasizes Ideology

Primakov's influence brought about a cautious, well-thought-out, and realistic Russian policy in the Middle East. The de-emphasis of ideological positions, (the defeat of their client state, Iraq, notwithstanding) has obtained a greater respect and influence for the Soviets in the Middle East than they have enjoyed since the days of Abdel Nasser. Primakov, in his doctoral dissertation, written in the late 1960s, maintained that the Soviet Union's favorite "comrade" in the Middle East, Gamal Abdel

Nasser, had no love either for communism, or for the Soviet model of socialism. Nasser's cordial relationship with the Soviet Union was based more on realpolitik than a desire to introduce socialist concepts into the body politic of Egypt. He urges his colleagues in the International Department to practice this same kind of realpolitik today.

The experienced Arab-hand, Euvgeny Primakov, an advisor to Russia's leaders for so many years and still going strong, in all matters excepting his hatred of America, represents the moderate center.

INDEX

BIBLIOGRAPHY

Ahmed, Nafeez Mosaddeq. *The War On Truth: 9/11, Disinformation And The Anatomy Of Terrorism*, Olive Branch Press, 2005

Baer, Bob, *Sleeping with the Devil. How Washington Sold our Soul for Saudi Crude*, (Random House) 2003

Bascio, Patrick, Novikov, Euvgeny. *Gorbachev and the Collapse of the Soviet Communist Party*, Chapter Ten: Soviet Islam, Peter Lang, 1994

Bawer, Bruce. *While Europe Slept: How Radical Islam is Destroying the West from Within*. Doubleday, 2006.

Bennigsen, Alexander and Broxup, Marie. *The Islamic threat to the Soviet State* New York: St. Martin's Press, 1983

Bergen, Peter. *Holy War, Inc.: Inside The Secret World of Osama Bin Laden*. Publisher: Free Press, 2001

Peter Bergen *The Osama bin Laden I Know: An Oral History of al Qaeda's Leader*: Free Press, 2006

Chomsky, Noam. *World Orders Old and New* Columbia University Press, 1994.

Cooley, John K. *Unholy Wars: Afghanistan, America and International Terrorism* Publisher: Pluto Press; 3rd e., 2002.

Dennis, Anthony J. *Osama Bin Laden: A Psychological and Political Portrait* : Wyndham Hall Press, 2002

Dennis, Anthony J. *The Rise of the Islamic Empire and the Threat to the West* (Wyndham Hall Press) 2001

Herman, Edward. *The Real Terror Network: Terrorism in Fact and Propaganda*, South End Press; 1st edition. 1982

Hoffman, Bruce. *Inside Terrorism*, Columbia University Press, 1999.

Hopkirk, Peter. *The Great Game: The Struggle for Empire in Central Asia,* Kodansha Globe; Reprint edition April 1994.

Hopkirk, Peter. *Foreign Devils on the Silk Road: The Search for the Lost Cities of Central Asia*. University of Massachusetts Press, 1980

Motyl, A Sovietology. *Rationality-Nationality Coming to Grips with Nationalism in the USSR*, New York: Columbia University Press, 1990.

Norval, Morgan. *Triumph of Disorder: Islamic Fundamentalism, the New Face of War*, Sligo Press Inc., 1999

Qutb, Sayyid. Milestones *The Myth of Islamic Tolerance: How Islamic Law Treats Non-Muslims* Prometheus Books, 2005

Rywkin, Michael. *Moscow's Muslim Challenge: Soviet Central Asia,* Rev/ ed/, Armonk, NY: M.E. Sharpe, 1990

Tillich, Paul. *A History of Christian Thought*, London: S.C.M. Press, Ltd., 1968

Wright, Lawrence. *The Looming Tower: Al-Qaeda and the Road to 9/11* (Knopf) 2006.

Khalid, Abdeed, *The Politics Of Muslim Cultural Reform: Jadidism In Central Asia*, University of CA Press, 1998.

Web sites

www.lailatalqadr.com/stories

www.pbs.org/wgbh/pages/frontline/shows/front/, PBS Frontline: Al Qaeda's New Front

www.loc.gov/rr/frd/terrorism.html. Library of Congress, Federal Research Division: Terrorism and Crime Studies, Official reports including the September 1999 'The Sociology and Psychology of Terrorism: Who Becomes a Terrorist and Why?'

http://dannyreviews.com/h/Terror_God.html. The Global Rise of Religious Violence -A review of Mark Juergensmeyer's book, "Terror in the Mind of God", February 20, 1999

http://www.cato.org/dailys/02-20-99. A Foreign Policy for Terrorists by Doug Bandow

http://www.americamagazine.org/terror.htm. "War in Afghanistan," America Editorial, Oct. 29, 2001

http://www.nsi.org/Library/Terrorism/usterror.htm. Terrorism: How Vulnerable Is The United States? -Stephen Sloan

http://www.pakistan-facts.com/article. Pakistan Facts - Jihad Recruitment on the Rise

http://www.theatlantic.com/issues Thinking About Terrorism -/86/jun/obrien.htm

http://www.emergency.com/cntrterr.htm. Summary of world-wide terrorism events, groups, strategies and tactics.

News Agencies: RIA news agency, Moscow

Articles

Abu Nidal Organization (Iraq, extremists), Council on Foreign
Relations,Updated October 2005

Ball, Carlos. "Antagonizing Traditional Friends,"
Techcentralstation.com, November 17, 2003.

Benjamin, Robert, Should We Negotiate with Hamas? Interview
with Former Israeli Foreign Minister Shlomo Ben-Ami,
February 14, 2006, Mediate.com

Halaby, Jamal. "Members of Terror Leader al-Zarqawi's Clan
Disown Him", ABC International, Nov 29, 2005.

Kaplan, Eben, Gauging the "War on Terror", Council on
Foreign Relations August 28, 2006

Kaplan, Eben. The Al-Qaeda-Hezbollah Relationship, Council
on Foreign Relations, August 14, 2006

O'Neil, Patrick. "Lenin offered to help Afghan struggle against
Britain", New York Militant, Vol. 65, No. 43, November 12,
2001.

Rotberg, Robert I. "The Failure and Collapse of Nation States:
Breakdown, Prevention and Repair," in When States Fail:
Causes and Consequences, ed. Robert I. Rotberg (Princeton,
N.J.: Princeton Univ. Press).

Stalinsky, Stephen. "The Islamic Affairs Department of the
Saudi Embassy in Washington, D.C.", MidEast Media
Research Institute, No. 23, 26 November, 2003

END NOTES

[1] The ethnic makeup of Astana is quite diverse, including a Russian community.

[2] Sergie Blagov article "Putin's Push for a Strategic Triangle," Asian Times, 8 December 2004.

[3] Initial reports stated that the number of insurgents numbered 50-60, but since many eventually escaped capture and about 100 were captured, this initial figure was obviously inaccurate.

[4] The figure was later greatly revised

[5] Bukhara, which is situated on the Silk route, in Uzbedkistan, is more than 2,000 years old.

[6] The overthrow of President Askar Akayev in Kyrgyzstan

[7] Freedom House was founded more than sixty years ago by Eleanor Roosevelt and Wendell Willkie

[8] The Wahhabi staff about 600 out of the official total of 1,200. However, there are numerous and scattered small mosques around the nation.

[9] Simon, Mafoot, "A Sufi Muslim Takes on Wahhabism," Sunday Straits Times,

[10] As reported on saudiembassy.net

[11] "IDB Allocates $202 Mln to Finance Islamic Development Ventures," Arabic News, 1/25/2000.

[12] Saudi Embassy Press Archive, July 8, 1995.

[13] Ibid, March 5, 2000

[14] Stalinksy, Steven, "The Islamic Affairs Department of the Saudi Embassy in Washington, D.C.," MiddleEast Media Research Institute (MEMRI), No. 23, 26 November 2003.

[15] At a Freedom House Conference in February, 2004

[16] The word hawala comes from Arabic and is defined as a bill of exchange or a promissory note. It is also used in the expression hawala safar, traveler's check.

[17] See much more about him in Chapter Twelve.

[18] The condemnation of other Muslims

[19] Annual Report on International Religious Freedoms 2004

[20] It is certainly not ancient history to speak of the Nazi Holocaust where it was reported that the Nazis minding overseeing the burning alive of Jews in ovens listened to Bach, Mozart and Beethoven.

[21] The sayings and deeds of Mohammed. They are as important as the Koran itself.

²² Based in Doha-Qatar.

²³ The Ottoman Empire was a multi-ethnic state that existed from 1299 to 1923 (624 years), one of the largest empires to rule the borders of the Mediterranean Sea.

²⁴ 14 U.S. Commission on International Religious Freedom, Report on Saudi Arabia, May 2003.

²⁵Stalinksy, Steven, "The Islamic Affairs Department of the Saudi Embassy in Washington, D.C.," MiddleEast Media Research Institute (MEMRI), No. 23, 26 November 2003.

²⁶ For a defense of the Wahhabi movement, see: The 'Wahhabi' Myth by Haneef James Oliver.

²⁷The Deobandi Movement, founded in 1860, was named after a small town in the Indian Himalayas where the movement was founded during the period of British rule in India. Like Wahhabism, it is a very strict form of Sunni Islam. The followers of both the Deobandi movement and the Wahhabi movement reject secular human knowledge. Deobandi philosophy has helped spawn many fundamentalist groups in the Muslim world.

²⁸ The Hadith and the Koran make up the Sunnah, the base of Islamic law.

²⁹http://www.state.gov/s/ct/rls/fs/2001/index.cfm?docid=6531 .)

³⁰ His full name is: Sheikh Osama Bin-Mohammed Bin-Laden

³¹ Abu Buraydah, a top al-Qaeda lieutenant captured in Pakistan, told US investigators in April 2002 that al-Qaeda had worked on building a dirty bomb. In November 2001, bin Laden told a Pakistani newspaper that al-Qaeda had nuclear weapons.

³²The Wall Street Journal, January 14 and 16, 2002.

³³ This sounds like fiction to the ears of the average Westerner, but to Russians it is the stuff of which their lives have been since Lenin ruled the Soviet Union.

³⁴ www.lailatalqadr.com/stories/p4180402, April 18, 2002.

³⁵ During a failed attempt to assassinate a top official of the Egyptian government, a young girl who was in the vicinity was killed. It was a public relations disaster for Zawahiri.

³⁶Al-Sharq Al-Awsat, December 6, 2001

³⁷ The more precisely the position is determined, the less precisely the momentum is known in this instant, and vice versa. --Heisenberg, uncertainty paper, 1927. We always know where an atomic particle was by its footprints, but not where it is.

³⁸ Meaning of Hadith: Since the word hadith will come up throughout one's study of Islam, it is a word the meaning of which is important. In works on Islam the word "hadith" usually refers to the

sayings or "traditions" which have been transmitted from the Prophet. Muslims hold these to be the most important source of Islamic teachings after the Koran. The word hadith for Shiite Islam and Sunni Islam differs. The fundamental distinction to be made between Shiite and Sunni hadiths is that in Shiism the traditions are not limited to those of the Prophet, but include those of the Imams as well. The Shiite collections, such as that of al-Kulayni, also contain sayings transmitted from and about the twelve Imams.

[39] How similar to the scenes the Roman population witnessed in the Coliseum "games."

[40] During Mohammed's time there was fierce competition between the Muslims and the Quraish. A truce between the two groups was formalized in the Treaty of Hudaibiya.

[41] It is necessary for the United States to seek greater development of its own domestic petroleum resources, while also encouraging a reduction by American and other Western consumers of oil from the Middle East. This, together with a massive investment in alternative sources of energy, would reduce the flow of the money transferred to the Middle East and used to finance terrorism.

[42] Colonel Stanislav Lunev is the highest-ranking military officer ever to defect from Russia to the United States. He defected in 1992, and his information was deemed so that vital he was placed – and remains in – the FBI's Witness Protection Program. As one of Russia's top GRU agents in America, Lunev was involved in making Russian war plans against America. Some of Lunev's information was revealed in the 1997 bestseller "Through the Eyes of the Enemy" (Regnery). Among many revelations, Lunev reported that Russia's military – despite the end of the Cold War, continues to prepare for a war with the U.S.

[43]Nidal died in August, 2002, in Baghdad. His Palestinian guerrilla group was blamed for attacks in more than 20 countries that have killed hundreds.

[44]Peshawar lies just 70 km from the Afghan border. It has long been a transit point for arms, drugs, gemstones and smuggled electronic goods.

[45] The school of Deoband, a Wahhabi twin, was also an attempt to counter the influence of some Muslims reformists who advocated a mix of religious and Western education. For Muslims to do well, they reasoned, they had to learn the ways of their masters.

[46] The enormous amount of his followers

[47] The great illusion of the young

[48] Here is an area where the United States can be very helpful and should act expedtiously.

[49]Another "must do" on the part of the United States

[50] Vinson Synan, The Holiness-Pentecostal Movement in the United States (Grand Rapids, Mich., Wm B Eerdmans' Publishing Co., 1971,) p 25.

[51] Paul Tillich, A History of Christian Thought (London: S.C.M. Press, Ltd., 1968), pp.225-226. (From lectures first given in 1953.)

[52]Also known as "Lion's Milk" One can drink itstraight or with water, soda, or mineral water. Raki, aromatized with anise-seed, can be consumed as a cocktail, but, more commonly, is sipped while enjoying "meze" (Turkish hors d'oeuvres and appetizers)

[53]Lenin is not a popular figure among Islamic terrorists.

[54]Yacov Bin Efrat, "Afghan boomerang", Challenge, No. 70, November 9, 2001.

[55] Movement of Islamic Resistance of Palestine

[56] Muslim tight community evolving into a state

[57] On November 20, 2003 the final results of the controversial November 2nd parliamentary elections in Georgia, elections that mirrored the political profile of European nations.

[58] For a different perspective on HT, see Regional security expert Ahmad Rashid's, "Jihad: The Rise of Militant Islam in Central Asia." He says that the lack of political freedoms drive people in Central Asia to join radical groups.

[59] Energy Department, International Energy Outlook 2004 (Washington, D.C., Energy Information Agency, April 2004, p.50

[60] Euvgeny Primakov, World after 9/11, published by MISLJ, Moscow, 2002, page 10

[61] Ibid. page 14

[62] Ibid. page 14-15

[63] Ibid, page 15

[64] Ibid, page 19

[65] Ibid. page 19

[66] Ibid. page 25

[67]For a detailed analysis of the International Department, see Novikov and Bascio, Gorbachev and the Collapse of the Soviet Communist Party: The Historical and Political Background, (New York, Peter Lang), 1994.